Six World Faiths

Six World Faiths

Douglas Charing, W. Owen Cole, Riadh El-Droubie,
Anil D. Goonewardene, Nila Pancholi,
Piara Singh Sambhi

Edited by
W. Owen Cole

CONTINUUM
London and New York

Continuum
Wellington House, 125 Strand, London WC2R 0BB
370 Lexington Avenue, New York, NY 10017-6550

First published as *Comparative
Religions: A Modern Textbook* by
Blandford Press 1982
Published by Cassell in 1991 as *Five World Faiths*
This edition first published 1996
Reprinted 1998

British Library Cataloguing-in-Publication Data
A catalogue record for this book is available
from the British Library

ISBN 0–8264–4964–6

Typeset by BookEns Ltd, Royston, Herts
Printed and bound in Great Britain by
Biddles Ltd, www.biddles.co.uk

Contents

Introduction

W. OWEN COLE

The Purpose of this Book

When the authors of this book sat down to write their six different sections they had one major aim clearly in mind, to introduce the reader to what they considered to be the most important aspects of their particular religion. These six faiths were chosen because of their place in British society. The 1988 Education Act, for example, which covers England and Wales, states that syllabuses which each local authority provides to guide teachers about what should be taught in Religious Education, should:

> reflect the fact that the religious traditions of Great Britain are in the main Christian while taking account of the other principal religions represented in Great Britain. (Ch. 40, part 1, section 8)

The principal religions are those included in this book.

No religion is monochrome or mono–cultural. It may be an exaggeration to say that no two believers share the same faith but there may be nuances and emphases of belief which differ even if very slightly. Certainly Christians in Britain see their religion in a different way from those in South Africa or India. Jews in Israel have a somewhat different perspective from those in the USA.

It is not possible to say 'All Christians...', 'All Sikhs...'. We are now sophisticated enough in our understanding to recognize that within religions there are differences. Not all Sikh men wear the turban, not every Christian lays the same stress upon the eucharist as others do. We hope, however, that this book will provide readers with an understanding of core beliefs and values so that the variables may not confuse them too much.

Meeting Religions through Believers

When you have studied the religions through books you may wish to encounter them through people. You are likely to be met with a friendly and enthusiastic response. If I go to a mosque Muslims normally ask me to sit behind the men when they are praying, though I have been invited to join the prayer line. To explain that the purpose of your visit is to observe not participate and sit at the back of the room is a wise precaution but this attitude is one which Christians seem to find difficult to accept (I have found groups I have been taking encouraged to occupy the front pew which always seems to be left empty). Hindus also find their hospitality challenged by non-participants. They expect everyone to join in.

A meal follows Hindu and Sikh worship and services may be long. It is unwise to plan for an hour's visit and be in a rush to leave. It is impolite to refuse food which will always be vegetarian. Hospitality is a characteristic of many religious groups and you should be prepared for it. In some respects it is also the time when most learning takes place as someone chats with you while you are eating, you are taken on a tour of the building, your questions are answered, you see the community socializing, and friendships are made.

It is tempting to invite one of your guides to speak to a class of pupils or some association to which you may belong. Should you do this it is thoughtful to offer transport. Not everyone has a car and travel involving changing buses three times can be irksome and costly. Make sure that any food offered afterwards is acceptable. I have known a headteacher offer a rabbi ham sandwiches! Go vegetarian is always the best advice, and have some fruit available. To ask your visitor about any proposed meal is even better! Remember, many Christians are vegetarian nowadays.

Being a visiting speaker is daunting. It is bad enough if, like me, you are a teacher. I can never be sure that I am meeting the purpose for which I was invited unless I have a long telephone conversation with the secretary. For anyone else it must border on the terrifying. What can one say about Judaism in forty minutes to a Christian fellowship or school class which believes that the Jewish scriptures are the 'Old Testament' and obviously point to the coming of Jesus, for example. It appears that these unpaid speakers give 'value for money' but if they were better briefed and given realistic requests they could give even greater satisfaction.

Our Approach to a Religion

The students of religion, be they seeking only personal

satisfaction or a university degree, must adopt a proper stance to their subject. They must refrain from wanting to make value judgements or comparisons. (When we do that we are likely to compare the best in our own tradition, if we belong to one, with the worst in the other person's. When Christians ask questions about religious militancy their host may reply 'What about Northern Ireland?' To which the Christian has been known to respond, 'But Northern Ireland has nothing to do with religion!' Such special pleading is common to us all. We are never comfortable when we feel that someone is trying to find things to criticize in the things we hold dear. We should be careful not to do it to someone else.)

Comparisons are best avoided, even the legitimate exercise of comparing Islamic worship with Sikh. This requires much sophistication. Few of us possess it. It might, however, be a useful experience for Sikhs and Muslims (and others) to sit together and explain their worship to one another. One person might say, 'Why don't you have your scripture placed centrally in your worship as we Sikhs do?' This is a comparative enquiry of the best sort for its purpose is mutual understanding not points scoring.

Cultural Differences

'Is this religious or is it just part of your culture?' is often a western or Christian question to which there is no eastern or even Jewish answer. For example, the separation of men and women in many acts of worship has basic religious justification though the so-called liberals may mislead us by denying this. Opposition to women priests by some Anglicans and most Roman Catholics has the same fundamental origin. It is related to concepts of ritual purity and impurity not merely social custom, tradition and biblical teaching. Christians sitting separately upon the floor in a village church in Pakistan may have more to do with the tradition from which they came, Islam, than the ways of the missionaries, but theirs is one appropriate to their circumstances and should be understood not ridiculed or criticized.

Dress often has religious significance, for instance, the *kippur* or *yamulka* worn by a Jewish man, the Sikh's turban, the modest dress of Muslim and Sikh women, the hat which black Christian and Jewish women tend to wear when they attend public worship. In some traditions the head is covered, in others the covering is removed.

9

Diet has already been mentioned. Before we question the food fads of others we might consider our own. Why would most Britons look aghast at the suggestion that they eat horse meat? Perhaps it is a throw-back to their Celtic heritage, in that religion the horse was sacred, just as the cow is for Hindus! It was taboo as the pig is for Jews and Muslims. Beware of rationalizations! Those who don't eat pork may provide hygienic explanations for their position but even if all their objections are met, it is unlikely that they will eat the proffered pork chop any more than I will knowingly eat horse or dog.

Names Hindus tend to know what their names mean. They are carefully chosen. Jews in Britain and other countries have a Jewish name used in the family and synagogue, and another first name (don't say Christian name!) which they use in public life. Muslim names can be very complicated. Much depends on the country of origin. Sikh given names are often the same for males and females. Jaswant Sagoo may be a boy or a girl unless K (Kaur, female) or S (Singh, male) is included, e.g. J.S. Sagoo. Incidentally, 'Christian' name is a bit of an anomaly, they are usually not given at baptism but before it! The priest says, 'Name this child... Alexander, I baptize you ...'. Why then are they called 'Christian' names?

Religious Dialogue

One of the great developments which has taken place in the last 25 years is the growth of dialogue. People of faith meeting together to share their beliefs and to combine to face the challenges which face them all such as ecological matters or inner city decay. Some specifically religious areas which they may explore are:

Festivals – how they are celebrated, what they mean. This is a popular topic for groups and individuals coming new to dialogue.

Worship – its form and purpose.

Women – what beliefs are there in the religions about their role?

Prayer – how people pray, what prayer/meditation (are they the same thing?) mean to people of different religions.

Suffering – what answers they give to the problem of innocent suffering.

God, or Ultimate Reality – what do these mean to adherents of the religions?

War and peace, euthanasia, world poverty and hunger, ecology, salvation, could be added to an almost endless list.

The process of dialogue begins with believers knowing about their own culture, beliefs, practices and values. This doesn't require dogmatism otherwise the next step may become impossible, but it cannot be based on spiritual immaturity either, otherwise we may be tossed about by the latest idea which we encounter and become utterly unstable. Dialogue can be threatening for some people. For others an important consequence is the enriching of their own faith by the reflection which is demanded of them. The second step in dialogue is being willing to listen respectfully to what other believers have to say. Time and again when I visit India I am told of Christians who only went to preach, they had nothing to learn. This is, of course, a gross exaggeration, but there is some truth in it. If we have nothing to learn dialogue is not for us, neither, perhaps is growth in our own religion.

The third step? ... Dialogue is an exploration, its destination for the individual cannot be predicted.

Whether users of this book have a personal religious faith or not, if they really wish to understand any life stance, they could do no better than reflect upon the following words by Max Warren a famous secretary of the Church Missionary Society:

> Our first task in approaching another people, another culture, another religion, is to take off our shoes, for the place we are standing on is holy, else we may find we are treading on men's dreams. More serious still, we may forget that God was here before our arrival.

N.B. Instead of the Christian terms for dates, B.C. and A.D., the following abbreviations tend now to be used in the study of religions:

> B.C.E., Before the Common Era, the internationally used system of dating
> C.E., Common Era.

Religions in the UK: a Multifaith Directory, published in 1993 by the University of Derby, ISBN 0 901437 06 9, is an invaluable guide to anyone wishing to contact a local mosque, synagogue, mandir, gurdwara or vihara, plus Jain, Zoroastrian, Baha'i and other communities other than mainstream Christian. It contains addresses, phone numbers and general information. For Christians see Yellow Pages!

HINDUISM

NILA PANCHOLI

Introduction

The term *Hindu* is derived from *Sindhu* which is the Persian name for the river Indus. The *Aryans* (a Sanskrit word meaning noble) invaded India from the north west and settled in the Indus river valley around 1500 B.C.E. The Persians called India 'the land beyond the Sindhu' and the inhabitants – who were not Muslims – 'the people beyond the Sindhu'. (Words beginning with 's' are often pronounced as 'h' when spoken in Persian. Thus the people living in that part of the sub-continent were referred to as Hindus). In the past Hindu was merely a geographical term for an Indian. As there was no special name for their religion, and as their way of life and religion could not be separated, the word Hindu was eventually given a religious significance.

Many religions in the world are named after their founders to distinguish them from other religions and they date from a specific period. The Hindu religion differs from other religions in this respect. The basis of belief is *Sanatana Dharma*. *Sanatana* means eternal, but the word *dharma* is very difficult to translate into English as there does not seem to be an exact word for it. To a Hindu dharma means that which prevents one from going down, ruining oneself in any manner and which makes for one's welfare, progress and well-being all round. Thus, dharma has more to do with the nature and behaviour of men than with their beliefs. It has numerous meanings in Sanskrit including right conduct, religion, duty, quality, law, justice and moral order. It is generally believed that dharma means right conduct, which may have different meanings. What is right conduct for one, may not be so for another, as for example, *Raja-dharma* (the duties of a king) will be different from *stri-dharma* (the duties of a woman).

Traditionally the king rules and a woman's duty is to marry and to raise a family. In this example *Raja-dharma* (the duties of a king) will be different from *stri-dharma* (the duties of a woman).

Hindus believe that there were no other religions when dharma began. This was the only moral order in the whole world, which taught humanity and righteousness to all mankind. It is said in the *Manu Smriti*, (2, 20) 'All the people of the world would learn from the leaders of this country the lessons for their behaviour'. In fact, all the living faiths of mankind had their origin in Asia – Hinduism, Buddhism, Jainism and Sikhism in India, Confucianism and Taoism in China, Zoroastrianism in Iran, Judaism and Christianity in Palestine (now Israel) and Islam in Arabia.

Sanatana Dharma allows the widest freedom in matters of faith and worship, absolute freedom with regard to beliefs in the nature of God, the soul, the creation and the form of worship. It does not force anybody to accept particular dogmas or ways of worshipping. Hindus may pray to their personal God in any form they desire to visualize him. Hinduism tells everyone to worship God according to his own faith, or dharma. Hence all sorts of religious faith, various forms of worship and diverse kinds of rituals and customs have found their honourable place side by side in Hinduism and are cultivated and developed in harmonious relationship with one another. Professor Radhakrishnan, a philosopher and President of India, wrote 'While it gives absolute liberty in the world of thought, it enjoins a strict code of practice. The theist and the atheist, the sceptic and the agnostic may all be Hindus if they accept the Hindu system of culture and life... what counts is conduct, not belief.' Thus, Hinduism is basically more a matter of conduct than of belief.

There is neither an exclusive, authoritative scripture, nor a 'church' to define and to teach the faith. It is, therefore, hardly surprising that a student finds the Hindu religion confusing. Many people consider that Hinduism consists of numerous deities with monstrous animal shapes, primitive beliefs, superstitions and magical formulae. Yet Hinduism has survived the pressure of Islam for 750 years and that of Christianity for over 150 years. Often it is believed that caste is a characteristic of Hinduism and yet there are recognized sects like the Lingayatas, the Arya Samaj and the Brahmo Sarnaj which do not accept the caste system and openly deny the superiority of the Brahmins. As Gandhiji has said, 'Hinduism is a living organism liable to growth and decay and subject to the laws of nature. One and indivisible at the root, it has grown into a vast tree with innumerable branches.'

The ideas and doctrines which can be considered as characteristic of Hinduism are that God can be understood as the indescribable, Supreme Reality, or Brahman; or as Brahma, Vishnu and Mahesha (Shiva) representing creation, preservation and destruction; or as a personal God – Ishta-Devata – such as Krishna, Rama and Ganesh.

The ultimate aim of the Hindus is to obtain salvation (*moksha*), that is to attain union with God. In order to achieve moksha, a man has to free himself from the chain of births and deaths. The number of births he has to have is determined by his individual actions which he performs at every stage in his life. The duties and actions are termed *karma*. Actions, whether ritualistic, for example offering worship, or social, like caring for one's parents or children, invariably produce their own good and evil effects. The effects of all his karma are cumulative and these shape his life. He can change his future at any stage in life by changing his actions. A man has to control his karma by disciplining his mind and body so that he can break the chain of rebirth. Hinduism teaches that all souls have the chance to attain moksha (salvation) by controlling their karma (actions).

In order to control his activities, disciplines are laid down in Hindu religion for his guidance. A life-span is divided into four stages called *ashramas*. *Brahmacharyashram* is the period of training, discipline and proper education. *Grahasthashram* is the life of a householder and active worker where he fulfils his obligations to society. *Vanaprasthashram* is the life of retirement when the bonds of attachment are being reduced. A person in this stage advises and guides younger people. Finally, a person becomes a *Sanyasi* or a recluse. A *Sanyasi* does not own anything but relies solely on the charity of others for his well-being. He tries to seek his ultimate union with God. Although these divisions of life are ideal and accepted, not many people follow them in practice.

In order to attain moksha, a person must achieve three objectives in life (1) *Dharma* (righteous conduct), (2) *Artha* (acquisition of economic welfare, the life of earthly prosperity) and (3) *Kama* – worldly pleasures, enjoyment of good things in life. The right balance of these three objectives is known as the ideal life in Hinduism. After achieving these three objectives, every individual's aim should be to achieve moksha (liberation) and reunion with God.

Another important doctrine of Hinduism is that of *Avatar* or incarnation. It is said in the *Bhagavad Gita*, 'Whenever there is a decline of *dharma* (righteousness) and rise of *adharma* (unrighteousness), I incarnate myself. For the protection of the good, for the destruction of the wicked and for the establishment of righteousness, I come into being from age to age' (*B.G.* 4, 7 & 8). Thus, Hindus believe that each follower has a spark of 'divinity' in himself and since each has this spark it can be assumed some can have it to a greater extent than others. Those who possess more divine qualities, such as religious teachers of special sanctity, are considered as *avataras*. Hence, Hindus accept the prophets of all religions as manifestations of God, as avataras for re-establishing dharma, or reorganizing society. They would cite Mahatama Gandhi, Jesus or Muhammad as examples of avataras.

The Sanatana Dharma pays respects to all religions. God, according to Hindus, is Infinite, Omniscient, Omnipotent and Omnipresent. He may appear in different forms to different people. There are many ways of reaching Him. Lord Krishna has said in the *Bhagavad Gita* (4:11), 'However men approach me, even so do I welcome them, for the path men take from every side is mine.'

Family Life

To a Hindu, religion is closely related to family life, as the *Bhagavad Gita* says, 'If the family breaks up, the religion will be lost as well.' Most families are extended, which means that children, parents, grandparents, uncles, aunts, and cousins all live together, help each other and make decisions bearing one another's needs in mind, but outside India many Hindu families are now nuclear and some people miss the fun and support of living together.

Just as the State helps the life of people in Britain, a Hindu family is, in essence, a state in itself and helps its members both in difficulties and in pleasure. The size of the joint family may be very large as it may include married brothers, their wives and families, in addition to unmarried brothers and sisters. The whole family lives under the headship and direction of the father, or the grandfather (father's father). Age is respected to the highest degree. If the family house is large enough, all the members of the family live within it. All the belongings are shared between the families. All orphans, widows and aged mothers have the utmost care from other more fortunate members of the family. The head of the family has a very high level of authority over all others, including married sons who may be fathers themselves.

When a male child attains maturity he does not leave the family and start his own life separately, he remains part of the joint family and gives all his loyalty and faithfulness to the family. No child of even very poor families feels neglected. The duties and burdens are shared. Selfish, individualistic motives are not fostered for each contributes to the welfare of all the others. If a son obtains success, his income brings extra comfort to the whole family. Each feels responsible for all the others. In every household the woman is the mother to all the children in it. Cousins feel as if they are really brothers and sisters. In fact the child in a Hindu family does not know the word 'cousin'. When a child mentions to the teacher that he has eleven brothers or sisters in a family, this should not be

17

taken literally as he would automatically include all his cousins as well as his brothers and sisters in the total.

In the event of a death of a father, the eldest son considers it his duty to look after and to care for the joint family. He makes every effort to sacrifice his own personal interests for the sake of the family. A Hindu child can look on the relative who has his welfare very close to his mind as his father. If a child's father is working on the night shift, the child's teacher may be visited by a relative of the family at a school open evening. In this case it should not be taken that parents have no interest in the child's education.

Any new venture is undertaken by the family as a whole. It becomes easier for a family to start a new business because there is a complete exploitation of the personal and family resources in complete harmony and understanding. This explains why many Hindus in this country have been successful in establishing private businesses.

Viewed against this background it becomes clear why marriages are arranged. When a male becomes of marriage-able age, looking for a bride is one of the pleasures of the family. Relatives and friends look for a girl who not only has to perform the duty of a wife but also has to look after the whole family. Account is taken of caste, sub-caste, kinship and horoscope and these are matched before the consent of either party is obtained. Arrangement of marriage is preceded by exhaustive and careful enquiries regarding the family tree and educational, financial and social background of the prospective bride and bridegroom. A marriage is arranged by the relatives of both sides but the groom and the bride are kept informed of all the activities in this connection and given first say in the event of not liking each other. The involvement of more than one generation in the arrangement of a marriage is a good thing as all the members of the family can give their opinions.

The motive behind an arranged marriage is concern for stability; this is not always appreciated by westerners. The bride will make her new home with her husband's parents on her wedding day and it is therefore essential that she comes from a similar background so that adjustment may be as easy as possible. It is romantic to think of a princess marrying a pauper but in practice she would find life sharing a kitchen and the domestic chores with four or five other women difficult if she moved to his house. The family living in the palace might find the intrusion of the pauper uncomfortable and disconcerting, however much he might like the change. At a more everyday level a highly educated only child, brought up in Delhi, might find it difficult to join in a like family of farm workers in one of India's villages. Parents, out of love for their children and concern for the cohesion of this family, would be unlikely to arrange such an ill-considered marriage. Arranging the marriage is not the end of the story, support for the couple and responsibility for their happiness remains the task of the parents long after the wedding day.

Marriage

It is important to remember that the success of the arranged marriage lies in the bride having considerable tolerance and learning to adapt herself to the ways of life of the bride-groom's household. In any good household this is taken into account; every effort is made to make the life of the bride happy but it is usual for the bride to adjust considerably more than the groom's household. A Hindu girl understands this and she normally accepts the whole situation, making herself happy and, in turn, tries to make the groom's household happy. She would eventually take the role of a mother in the joint family system.

At this stage, it should be pointed out that women were, and still are, highly regarded in Hindu society. This esteem temporarily disappeared during the Muslim and British rule. Hindu women have played a significant part in the building and preservation of Indian culture. They have maintained the harmony of Hindu homes and have created beneficial influences upon men. Women have functioned in responsible positions such as queens, teachers, administrators, philosophers, mystics, scholars, poets and politicians. In all these positions Hindu women exhibited calmness, patience, dignity, grace, femininity and a happy family life.

Marriage is considered to be a religious duty in order to provide sons for the joint family system. A Hindu family believes that the bond of marriage is not soluble and this bond continues in the life after death. Divorce in Hindu families was unknown at one time. The laws of India allow this now and western influences seem to be slowly affecting the life of Hindu families in the matter of divorce but it is still regarded as a tragedy, bringing disgrace upon the family.

It would be incomplete if a mention were not made of the emerging change in the practice of arranged marriages among

Hindus now living in the West. In the sub-continent of India, boys and girls have no opportunities to mix socially and the system of arranged marriages works as a whole, though occasionally there are a few exceptions and there may be a few love marriages. In Britain, the structure of society is different. Democracy seems to find its way in youngsters. Boys and girls meet each other socially and at schools and colleges. Provided the educational and social background is satisfactory, the parents are usually pleased to arrange marriages to suit their children. The parents wish to approve of their children's partners even if they do not choose them. At the same time, they would discourage a 'love marriage' if the family background was unsuitable. Thus, an era of semi-arranged marriages seems to be emerging among Hindu families in the West – and sometimes even in India.

Hindu Worship

The worship of God helps to keep material progress balanced by spiritual progress. In order to achieve peace of mind various outer and inner observances are laid down in the scriptures. There must be absolute faith in God, intense love for him and a complete surrender at his lotus feet.

Worship in the Home

Home is the most important place of worship for Hindus. They may have a room, a corner or an alcove set aside for worship (*puja*). This place consists of pictures and images of their chosen God, decorated with tinsel and lights. The mother is usually the person responsible for carrying out daily puja. She rises early in the morning, usually has a quick shower, or a bath, while chanting the name of God, and puts on clean clothes because cleanliness is very important in Hinduism. She may worship God in many ways, such as by washing, dressing or decorating a statue, offering it flowers, incense, light (*diva*), food (*prasad*) and prayers. It is essential to realize that the statue is not worshipped but it is taken as a representation of God. (This is discussed in the section on Image Worship). Vinoba Bhave, a modern Hindu and disciple of Gandhiji says the worship of an image is 'the art of embracing the whole universe in a little object'. As the image of God's *murti*, or form, made manifest for his worshippers, it is treated as one would treat God himself. This statue, as God's representative in personal form, is fundamental to the meaning of puja and is always preserved in rituals.

Prasad is food which has been sanctified by special selection and preparation and then offered to God in love and devotion. As the Lord has created everything for our use and enjoyment, Hindus believe that we should acknowledge our debts to him before beginning to enjoy these things. God provides us with food and if it is consecrated by being offered to him first, we benefit by eating it because we need God to give us strength and provide us with energy to do work to obtain food. It is not that God needs food! In *Bhagavad Gita*, Lord Krishna says, 'If one offers me with love and devotion a leaf, a flower, fruit or water, I will accept it' (*B.G.* 9, 26–27). The Lord is not hungry for our food, but for our love.

In the West, a person may not have time to perform all these rituals every day in which case a *diva* (a wick of cotton wool dipped in ghee and placed in a container) and incense sticks are lit and the prayer said, or the *japp* (repetition of mantra e.g. Om, Namah Shivay or Om, Namah Bhagavate Vasudevaya) chanted while the person is on his or her way to work. A man usually says the Gayatri mantra at this time. This is taken from *Rigveda* (3, 62, 10) 'Let us meditate on the most excellent light of the Creator. May He guide our minds and inspire us with understanding.' This prayer is just as important to the Hindus as the Lord's prayer is to Christians. Sometimes a record of prayer may be heard while the family has breakfast. Usually only when the puja is completed does an orthodox Hindu eat and carry out the duties of the day.

In the evening when we need to light our rooms, the diva is lit before other lights are switched on. At this time some families get together and pray. In this way, the traditions of puja among Hindus may be passed to the young. From what has been said so far it can be seen that home worship is extremely important. In fact, worship is an essential aspect of Hindu family life. Going to the temple (*mandir*) is far less important and plays no part at all in the religion of some Hindus.

Temple Worship

Temples in India may be very large, beautifully designed and wonderfully built in carved stone, or be very small and simple. The latter are called *dehris*. In the middle of the temple is the central shrine, known as *garbhagriha*, the home of the chief divinity, perhaps Krishna with his wife Radha. The ceilings are beautifully carved or decorated with paintings from Hindu mythology. The temple might also contain a large hall where the sacred literature is recited for all who wish to listen. Large temples in India also provide a rest-house for pilgrims. In the West, however, schools, church halls or other premises are bought and converted into temples. The shrine, or garbhagriha, may be at one end of the room on the platform and the ceiling may be gaily decorated with tinsel and coloured lights. On the shrine, one would see fruit and

A room in a house has been converted into a temple. Here Hindus gather in front of the shrine to worship God by singing hymns.

flowers which have been offered, *ghee* (clarified butter), diva, incense sticks for burning, *kumkum*, (red paste used for symbolic marking on the foreheads of worshippers), a fivefold lamp, bells to ring to call the deities' attention and slots in which to make a financial offering.

In the hall of a temple there are shelves or pigeon-holes to keep the shoes which must be removed before entering the shrine room. Leather (especially in the form of footwear) is polluting and should not be brought near the area where worship is to take place.

A temple, or church, has some kind of community or social function in the West, whereas in India it may only be used for individual worship. This is because a Hindu in Britain has no time to socialize with his own people and keep in touch with his culture at work so the temple is the only place for him to do this. In India socializing takes place both at work and in the village during the general routine of life. In the West, rituals themselves require a gathering of people. The people are drawn together in the temple on festive occasions when they have a chance to dress up and to meet their friends. A *mandir* is usually used for weddings, for language classes such as Gujarati, Hindi and English, for giving discourses by the eminent religious speakers – Gurus or experts who have a deep knowledge of Hinduism – and occasionally for youth activities. A priest has to perform rituals in a temple similar to those performed by a Hindu householder, that is to awaken, bath, dress and feed the statue before visitors arrive to worship. *Arti* is performed twice a day.

Ritual of Arti

Arti is a ritual in which a fivefold lamp and incense sticks are lit. The worshippers stand up facing the shrine and the priest rotates the fivefold lamp around the shrine with one hand and rings a bell with the other hand. Other worshippers join him in ringing bells, beating drums, blowing a conch and playing all sorts of percussion and other musical instruments. Everyone sings the arti prayer. Five symbolic features are represented in arti, namely fire, water, sound, smell (incense) and ether. When the arti prayer is finished, the priest spoons water round the lamp, turns towards the worshippers and directs the purificatory powers in their direction by waving his hand across the top of the flame. The lamp in the plate is afterwards passed on to the worshippers who pass their hand over the flame, then over their faces, eyes and heads after putting their contribution in the plate. The offering of food (prasad) to God is given after the ritual and later worshippers are given their share.

Arti should usually be conducted between about 20 minutes before and after sunrise and sunset. These times, however, cannot be adhered to because they do not suit the working community in western countries and so they have to be changed. Arti may not be attended by many people in the West due to the cold weather, distance and time involved in travelling to a mandir and the problems of working on a shift basis where time off for temple worship is not regarded as essential.

Throughout the ritual, children are not reprimanded for fidgeting, talking, walking about or leaving the room as they are at liberty to do what they like. Major services at a temple are usually held on Sundays in Europe, America and Africa to enable as many people as possible to attend.

Yoga

Some people worship by practising yoga. Yoga is not just a system of physical discipline with difficult postures and breath-controlling exercises, as believed by westerners. The word *Yoga* is derived from the Sanskrit word *Yuj* to join or concentrate, so yoga is the way by which the soul is released and united with God. By practising meditation they surrender themselves unto God and control their thoughts. They may also chant the sacred symbol for God – *Om*. The aim of Yoga is to attain supreme consciousness with sound mind and healthy body. There are other kinds of Yoga, e.g. Karma Yoga (Yoga of action), Bhakti Yoga (the Yoga of love and devotion) and Jnana Yoga (the Yoga of knowledge), each aiming at the uplift of mankind and eternal liberation.

Image and Symbol Worship

To a Hindu, every physical object is a manifestation of God. Any form can be used for the focus of worship if it symbolizes divinity for the devotee. As a matter of fact, almost everybody, Hindus or non-Hindus, uses some kind of symbol during the time of worship: for example, a church is a symbol. Mahatma Gandhi said, 'I think that idol worship is part of human nature. We hanker after symbolism. Why should one be more composed in a church than elsewhere? No Hindu considers an image to be God. I do not consider idol-worship a sin.'

Westerners often wonder why Hindus worship 330 million gods. To a Hindu, the millions of gods are really the manifestation of the many aspects of one truth – *Brahman* (God). The goal of every Hindu is to achieve *moksha*, union with Brahman. Symbols or images are merely external aids for the upward march of the soul.

Images are usually used in worship to represent God. All the organs and instruments of any god are symbolic. It is the duty of the devotees to take the meaning of these in the spirit of righteousness.

Lord Ganesha

According to Hindu scriptures Lord Ganesha, or Ganapati, the first son of Shiva, is the remover of obstacles and bestower of fortune. He is the god who is always worshipped first in all

Hindu shrines are often rich in their variety. The ten-armed goddess Durga is a reminder that divinity is not limited as we are, and may be female as well as male – though transcending both. The Buddha, and sometimes Jesus or Guru Nanak, may have a place in the shrine, as well as such symbols as Om or the swastika.

functions, rituals, ceremonies and every important undertaking.

Even followers of Buddhism and Jainism, which exclude worship of God, pay homage to Ganesha. The very popular image of Lord Ganesha has four hands. In the right hands he holds a rosary (*mala*) and a goad (*ankusha*). The rosary represents the encircling time, or *kala*. According to the Eastern thinkers, kala is also called the presiding deity of Death. The rosary in the hand of Ganesha indicates that he controls Death, giving assurance to the devotees. As the elephant driver uses the goad to control the elephant, so Lord Ganesha uses the goad to regulate the activities of all beings. The goad in the hand of Lord Ganesha indicates that the fate of a person is in his hand. So, all should worship him for a better future. In his left hands, Lord Ganesha holds a hatchet for the destruction of ignorance, and round sweetmeats as a reward for those whose ignorance is destroyed.

The snake, the representative of death, under his chin, denotes that he is the controller of death. His big belly denotes that the devotee should be firm and solemn, he should digest different arguments like food. The fact that his body is that of an elephant and his vehicle is a mouse, indicates that he is the master of all creatures, from the tiny mouse to the biggest elephant. His sacred face represents Om, the sacred syllable, which is chanted before all vedic hymns. The big ears indicate that he has heard many *shastras* (scriptures) and the small eyes show that he is very meditative and possesses sharp sight. Thus this symbol silently teaches the devotee that he should listen more and be watchful. Shiva, Vishnu and other gods also carry certain symbols which are significant.

It is interesting to note that God is also worshipped as Mother in Hindu religion. This concept of God as Mother is alien to westerners who use male terms such as Father to describe God. Goddess Sarasvati, Lakshmi and Parvati are inseparable powers of Lord Brahma, Vishnu and Shiva – Trimurti of Hindu religion. The mother goddess has several names and forms: Durga, Kali, Ambika, Lakshmi, Sarasvati, Bhadrakali and Bhuvaneshwari.

Goddess Durga is seated on a lion, with ten hands, each with some weapons or gift. In her right hands, the mother is holding a disc, a sword, a bow and a rosary. The disc represents the wheel of time. Time is indeed the great killer, but in the hand of Goddess Durga it is under her control and she herself is beyond time. Those who are devoted to the Mother shall conquer time and become immortal. It further indicates that the Mother shall destroy any force that may obstruct the progress of the devotee. The sword is regarded as the weapon that destroys ignorance, indicating that she is the bestower of knowledge and destroyer of ignorance. The bow assures the devotees against any demon. The rosary in the Mother's hand reminds the devotee that he should perform the chanting of mantras with a rosary always in his hand. In her left hands, the Goddess is holding a conch, a mace, the lotus and a trident, the famous weapons of Lord Rudra. The conch represents the four kinds of sound described in the vedas; in the hand of the Mother it indicates that the voice and the life of all creatures is in her hand. The mace, the instrument of destruction, shows that those who surrender at her feet have no fear of death. A lion, the king of animals, is seen lying ready for the service of the Mother.

The lotus is an ancient and favourite symbol of the cosmos, and of man. The lotus seeds, even before they germinate, contain perfectly formed leaves in miniature. The roots of the lotus in the mud represent material life, the stalk passing through the water typifies existence in the astral world and the flower, floating on the water opening to the sky, is emblematic of the spiritual being. The lotus in the hand of the Goddess indicates purity, love and harmony – qualities which are the essence of righteousness. The lotus in the hand of Durga reminds the devotees that if they desire the favours of the Mother Almighty, they must possess a pure and tender heart.

During the festivals of Nava-Ratri and Chaitra, Goddess Durga is worshipped systematically in every part of India.

Lord Vishnu

Lord Vishnu is widely worshipped. He is called upon for the preservation of the universe, for the protection of the good and for destruction of evil-doers. He is thought to descend to earth in a human or animal incarnation (*avatar*) to save the world from the imminent danger of total destruction. The ten incarnations of Lord Vishnu are as follows:

The Fish (*matsya*). Lord Vishnu took the incarnation of a fish when the earth was overwhelmed by a universal flood. He became a one-horned small golden fish and grew until he was enormously long. He is said to have saved the human race by towing a ship with a rope attached to the horn.

The Tortoise (kurma). Many divine treasures were lost in the universal flood, most importantly *amrit* (nectar), the divine elixir of immortality. Gods and demons looked for nectar by churning the cosmic ocean, using the mountain Mandar as a churning stick. Lord Vishnu came down as a tortoise to help the weaker gods. Lord Vishnu as a tortoise supported the mountain on its curved back which enabled the gods to obtain nectar.

The Boar (varaha). This incarnation was to destroy the demon Hiranyaksha who had persecuted men and gods, casting the earth once more into the depths of the cosmic ocean. However, Hiranyaksha had obtained a boon from Lord Brahma by which he could not be killed by any god or animal, with the exception of the boar which he had forgotten to mention. Therefore, Lord Vishnu took the form of a boar, killed the demon Hiranyaksh and raised the earth out of the ocean on his tusks.

The Man-lion (nara-simha). Lord Vishnu assumed the form of a man-lion to kill the demon Hiranyakasipu. This demon king had prohibited the worship of Lord Vishnu and insisted that he be worshipped instead. His son Prahlad was a great devotee of Lord Vishnu and refused to give up the worship of God. Hiranyakasipu tortured his son Prahlad in many ways but Prahlad did not yield. Hiranyakasipu also had secured a boon from Brahma – he could not be killed by god, man or beast, either by day or night, either inside or outside his house. Hence Lord Vishnu as man-lion killed him at twilight on the threshold of his doorway and delivered his devotee Prahlad from his father's tyranny.

The Dwarf (vamana). The fifth incarnation was of a dwarf. The demon king Bali had conquered the celestial kingdom and driven the gods out of their native land. The harassed gods approached Lord Vishnu for his help and he came down to the earth in human form as the dwarf King Bali who used to give alms to Brahmins. Vamana, dressed as a Brahmin, approached Bali and requested as much land as he could cover in three strides. As soon as the request was granted, Vamana grew so terribly tall that in two strides he measured the whole kingdom of Bali. There being no place for the third stride, it was put on Bali's head. Surrendering completely, Bali was exiled from his kingdom. Thus the earth and heaven were won back for men and gods by Lord Vishnu.

The Rama with axe (Parasurama). At one time the warriors had become very powerful and were exercising tyranny over all men, even persecuting the Brahmins. Then Lord Vishnu took human form to protect the Brahmins and came into the world as Parasurama. He destroyed the whole race of Kshatriyas in twenty-nine campaigns.

Rama. The seventh incarnation was of Sri Rama, to save the world from the tyranny of the ten-headed demon king, Ravana, who ruled Sri-Lanka. Ravana had obtained a boon from Lord Shiva in which he could not be killed by the hand of gods, or demons. Thus protected, he had waged war on gods, persecuted sages and ravaged the people. The gods requested Lord Vishnu to destroy Ravana. Lord Vishnu appeared on earth in human form as Rama, because Ravana had been too proud to ask not to be killed by a man!

Krishna. Incarnated as Krishna, Lord Vishnu destroyed the demons Kansa and Shisupala. Krishna is the most popular and beloved of all the incarnations and there is no Hindu who does not know his name. Lord Vishnu manifests himself fully; in Krishna, we find the ideal child, the ideal youth, the ideal lover, the ideal soldier, the ideal statesman and the ideal philosopher. He gave us the *Shrimad Bhagavad Gita*, the cream of Hindu philosophy, which teaches us the path of devotion and the philosophy of action. The *Bhagavad Gita* is considered by the Hindus the greatest teaching on ethics and morals.

Lord Buddha. The ninth incarnation was the Lord Buddha who taught doctrines to bring back the people who had gone astray. There are two outstanding features in him. Firstly, he claimed no superhuman origin, nor did he ever say he was in communion with any supernatural being. Purity, love and service were his characteristics. Secondly, he upheld the truth that man is the maker of his own destiny.

Kalki. The tenth incarnation, that of Kalki, is yet to come. It is believed that in this present age of evil (*kaliyuga*) men will degenerate so much that even Lord Vishnu will not be able to save them except by destruction and building a new world. It is believed that for this purpose Lord Vishnu will appear as Kalki riding on a charger, waving the sword of destruction in his right hand.

These incarnations are significant to Hindus as they are also based on evolution, representing forms of life from the lowest to the highest.

The *Aum* Symbol (*Om*)

The word and symbol *Aum* in Sanskrit is fundamental to Hinduism. The scriptures say that *Aum* and *Atha* were spoken by Lord Brahma, the creator. According to the *Bhagavad Gita*, Aum is the best name for God and it must be uttered regularly. The symbol is composed of three basic letters A, U, M, from which it is said the alphabet and language were developed.

Everything is pervaded by Aum and Aum is identical with God. According the Acharya Vinoba Bhave, the Sanskrit word *Aum* and the Latin word *Omne* are both derived from the same root. Both these words convey the concept of omniscience, omnipresence and omnipotence.

Aum is used in the praise and prayer of all deities. Realizing the importance of Aum, the devotees may say the mantra *Aum Namah Shivaya*. The meaning of the word Aum is vast and abstract. By using it the devotees concentrate and unify their senses, will, intellect and emotions on the name of the Lord to meditate on the full meaning of prayer.

Religious Practices

The important precepts of Hinduism are that 'You must respect your mother as God, your father as God, your teacher as God and your guest as God.' this gives us the idea that family life is of paramount importance in Hinduism and awareness of God can be attained by performing one's duty towards the family first.

Hindus believe that one should try to find God who is hidden within the heart of every being. Thus Hindus will offer food and water even to the unknown persons coming to their house. The scriptures say 'Offering food to others is the best among all donations because food is the primary need of all the living beings. None can do without, even for a day. Hence, the best donation is to offer food to the needy.' In fact the Sanskrit word for guest is *Atithi* which literally means 'undated'. The person who comes without making any prior appointment is regarded as the honoured guest. Every pious Hindu is expected to keep some food aside for the arrival of an unexpected guest so that no one should be turned away hungry from his door. A Hindu will keep some portion of food from his own plate for animals (especially cows), birds, insects and even ants. The ancestors are not forgotten and special food is offered to them on certain days by Hindus.

There are sixteen *samskaras*, or purificatory rites, associated with certain major events in a person's life, from conception to beyond cremation, prescribed for Hindus and most of them take place at home, except that of *sanyasa*, or renunciation and cremation. Even the wedding ceremony can take place at home if the house is large enough. This is often the case in India. In the West, however, the marriage ceremony takes place at home first and then the remainder of the ceremony is conducted in a temple or a hall. Hindu life is therefore more home-centred than temple-centred.

Birth

When a baby is born in a Hindu family there is great rejoicing

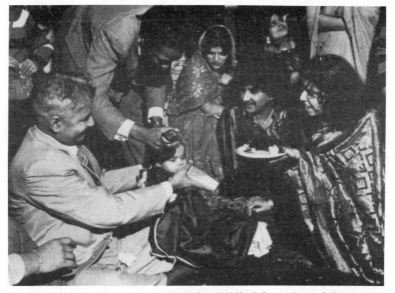

An important ceremony in a Hindu child's life is that of shaving the hair – the rite of mundan. *It removes the last vestiges of birth pollution and is a joyful family celebration.*

and the Brahmin priest is informed of the date and exact time of its birth. This information is very useful in preparing the baby's horoscope. Hindus accord significance to astrology at the important stages of their lives. The priest will then suggest suitable syllables from which the parents select a name for the baby. This is one of the reasons why Hindus do not register their baby's name immediately in western countries.

Many boys go through a ceremony when they have their first haircut. The symbolic meaning of this ceremony is that bad *karma* (actions) from the previous life are to be removed in the present one.

Upanayana

One of the important ceremonies is the *Upanayana*, or sacred thread ceremony. This is regarded as very important in the life of a Hindu boy, especially to one in a Brahmin family. In this ceremony, the boy who is ready to receive religious education from his spiritual teacher (guru), is given a thread with three strands, which he wears on the left shoulder across

33

the body to the right hip. There are many reasons why there are three strands: they may be to remind the wearer to control his mind, speech and body; they can also stand for the major Hindu deities, Brahma Vishnu and Shiva, or the states of wakefulness, dream and sleep. The sacred thread is a symbol of his second birth; the first birth is when he is born from his mother, the second when he begins to learn from his guru. In previous times the boy would have left his home for a few years at the age of eight or nine to receive education from his guru. Now the custom has been modified to suit present day circumstances and, instead of leaving his family, he stays at home. So the custom is for him to say goodbye to his family, 'beg' for food from his mother, set off for a few moments on a simulated journey to his guru with a staff and begging bowl and then return home.

Marriage

The marriage ceremony takes place at the bride's home, or the hall hired by the bride's parents. The marriage day, and time, are fixed by the priest by referring to the religious calendar. A great amount of preparation takes place before the wedding. Although it is illegal to give a dowry, the bride's parents try to give as much as they can afford to their daughter. Many saris are bought for the bride, as well as for the bridegroom's relations, by the bride's parents. Many relations of the extended family arrive a few days before the wedding to help in the preparation. The bride takes a special bath and the hands and soles of her feet are decorated with an orange plant dye, henna, in very intricate patterns. The wedding dress and jewellery vary from region to region, but usually the bride wears a red sari with gold thread embroidered throughout. For the wedding day, the bride is as resplendent as her family can make her.

At the beginning of the ceremony, Lord Ganesha is worshipped. A special canopy (*mandap*), decorated with tinsel, balloons and coloured lights, is erected for the wedding ceremony. When the bridegroom's party arrives, they are welcomed by the bride's mother as well as a girl from the family, who carries a little pot and a coconut on her head, and they perform a welcome ritual. The marriage ceremony is performed by the priest in the presence of the relations of both the bride and bridegroom. The parents of the bride

At a Hindu wedding two families rather than only two individuals are united. The couple sit surrounded by relations.

welcome him in the same way as they would welcome God, by washing his feet and giving him the best of everything. When the bride is given away by both the mother and father, the genealogy of the bride and bridegroom is recited. The sacred fire, *agni*, the witness of the ceremony, is then lit and many fine offerings are made while reciting mantras from the *Vedas*. A white cord is attached to the shoulders of the couple and seven steps (*saptapadi*) are taken around the fire. Each step has a meaning – 'One step for food, two for strength, three for increasing wealth, four for good fortune, five for children, six for the seasons and seven for everlasting friendship.' At the end of each complete round the bride is told to touch a stone (*pashana*) and remain stable like the stone, that is renouncing the attachment of her own parents and family and, instead, loving the bridegroom's family. Prayers for good fortune and peace conclude the ceremony. There are then celebrations for family and friends in which a great deal of money is spent.

Death

Antyesti, the last rite, is a funeral oblation. Hindus believe that bodies should be cremated and not buried. The eldest son, or nearest male relative, lights the funeral pyre. Outside India he may just stand by the coffin and see it pass into the furnace. Verses from the *Bhagavad Gita* are chanted. Hindus believe that 'as a man leaves his old clothes and puts on new ones, so the soul leaves his body and moves to a new one', as stated in the *Gita* (2, 22). Thus death is nothing to be afraid of. On the third day after the cremation (or at any other convenient day) the ashes of the dead are thrown into a river, preferably the river Ganges. The last Antyesti rite is performed on the tenth, eleventh and twelfth day after cremation when offerings of rice balls (*pinda*) and milk are made to the dead, usually by the eldest son.

Hindus consider all days as holy days and they have no day of rest in the week. Astrology plays a large part in observing these holy days. Certain observances are carried out on one chosen day during the week, e.g. Monday is dedicated for the worship of Lord Shiva, for getting a good husband, wealth and knowledge. Tuesday is for worship to Goddess Durga, for progeny, health and wealth. Thursday is dedicated to the Guru or spiritual teacher. Saturday is dedicated to Hanumanji. On the day that is chosen in the week, the people eat only one meal a day. Besides these weekly observances people also observe *Ekadashi* (eleventh day of all fortnights). On these days people only eat fruit and nuts as no grain is allowed. Thus Hinduism is a way of life, practised day by day so each day has a meaning.

Hindu Scriptures

The Hindu scriptures are divided into two parts, the *shrutis* (what is heard) and the *smritis* (what is remembered). The *vedas* are the *shrutis* and the *Puranas, Ramayana, Mahabharata* and *Dharma-shashtras* are the *smritis*.

The *Shrutis*

The vedas, the oldest books in the library of man, are divine knowledge and were revealed by God to the great ancient *Rishis* (seers) of India. The word 'veda' is derived from the sanskrit *vid* to know, hence veda means knowledge. The vedas are a record of inspired wisdom and deep inner experience. They are written in poetic form, invested with deep inner meanings and magical potency. The four vedas are: *Rigveda, Yajurveda, Samaveda* and *Atharvaveda*. All four vedas contain high philosophical and divine knowledge. Their aim is permanent peace, prosperity and eternal liberation.

The Rigveda is the main book of hymns. In the Yajurveda there are mainly sacrificial formulae in both prose and verse to be chanted at a sacrifice (*yagna*). The Samaveda is composed of many verses from the Rigveda set to music for singing during the sacrifice. The Atharvaveda abounds mainly in spells and incantations in verse to be used for many other purposes than the spiritual.

There are four *Upa-vedas*, or subordinate words of the vedas. *Ayurveda* deals with the science of medicine and is the combination of anatomy, physiology, hygiene, sanitary science, surgery and other curative and preventative sciences. *Dhanurveda* deals with military science such as the science of archery. This was necessary to protect the country, but by fighting only in self-defence. *Gandharva veda* deals with the science and art of music and dance such as Bharat Natyam. *Sthaptya veda* covers engineering, architecture, sculpture, painting, drawing and higher mathematics of every type. Thus the vedas give an all–round knowledge of both secular and spiritual life.

The *Upanishads* come at the end of the vedas, being the fourth and final section. They are also known as *Vedanta* (the end of the vedas). They refer back constantly to the vedas, saying 'Thus have we heard from sages of old'.

'Upanishad' means sitting down near the preceptor. This refers to the disciple sitting near his guru (teacher) to gain vedic wisdom. They are in question and answer form between the guru and pupil. There are 120 Upanishads but only ten are of great importance. The Upanishads give the most important teaching of the Hindu religion – the doctrine of the Brahman and the Atman (God and the soul).

The *Smritis*

The *smritis* take the form of epics and, in contrast with vedas, are thought of as human in origin. They narrate events which actually happened, thus they are known as *Itihasa*, or history, in India. In the evenings, people gather to listen to stories from the epics, by specially trained story-tellers. Even the most illiterate labourer would know them.

The story of the *The Ramayana* represents, through Lord Rama, an obedient son, a grateful disciple, a generous brother, an ideal husband, a man of true promise, a dutiful king, a great warrior, a forbearing personality and a perfect human being. He can never be forgotten by any Hindu, to whatever caste or creed he may belong. It narrates the unjust exile of Rama, the capture of Sita by the demon king Ravana, and the rescue of Sita by Hanumanji – the monkey God. Rama administered his kingdom ideally for the benefit of mankind, bringing peace and happiness to all the people. *The Ramayana*, written by Valmiki, and a later version by Tulsidas, is a poem containing 48,000 lines which is a source of guidance and instruction to the millions of people in India. *Ramayana* is not only a literary work but is a cultural analysis of the highest of ideals of the Hindu life.

The *Mahabharata* is the longest poem ever written containing 100,000 verses, making it probably seven times the length of Homer's *Iliad* and *Odyssey* combined. It is often called the fifth *veda*. There is a saying in Sanskrit, 'What is not in this epic, is not in India', showing that it is the ocean of Hindu knowledge. As well as being an epic, it contains philosophy, rituals and mythology. It describes the war between two families, the Pandavas and the Kauravas who were cousins. The Pandavas were five brothers renowned for their faith in dharma and the Kauravas were a hundred brothers who were evil-minded. A historical battle was fought at Kurukshetra in the Punjab and was won by the Pandavas. According to the *Mahabharata*, righteousness is the source of progress of a nation and wickedness is the cause of peril.

The epics have been used as material for dramas, literature and songs for thousands of years. They have been translated into various languages to familiarize millions of people with them. They represent the civilization, advanced in morality, spiritualism, science and technology, of the ancient Hindus. Sri Jawaharlal Nehru rightly said 'I do not think any person can understand India or her people fully without possessing a knowledge of the two magnificent epics that are India's pride and treasure'.

The *Bhagavad Gita* can be said to be the cream of Hindu philosophy. It is a poem of approximately 700 verses and is part of the *Mahabharata*. It is a dialogue between Arjuna and Lord Krishna in the battlefield of Kurukshetra. Arjuna was stricken with grief, compassion and doubt at the thought of killing friends, relatives and teachers in the army of his enemies. Krishna told Arjuna about the immortality of the soul – the body may die but the soul is indestructible. He told Arjuna that as a member of the Kshatriya (warrior) caste his duty was to fight without thought of the consequences. Thus the Gita teaches one to do one's own duty to the best of one's ability yet not get caught up with the fruits of the work.

The *Gita* teaches the way of knowledge (*jnana-yoga*), the way of works (*karma-yoga*) and the way of devotion (*bhakti-yoga*) to a personal god. The last is the easiest and most effective way of God-realization because one comes into contact with an *avatar* (God-incarnation) and remains under his guidance.

The *Gita* teaches the social nature of man and does not say that people should seek salvation in lonely forests but in the midst of life. It teaches that the most important way of life is to work and to dedicate all the fruits to God – by complete surrender to him.

There are 18 principal *puranas* and 18 less important ones. Each one is a mixture of mythology, history, philosophy and geographical knowledge. They also give accounts of the creation of the world.

The *Dharma-Shastras* (scriptures of the *Dharma*) are known as smritis explaining the religious codes of the Dharma, the foremost of which is the *Manu-smriti*. These books, as well as the epics and the puranas, are guides to social living under different circumstances and in different times.

There are many Indian poets who have written hymns and devotional songs such as Jayadev, Mirabai (1504), Narsinha Mehta (1415–1481), Chaitanya (1485–1533), Namadeva, Tukaram (17th century) and many others.

The Hindu scriptures contain a vast range of knowledge, the quality of which is truly remarkable. For instance, the stories of the universe contained in the hymns of the Vedas relate to our present-day understanding of the cosmos, in spite of the fact that they were known as early as 2500 B.C.E.. (It is interesting that they reveal such a remarkably sophisticated knowledge of the universe 4,000 years before the invention of the radio telescope.) The Hindu knowledge of mathematics, psychology and metaphysics revealed in the scriptures is also considerable.

Class and Caste System

The Classes

Hindu society is divided into four classes which are termed *varnas*. (*Varna* means colour in Sanskrit). The earliest reference to the four classes is in the Purusha Sukta of the *Rigveda* (X, 90, 11–12) where they are described as having sprung from the body of Brahma, The *Brahmins*, the high class, are said to have originated from the head of the Brahma, the *Kshatriyas*, the warrior class, from his shoulders, the *Vaishyas* or business and trading communities, from his thighs and the *Shudras*, or labouring class, from his feet.

As the head of the social hierarchy, the Brahmin's traditional duty is to study and teach, to give and receive gifts and to perform religious ceremonies. He is devoted to intellectual, mental and spiritual activities. The *Kshatriya* maintains law and order and protects the territory from enemies and internal troubles. He is the leader, and the arm of society. The Vaishya's chief function is to breed cattle, to till the earth, to pursue trade and to lend money. He is the source of economic welfare. The Shudra belongs to the menial and labouring class which serves the other three classes and is known as the working class. Thus each person has a place in society and a function to fulfil. It is said in *Manu Smriti* (X, 97) 'It is better to do one's own duty (*dharma*) badly than another's well.'

The principle of the class system has a lot of influence on duties in life. The Brahmin's dharma is to lead a disciplined, religious life. It would be sinful for a Brahmin to kill in battle, while it is the normal duty of a Kshatriya to fight, or to take life in hunting. It is natural for a Brahmin to study and to repeat the vedas, but it would be a sin for a Shudra to do so. On the other hand, a Shudra may drink alcohol, which is considered to be a great sin for a Brahmin. Thus each class has its own standards of conduct.

Even in classless societies, people are divided into intellectuals, or saintly persons, soldiers, business people with commercial abilities, and humble people who can serve the society best with their manual labour. These four divisions of labour, or duties, have existed for a long time in human society. Western society is not free from a class system.

The *Gita* (4:13) says 'The fourfold *varnas* have been created by Me on the basis of quality (*guna*) and action (*karma*)'. Lord Krishna indicates that each should do the job to which he is best fitted. The emphasis here is on guna (quality, aptitude) and karma (action, function) and not birth.

This doctrine of guna is one of the basic notions of Hindu thought. There are three basic qualities which make up a human personality. These are termed *Satva, Rajas* and *Tamas*.

Satva is the state of mental purity, the state of equilibrium – the balanced personality, with the qualities of serenity, purity and forgiveness. Anyone with these qualities is termed *Satvic*. The Brahmins are dominant in the *Satva guna*. They have serenity, purity, forgiveness, knowledge and realization and belief in God.

Rajas is energy, restlessness, misery, greed, fighting ability in the face of aggression; in fact, a personality where the egoistic characteristics predominate. The Kshatriyas exhibit lordliness and fighting ability in battle.

The third guna, *Tamas*, represents qualities of restlessness, impurity, sleep and lethargy where all evil qualities predominate. Vaishyas are in the mode of passion and dullness.

These qualities are compounded in different proportions in all individuals as a result of one's actions in previous existences and environment. The fourfold division of Hindu society was based on the predominance and combination of these three qualities, or gunas. Within this fourfold division each individual has to follow his own inborn nature and thus arrive at his possible perfection. According to the *Gita*, the four classes are not determined by birth but by psychological characteristics which fit a person for definite functions in society.

In religious scriptures, class is not looked upon as a matter of birth but is determined by conduct and character. This is illustrated in *Mahabharata*, Vana Parva, 180, where Yudhisthira defined Brahmins in terms of their behaviour (truthful, forgiving, kind, and so on) and pointed out that a person should not be considered a Brahmin just because he was born in a Brahmin family, or he need not be a Shudra even though he came from a Shudra family. It has been noted that Shudras were scholars, statesmen or saints, whilst Brahmins have been known to have engaged in non-intellectual trades.

Gandhiji, in talking about *Varna-dharma* said, 'By their discovery and application of certain laws of nature, the peoples of the West have easily increased their material possessions. Similarly, Hindus by their discovery of this irresistible social tendency (*Varna-dharma*) have been able to achieve in the spiritual field what no other nation in the world has achieved. 'It should be remembered that Gandhiji's defence of Varnasrama-dharma does not mean that he supported the caste system as it existed in his time.

Caste System

The Indian class structure existed 5,000 years ago. With the passage of time, many different tribes came under the influence of Hindu religion and culture and the caste system developed out of the multi-racial nature of Indian society. This began when sons adopted their father's professions and occupations even though they did not possess the required qualities, or guna. It is essential at this stage to distinguish between classes (*varna*) and castes (*jati*). There are only four classes and they are stable, but castes are innumerable. Castes rise and fall in the social scale, sometimes old castes die out and new ones are formed, but the varnas (classes) remain the same.

Both classes and castes seem to have different origins. It is very difficult to trace the origin of the caste system. It may be the response of many small and primitive peoples who were forced to come to terms with a more complex economic and social system. When wave after wave of invaders came into India, Hindu society was not strong enough to withstand the repeated pressure on the Hindu religion. The people started to form groups on the basis of occupation, locality and relation-ship to ward off conversions. The groups also introduced the fear of exclusion from the caste group, producing a kind of social boycott. Thus grouping into castes and sub-castes took place and worked against many invasions. Eventually the system became rigid. Only now is that rigidity diminishing.

The main features of castes are (1) *Heredity* i.e. one cannot change one's caste by choice, it is determined by birth; (2) *Endogamy* i.e. every member of a caste must marry a member of the same caste and may not marry outside it; (3) *Commensal restrictions* – these are regulations regarding the acceptance of food and drink from members of other castes, e.g. a Brahmin

43

may not eat with, or accept food from, a *mistry* (carpenter, or joiner).

There exists a complex hierarchy of castes, each maintaining a distant relationship with the other castes. It is thought to be impure to deal with certain work e.g. clearing night-soil, tanning leather, disposing of animal corpses, butchering, brewing alcoholic liquor. The people who did these kinds of jobs were described as untouchables. Members of this caste were not allowed to make contact with those of the higher castes. Unfortunately, by the nature of their work, they remained unclean and unhygienic and they had to dwell in special quarters outside the village boundaries and were not allowed in places of worship and public places. Gandhiji attempted to change the status of untouchables naming them *Harijans* – 'children of God'.

The caste system as social order had some advantages. Each caste had a vocation of its own. Every member could get his occupation as a birthright which could solve economic competition and unemployment problems. Each caste attained skill through working hard for generations in the same type of work. Along with the institution of the Hindu family, caste has preserved the Hindu race and its civilization. Caste has done the same work for many centuries as was done by the medieval trade guilds in Europe. Caste preserved religious learning by isolating the Brahmin caste and giving them the exclusive duty and privilege of teaching. It also preserved manual skills and knowledge of the arts and industries by compelling boys to follow the profession of their fathers.

In the two epics, *Ramayana* and *Mahabharata*, birth has not been given much importance. Janaka, a Kshatriya (by birth), a king in the Ramayana, was the most famous *Rishi* (seer or religious man) of his time, and Parashurama, a Brahmin by birth, was the most renowned warrior. Drona was the preceptor of archery and military science, while Vidura, the king's brother, was the most highly respected devotee and sage. It is also noteworthy that in Hindu literature most admired characters were half-castes, e.g. Vidura was the son of a Shudra woman. Vyasa, the compiler of the Vedas, was born of a fisherwoman, Parasara of a Chandala woman, and Vasishtha was the son of a prostitute.

In the scriptures, inter-caste marriage was frowned upon though *anuloma* (marriage where the husband was of a higher class than the wife) was not completely disapproved of. On the other hand, *pratiloma* (marriage where the wife's status was higher than that of the husband) was always frowned upon. For example, in the *Mahabharata* (Adi Parva) King Yayati marries Devayani, daughter of the Brahmin guru Sukra-charya. There are some other examples of pratiloma marriage in Hindu literature. This may be compared with the situation in Victoria England when, for instance, a peer married an actress; he would not incur the same scorn as the lady who married her groom.

There is a great variation in the number and nature of the castes in each village. Caste customs and rules vary greatly from region to region. The pollution attached to the low castes could be transmitted to higher castes in many ways, such as by touching, by eating prohibited foods, etc. Each caste regards certain other castes as a source of pollution under certain circumstances. A caste prohibits the polluting influences of lower castes by endogamy and commensality.

The Buddha, Guru Nanak, Kabir, Tukaram, Ram Mohan Roy, Gandhiji and many other reformers have been opposed to caste-divisions and many anti-caste movements have taken place throughout Indian history.

The caste system is now outlawed by the Indian constitution. Untouchability has been made illegal and places of worship are open for everyone. Under the new law, marriages between Hindus of all castes have been made legal, e.g. an untouchable man may now marry a Brahmin girl. Special places and scholarships at colleges and universities and government appointments are reserved for low caste people. There is an untouchable who was a cabinet minister in a recent government and in future more will attain high office. Life in the cities and in the growing industrialized areas makes the observance of caste distinction increasingly difficult.

Caste consciousness still exists in many aspects of daily life, e.g. the area in which one lives, whom one invites for a meal or to a wedding or naming ceremony, but, above all, whom one may marry. Parents would like their children to be married in the same caste and with the person of the same social status. A Brahmin father may not like his son marrying a *chamar's* (shoe-maker's) daughter. There are some instances where the parents will break off their relations with the couple when such marriages take place. In modern India and the West, young boys and girls from different castes often meet and marry. When the families are not orthodox and are forward-looking, they may accept such unions. However, there are a number of cases where the young couple have been rejected by both families, in which case the couple have to find their own way in the world. This is not very easy, as the support and help of the family is essential for the success of a Hindu marriage.

Finally, the subject of the caste system should be treated with extreme caution; one has to beware of generalization. The barriers between castes are breaking down and there are a few examples of inter-caste marriages. This is true not only of India but of any traditional society.

Hinduism is a dynamic, living religion. Class and caste have been important in giving Hindu society both stability and cohesion. However, as has been mentioned, they have had their critics within the Hindu tradition and, in 1951, the discriminatory aspects of the system were declared illegal by the Indian constitution. Hindu society now seeks unity in other ways, through democracy and a sense of national pride, but marriages and other aspects of life, especially in the villages, are still influenced by beliefs, almost 4,000 years old, which lie at the very roots of Hindu culture.

Festivals

Festivals and celebrations are held throughout the year, bringing laughter, joy and spiritual security into Hindu life. A festival is a time for feasting and enjoyment, an occasion for family rejoicings and community celebrations. They commemorate important events, birthdays of national heroes, the cycle of the seasons and the harvest. Some festivals like Diwali (the festival of lights) are connected with the symbolism of light – darkend lamps are lit to ward off evil spirits – while other festivals like Holi are celebrated with riotous behaviour – a change from normal life where women beat men, and caste observances are forgotten. Festivals vary from area to area and community to community. The main festivals are described here. Exact Gregorian dates cannot be given for they are based on a lunar calendar. According to this, a lunar month is divided into two fortnights, bright and dark respectively. For the western readers, approximate English months are given as a guide.

Makara Sankranti (14 January)

This festival is the only one to come on the same day every year which is when the sun enters Capricorn and begins to move on a northward path. According to Hindus, the northward path is the Godward path, or noble path. Bhishma Pitamaha (a great character in the *Mahabharata*) waited to die in this auspicious period.

On this day, people distribute *til ladoos* (balls of sesame seeds made with sugar) to the Brahmins. The children, young and old, enjoy themselves by flying kites on their house tops and competitions are held. Hindus believe that any donation made on this day brings in the highest results. In Maharashtra, people give grains of multi-coloured sugar and sesame seeds and exchange the greeting which means 'Let there be only friendship and good thoughts between us, from now onwards'.

Vasant Panchami (January–February)

On the fifth day of the bright fortnight of the month of *Magha*, this festival is celebrated, particularly in North India. Spring is the happiest time of the year as nature seems to be smiling over all. Trees begin to bud and plants begin to sprout; mustard fields are full of yellow flowers; people rejoice at hearing the cuckoos sing. This season is an occasion of social gathering. As the trees have already shed their old leaves and are beginning to grow new ones, so people should discard their old bad habits and turn over a new leaf.

From the astrological point of view this is a very auspicious day. On this day, Goddess Sarasvati (the goddess of learning) first appeared on the earth. In the city of Patna (in Bihar) there is a procession carrying the image of Goddess Saraswati through all the main streets.

Maha Shivaratri (January–February)

This festival is on the fourteenth day of the dark fortnight of the month of *Magha*. People fast on this day and worship Lord Shiva in his emblem of the *lingam*, day and night. The fasting and vigil of the night are believed to bring one great merit and to release one from the cycle of birth and rebirth. This is the day when Lord Shiva appeared for the first time as an emblem of blazing fire (*lingam*). He came in this form to harmonize the conflict between Lord Vishnu and Lord Brahma as to who was the greater. When he appeared as the lingam the gods Brahma and Vishnu worshipped him in that form and from that day the Linga worship has been practiced by Hindus all over India.

On this day people worship Shiva by offering him milk, water and bilva leaves and by the chanting of the *Rudra-Ashtadhyayi* and vedic hymns.

Holi (March–April)

This is the most popular of all the Hindu festivals. It is on the fifteenth day of the bright fortnight of the month of *Falgun*. Logs of wood are collected and set on fire by a large gathering of people in every village, amidst joyous shouts and merrymaking as they remember the mercy that God's name can bestow on his devotees. Holi is a harvest festival. People eat new corn of grain or wheat cooked in the fire and enjoy themselves.

On the second day of Holi people squirt each other with coloured water and powder. All people, without distinction of caste or sect, celebrate by indulging themselves in this innocent pastime. Children parade streets with syringes threatening passers-by; mischief and frivolity reign all day. Some say that Lord Krishna started this custom by spraying the cowgirls (*gopis*) for fun on this day. In Mathura, (Lord Krishna's birthplace), Holi festivities last several weeks and pilgrims flock from all over India.

The hot, dry season in India starts at Holi. This is the time when people sleep in the open air, sometimes on their flat roofs, so the places outside the homes need to be cleaned. Many harmful germs are destroyed by burning fires and by sprinkling coloured water in every corner of the village. This is the only festival in which even the poorest have a chance of great enjoyment.

Rama Navami (April–May)

On the ninth day of the bright fortnight of *Chaitra*, Lord Vishnu incarnated himself as Lord Rama – the embodiment of virtue and morality. People fast and worship Lord Rama on this day. They go to the temple at noon, the time of Rama's birth, and a special Arti is performed all over India and elsewhere. continuous reading of the *Ramayana* (throughout the day and the night) is also carried out.

Guru Purnima (July–August)

The fifteenth day of the bright fortnight in the month of *Ashadh* is the special day for worshipping the Guru, or spiritual guide. Originally, Veda Vyasa, the Guru of all the Hindus was worshipped on this day. Hence, it was called *Vyasa Purnima*. Veda Vyasa systematized the Hindu beliefs and showed the path of salvation to all. This festival is specially observed by Sanyasins all over India.

Raksha Bandhan (August–September)

The fifteenth day of the bright fortnight of *Shravana* is called Shravani or Nariel Purnima. On this day, *Raksha Bandhan*, the changing of the Sacred Thread, and the Coconut Day, are celebrated. *Rakhis* are multi-coloured silken threads of various sizes and shapes for protection from evil sources. On this day, after having a bath, a sister ties a rakhi on the right wrist of her brother reciting a holy mantra – often the *gayatri* mantra. In return her brother gives her a gift, usually a token of money. If a girl's brother is away, she sends the rakhi to him by post. However, if a girl has no brother, she ties a rakhi to her cousin who she regards as brother, or adopts a brother outside the family. Thus, Rakhi is a sign or love and a plea for eternal protection.

Legend has it that Indra (the vedic king of heaven) was driven away from his kingdom by demons. Sachi, his wife, asked Lord Vishnu for his help. The Lord gave her a thread to tie on her husband's wrist for luck. It is said this amulet protected Indra and he won his celestial abode.

The significance of tying a rakhi is that the weak and the poor are protected by the brave and the rich. It is said that the Hindu Rajput queen, the Rani of Mewar, sent a rakhi to the Mogul Emperor Humayun when she needed help to save her kingdom. Humayun accepted the rakhi and sent immediate help to the Rani.

On this day the Brahmins change their 'sacred thread'. This rite of changing threads is known as *Upakarma*. The new thread is consecrated and is worn first and then the old one is removed. The verses from the vedas and the Gayatri mantra are chanted throughout the ceremony.

The day is also known as *Nariyal Purnima*. This is celebrated by fishermen especially in Maharashtra and Bombay. In Hindu religion the coconut is used on many occasions. When starting a new enterprise, or in the event of important ceremonies such as weddings, or when a person goes on a journey, a coconut is given as a symbol of good luck. Coconut is a nutritious natural food. It provides milk, carbohydrate and protein – a complete food in itself. When a coconut is offered it is implied that a person has given his most valuable thing to show his love and affection for the other person. On this day, the fishermen paint their boats and decorate them with flags. With much rejoicing, they offer a decorated coconut to the sea.

Janmashtami (August–September)

The birthday of Lord Krishna is celebrated on the eighth day of the dark part of the *Shravana* month. Hindus fast on this day and spend a lot of time in singing *bhajans* (hymns). The birthday is celebrated at midnight by the ringing of bells and the blowing of conch shells in the temples. The image of the baby Krishna is placed in a beautifully decorated cradle and sweets are distributed and eaten after first offering them to the image of God. There are most noteworthy celebrations in and around Mathura where Lord Krishna was born.

Ganesha Chaturthi (September–October)

The fourth day of the bright fortnight in the month of *Bhadrapad* is the incarnation day of Lord Ganesha. According to Hindu scriptures, this elephant-headed God is known as *Vighneshwara*, the remover of obstacles, and is worshipped at the beginning of any ceremony or at the start of any important projects. He is the God of prosperity and good fortune; his birthday is celebrated all over India. It is celebrated with great enthusiasm and pomp in Bombay and Maharashtra for more than ten days.

On this day, an idol, or clay image of Ganesha, is brought into the home, installed and worshipped with special prayers. For ten days Ganesha is worshipped with music, feasting and dancing. Many cultural programmes are also organized. On the last day, the clay image is taken out in a procession with cries of 'O Lord Ganapati, come soon next year', accompanied by bands and music. Finally, the image is submerged in a river, or the sea.

Children start school for the first time on this day because Ganesha Chaturthi is considered to be the most auspicious day of the year.

Nava-Ratri (October–November)

The festival of nine nights, which is celebrated, especially in Gujarat, with great enthusiasm and gaiety, starts from the first day of the month of *Ashvina*. At this time, the goddess Durga (or Ambaji, as she is known in Gujarat) is worshipped. An image of the goddess is placed in a specially decorated canopy and men and women dance around it in a large circle. An earthen pot with a design of holes (known as *garba*) and a lamp placed inside is kept beside the canopy. Men and women dance together in harmony with drums, rhythmically clapping their hands and singing traditional songs. They also dance using specially decorated short sticks with increasing speed, vigour and with lots of excitement. In India this dancing takes place outside, but in Britain school halls are hired for this purpose. Young girls have an exciting time as they have a chance to dress in saris.

In Bengal *Durga Puja* is the most colourful festival. The goddess Durga is also known as *Mahisha mardini* – the killer of the buffalo demon. She is supposed to have ten hands, each one holding the symbolic weapon of destruction. Beautiful statues of the goddess Durga are made and worshipped for nine days. This is a cultural festival of music, dance and drama. On the tenth day, goddess Durga is taken out in a procession and immersed in the Hooghly river.

Dashera (October–November)

This festival is celebrated in various ways throughout the country. It is also known as *Vijaya Dashami*. 'Vijay' means victory, and any activity started on this day brings success. Lord Rama killed Ravana, and goddess Durga killed the Mahishasura on this favourable day. In the north of India, the story of Lord Rama (the hero of *Ramayana*) is acted out for nine days by young boys dressed as different characters. On the tenth day, huge effigies (stuffed with crackers) of Ravana, his brother Meghanad, and his son Kumbhakarna, are erected in a large area of open ground. There, Rama, an ordinary actor, shoots arrows of flames until all three effigies burst into flames. The cheering crowd shouts 'Victory for Lord Rama'. This is a festival of the triumph of good over evil.

In Mysore this festival is celebrated with great pomp and pageantry; elephants lead a procession through decorated streets which attracts large crowds of people. *Shami*, a kind of tree, is also worshipped on this day.

Diwali (October–November)

It is observed on the fifteenth day of the dark fortnight of the Hindu month *Ashvina*. The word *Diwali* is derived from the Sanskrit word *Deepavali*, meaning rows of light. This is one of the most joyful Hindu festivals and is celebrated in all parts of India. It is a festival of illuminations, display or fireworks, and the festival of sweets.

Long before this festival starts many activities take place in the home. Women spring-clean the house from top to bottom. They prepare snacks and sweetmeats for the festive occasion. New clothes are bought for everyone and parents buy fireworks for children. Women decorate their front courtyard doors with Rangoli patterns by using different coloured powder. Hindus believe that the goddess Lakshmi visits only those houses which are clean and well-lit at this festive occasion.

The day after Diwali is celebrated as the New Year Day. People dress in new clothes, meet friends and relations and go to temples to pray for a happy and prosperous new year. Greeting cards are exchanged. Business people open new account books. On this day *Annakoot* – the mountain of food – is cooked and offered to God and later distributed to people. Thousands of years ago Lord Krishna sheltered the people from very heavy continuous rain (caused by Indra) by holding the Govardhana Mountain over them. The joyful people in return cooked various foods which they gave him. Thus, to commemorate this occasion there is Annakoot in many temples throughout India and in England.

Thus festivals are occasions in which people meet, dress up, sing, celebrate a special time and balance the normal daily world by temporarily forgetting the working life. The atmosphere in which people meet is special and different from the working one.

In conclusion, festivals play a major part in Hindu religion. They are fundamental to worshipping various deities. It seems that no other religion or culture puts such an emphasis on festivals. They depict the Hindu culture and show the way of life.

Hinduism in Modern Society

Although the homeland of the Hindus is India they also live in Bali, Fiji, Guyana, Sri Lanka, Mauritius and many parts of the West Indies and Africa. In the UK there are over 300,000 Hindus who have come from Gujarat, Punjab, Maharashta, the South of India, Kenya, Uganda, Guyana and other parts of the world. They have settled in or moved to all parts of Britain.

Emigrant Hindus, because they have left their homeland, are usually staunch in their belief and practice of Hinduism in contrast to their counterparts in India. This also applies to other emigrant national groups. Second generation Hindus, on the other hand, are under the influence of western society and they tend to move away from traditional practices, although a few of them do uphold their beliefs.

Today we live in a world in which violence is prevalent and in which many feel concerned about the decline of moral standards, or the lack of them. Hindus in western society have a strong sense of social duty. This was shown by their support of the Ugandan refugees in 1972 by helping them in their troubled times. Most of them came penniless and started with nothing in Great Britain. It was their deep religious faith which sustained them through adversity and helped them through their troubles.

There is a strong desire on the part of Hindus in the West to retain their cultural heritage. Language classes in Gujarati, Hindi and Punjabi have been set up in temples in many parts of the country as Hindus believe that religion, culture and language are inseparable; if the language is forgotten the culture will be lost.

Although Hindus have been slow to establish their places of worship, the mainstream Hindu Hare Krishna temple at Watford was one of the first, being founded nearly a quarter of a century ago. This phenomenon of keeping to religious practices can be clearly observed by the number of temples that are being established in the western world.

An example of this was the building of the new Hindu *mandir* (temple) which opened in Neasden, London on August 20, 1995, the cost of which has been met through donations from the Gujarati community. The grand opening ceremony which was attended by many prominent politicians including the British Home Secretary, received international media coverage. The whole project was inspired by his Divine Holiness Pramukh Swami Maharaj, spiritual leader of the Swaminarayan Hindu Mission.

A six day 'Festival of Inspirations' to celebrate the mandir's completion began on August 18 with a cultural parade through central London when thousands of people marched from Hyde Park to Trafalgar Square as sacred images to be installed in the mandir were paraded through the streets.

The creation of this mandir, with its carved domes, pinnacles and pillars, built according to ancient Hindu scriptures, has required 2,828 tons of limestone from Bulgaria and 2,000 tons of Carrara marble from Italy. These were shipped to India where it took two years for 1,500 sculptors to carve the individual pieces that comprise the interior; after which all the 26,300 numbered pieces were brought to London, where they were assembled on the Neasden site by a workforce of volunteers. The mandir has the only cantilevered dome in Europe not to have a steel structure.

Adjacent to the temple is the haveli, a cultural and social complex including a prayer hall, sports and crèche facilities, halls for conferences, exhibitions and weddings, a library, health clinic and kitchens which can cater for several thousand people. In contrast to the marble and limestone mandir, the haveli is made of carved Burmese teak, supported by an English oak frame thus showing the bonding of the products of different nations. The mandir also houses a comprehensive exhibition of Hinduism, which is intellectually stimulating, visually stunning and spiritually motivating.

The Swaminarayan mandir opens a new chapter for Hindus and the wider community in the UK and in Europe as a whole. It will become the source of inspiration and joy to the Hindu community for many generations to come. This magnificent mandir may encourage anyone seeing it to reflect that Hindus have made and will continue to make a great contribution to the culture and enrichment of this society. The mandir will restore faith for many Hindus, will illuminate the path for those who were lost and will allow

55

The Swaminarayan temple which was opened in Neasden in August 1995

Hindu children to experience their historical and living culture in all its glory and their own identity.

The Guru

Scriptures and temples, in themselves, cannot illuminate the minds of devotees. In the Hindu religion there is great emphasis on the need for a guru, a spiritual teacher. (The Guru is the one who dissipates the darkness clouding a person's mind and heart and brings enlightenment.) It is stated in Srimad Bhagavata 'The spiritual seeker must find proper instruction at the feet of a Guru who is well-versed in Vedas that lead to the knowledge of God' (Srimad Bhagavata 11.3.21). It is the Guru's duty (*dharma*) to pass on the heritage and guidance to the devotees who are struggling to search for truth. Traditionally, devotees always seek Gurus and having found them, give all their respect and devotion to them. An example of this is the founder of the Swaminarayan Hindu Mission of London, Shree Pramukh Swami Maharaj, the guru for the fastest growing Hindu sect of the last part of the 20th century.

The Swami practises celibacy (*Brahmacharya*), avoiding any kind of contact with women, not because women are considered inferior to men in Hindu religion. This means that he does not even see his own mother. Celibacy is one of the rules of the Swaminarayan sect and he has been following this rule for the last 60 years. As mentioned earlier on page 19, the status of women is high in Hindu religion. There is a feeling among westerners that Hindu women are submissive and are under the dominance of their husbands, but this is not true. They may not be as outspoken as their western sisters, but they do let their views be known. The foreign rule did not seem to contribute much to the advance of women in India but, since independence, they have been given equality in all walks of life. Even at a local level, they contribute to national development and today there is no activity or even a demonstration without women.

Normally Hindu religious traditions are transmitted to the children by the mother and the extended family. However, owing to the economic climate in the West, often both parents have to work and they do not have as much time to impart the cultural education as they would in India. Moreover, families in western society are generally nuclear and the children do not have the benefit of living with an extended family. Schools do not seem to play as much a part

57

as they should to improve the self-image of children. Thus the atmosphere is not suitable for spiritual nurture. However some groups have come into existence who have taken up the task of educating their children themselves although they lack financial resources. Nowadays the dietary rules for Hindu people are not as strict as they used to be. The most orthodox Hindu may not eat meat, fish, eggs and may even refuse to eat garlic and onions. Hindus believe that a person's constitution is made up of the food he eats; onions and garlic are supposed to create tamas guna – the qualities of restlessness, impurity, sleep, lethargy, anger and dullness. Beef eating is prohibited as the cow is considered sacred in Hindu religion.

Hinduism is changing by a steady process of adaptation. As it can be seen from previous chapters, the temple is used more as a social centre than as a place of worship. Hindus in western society celebrate their festivals at the weekends, rather than on working days, to suit the host society. However, the cultural tradition survives and if the present trends continue it will never be lost.

Festivals do not consist just of religious observances but incorporate many cultural and social activities. Typical of these are the Ganesha Chaturthi festivals in Maharashtra where people from all walks of life, intellectuals to village folk, participate in many activities with great joy. The advance of Hinduism has modernized the festivals and Hinduism will continue to change with changing conditions, without rejecting any part of its inheritance from the past.

When a westerner thinks of the Hindu religion, he usually thinks in terms of arranged marriages and caste, regarding both unfavourably. The mass media have played a large part in influencing views regarding arranged marriages. If any marriage does not work out, a big issue is normally made of it. In fact, thousands of arranged marriages have been successful over the centuries and many will continue to be so. The caste system is breaking down and many inter-caste and inter-national marriages are taking place. To a Hindu, the insight of the Guru and his blessing are more important than a Brahmin's rituals.

Hindus' outlook on life in modern society might be summed up in two words – dharma and karma. In the theory of karma, he would accept the circumstances surrounding him for example wealth, or poverty, or sickness, or whatever situation in which he finds himself. His dharma implies that he should concentrate on making the most of his circumstances by creating a new life for his family, which is better than his own and that of his generation. The classic example of this is Mahatma Gandhi who tried to persuade the ruling powers to understand this view-point and force a change of heart by open non-cooperation, but without harming anyone in the process. A modern Hindu in the West may follow Gandhiji's example when he is faced with racial discrimination in his job, housing and many other areas. Hindu religion does not allow him to accept the evils of society.

The message to a modern Hindu in the West must be a simple one – to develop an awareness of moral and spiritual sanctity, to give importance to self-analysis, self-criticism, self-correction, to cause no injury to any living being by thought, word or deed, and to seek the truth in all things.

It would be appropriate to end by quoting a well-known Hindu prayer:

> From the unreal lead me to the real,
> From darkness lead me to the light,
> From death lead me to immortality,
> *Brihadaranyaka Upanishad 1.iii.28*
> Om Shanti (Peace), Shanti, Shanti.

Shree Pramukh Swami Maharaj, the inspirer of the Swaminarayan Mandir in Neasden, is a famous Hindu Guru – a spiritual preceptor who brings enlightenment and spiritual liberation (moksha) *to his devotees.*

JUDAISM
DOUGLAS CHARING

Introduction

What is a Jew?

The Jewish religion teaches that a child born of a Jewish mother is a Jew, irrespective of upbringing. This means that, for example, a child of a Jewish father and non-Jewish mother is not regarded as Jewish, even though he may act as a Jew by attending synagogue, observing the Sabbath and festivals and mixing mainly with Jewish friends. On the other hand, a child of a non-Jewish father, and a Jewish mother, even if he is brought up as a Christian is still, from the Jews' viewpoint, a Jew, although, of course, his upbringing may have made him totally ignorant about Judaism. It is, therefore, not knowledge nor upbringing, but the religion of the mother which determines the status of the child according to Judaism.

It may be quite easy to say who is a Jew, it is far more difficult to say what a Jew is. Are Jews a race? Some people think of the Jews as a race. Many books written, say fifty years ago, often mentioned the 'Jewish race' or even 'Jewish blood'. (In Germany, in the 1930s, under Adolf Hitler, it suited the Nazis to regard the Jews as a separate, race. In fact, the Nazis thought of them as an *inferior* race that should be exterminated. The Holocaust, when some six million Jewish men, women and children died in concentration camps in Germany and Poland during the Second World War, was a direct result of these ideas.) Today Jewish people are no longer seen as a distinctive race. Indeed, it is difficult to see how they can be regarded as such when it is realized that there are yellow Jews from China, brown Jews from India, and black Jews from the West Indies and Africa.

Are Jews then a religious community? At first sight 'religion' seems the correct word to describe what ties the

Jews together. There are, however, some Jews who do not regard themselves as religious, some would even say they are against religion. Yet these same people would be proud to call themselves Jews. We cannot speak of a Jewish nation, since the majority of the world's Jews do not live in the Jewish State of Israel but in various countries throughout the world.

Perhaps the correct term is 'people' or 'ethnic group'. This would then cover the religious Jew, the secular Jew and the national, or Zionist, Jew. A Jew is not necessarily someone from Israel (Muslims and Christians also live there); someone who does not eat pork (Muslims also refrain from eating pork); or someone who observes every smallest detail of his religion.

It cannot be denied that it is their religion which has kept the Jewish people as a distinct community, although that religion has changed over the centuries. Certainly Judaism today is different in many respects from the Judaism of biblical times. Just as in the past there have been different religious groups, so today we have schools of thought which share some ideas and practices and differ widely in others. In Britain, religious Jews are either Orthodox or Progressive.

The Orthodox

The majority of Jews in Britain belong to an Orthodox synagogue, although they themselves may not be Orthodox. Some prefer the term 'traditional' since they believe they are practising a religion virtually unchanged for centuries. The truly Orthodox Jew accepts the views of God as developed in the Bible, and the rabbinic writings of the Talmud and Midrash, both of which contain the revealed word of God. He believes that every law and commandment is binding and is of equal importance, and that no law or ceremony can be changed or abolished. His prayers have also remained unchanged. Some ultra-Orthodox Jews will have very little to do with non-Jews, indeed they have almost no contact even with non-Orthodox Jews, and spend all their time in their own circle, to ensure that no 'foreign' influences tempt them away from their religion. The Orthodox Jew has no need or desire to 'up-date' his religion, for he feels that his religion in its present form is just as relevant today as it has been in the past. The life of a strict Orthodox Jew is a demanding one and requires great commitment and sacrifice. For this reason many Orthodox Jews are against other forms of Judaism, claiming that they have the authentic version and that other forms are only religions of convenience and will soon disappear through apathy and intermarriage.

The Progressives

There are some Jews who maintain that since Judaism has always accepted change and development, there is a need, from time to time, for a form of 'spring-cleaning', to sweep away the cobwebs of outdated laws and rituals. This would also include a reform of some ideas and practices, and the introduction of new concepts and ceremonies. They therefore do not feel bound to observe all the laws and commandments laid down in the Bible and the Talmud since they do not share the Orthodox view that this literature is of divine origin and that it is literally the 'word of God'. They believe that these writings have been interpreted by men who may have been divinely inspired but were subject to human error. Such Jews speak of a 'progressive' revelation, meaning that God still speaks to us today and that every generation has the right to make changes in the religion in order that it can speak to the present and future generation in a language it understands. Non-Orthodox Jews are sometimes known as Reform, or Liberal, or just Progressive. These Jews will observe the major customs but will ignore or even abolish those minor practices which they feel are no longer suitable in today's world. Their prayer book will include new prayers, and outdated prayers will be removed. They will seek dialogue not only with their Orthodox co-religionists, but will also be keen on inter-faith relations. Progressive Jews welcome the diversity amongst Jews and see this as a strength and not a weakness.

The Prophets

It is not easy to be a leader and people are often not very interested in the changes or reforms which are intended. Indeed, they may even be hostile towards you and your ideas. There is an ancient Jewish story which illustrates this well. It speaks of God addressing Moses: 'My children are obstinate, ill-tempered, troublesome. In assuming leadership over them, expect to be cursed and even stoned by them.' Many of the world's religions have enjoyed inspiring leaders who often have the title of founder. The Jewish religion, however, has not one founder, but three. The history of the Hebrews, who were later called Jews, can be found in the Hebrew Bible; Christians call this part of their Bible the Old Testament. You might expect the Bible to begin with the story of the Hebrews, but in fact it starts with stories about the creation of the world and the great flood. We have to wait until chapter twelve of the book of Genesis before we read of the first founder of the Hebrew religion and people.

Abraham

Abram, or as he was later called, Abraham, was the first believer in one God to be known by name. The Bible does not tell us how he came to believe in the one God, nor does it say anything about his boyhood. In all religions there are many stories about the childhood of the founder, and Judaism is no exception. These stories are found in a collection of books known as the *Midrash*, written by the early rabbis and teachers of Judaism.

One story tells how Abraham, being fully convinced of the existence of only one God, attempts to influence other people. It happened that Abraham's father, Terach, was himself an idol worshipper, and even owned a shop where he sold idols. He became a wealthy man because people came from far afield to purchase the many idols on display. One day he had to attend a meeting in a neighbouring town and left his young son Abraham in charge of the shop. He did not have to wait long before the first customer entered the shop. The man made his choice and then Abraham asked him how old he was. 'Fifty years,' answered the man proudly. 'Surely,' said Abraham, 'your brain can't be as old, for how can a man of your age bow down before a mere image that was just completed yesterday!' The man felt very ashamed and quickly left the shop minus his idol. Every time a would-be customer entered the shop, Abraham did his best to discourage him and to make him doubt the importance of idols. When it was time to close the shop, Abraham smashed all the idols with the exception of the largest one. In its hand he placed a hammer. When Terach returned he was profoundly shocked and wanted to know who was responsible for this outrage. 'It seems,' said Abraham, 'that the idols decided to hold a contest to see who was the strongest, and there is the winner!' His father replied, 'What nonsense! Idols can neither speak nor understand.' 'Precisely,' agreed Abraham. 'They have mouths, but they cannot speak, they have eyes but they cannot see, they even have hands, but they cannot move them. These have no power, unlike the true God, the Creator of heaven and earth.' Thus Abraham was to convince his family and neighbours of the need to turn from their false gods. Abraham lived to a ripe old age. His son, Isaac, and his grandson, Jacob, were also men of courage, and although Abraham was told by God to move to a new land, later to be called the land of Israel, circumstances made it necessary for Jacob and his sons, including Joseph, to move to Egypt.

Moses

At first, the Egyptians were good to the Hebrews, who were now known as Israelites. Indeed, Joseph had become Chief Minister. However, a new king refused to recognize the good that Joseph had done for the Egyptians. He decided to make slaves of the children of Israel and ordered all their male babies to be drowned in the River Nile. One family refused to do this and hid their baby son Moses in a basket which floated amongst the reeds in the river. The king's daughter found the baby and decided to adopt him. Moses therefore became a prince of Egypt, but his family knew what had happened and kept in touch with him so that he should not forget that he was also an Israelite. Moses was regarded as a leader for his people. According to the Midrash, God decided on Moses because as a shepherd he had noticed that a little kid had strayed, so he ran after it for fear that it would get lost and die of hunger and thirst in the wilderness. He searched for a long time before finding the kid, and seeing that it was so weak he carried it all the way back to the flock. God was greatly pleased and said to him, 'Deep is your compassion, Moses. Because of your kindness to this little animal you will be the leader of My people Israel, and are destined to serve as their devoted shepherd'. God told Moses to go to King Pharaoh and say to him, 'Let My people go, so that they can serve Me'. According to the Bible, many bad things happened to the Egyptians before Pharaoh would allow them to leave. After leaving Egypt (we call this the Exodus) Moses' leadership was to be of even more importance. Many of the people were dissatisfied, some even thought life in Egypt was tolerable. Others questioned the authority of Moses. It took Moses and the people some 40 years to reach the Promised Land, and only the children of the slaves were able to enter it. Even Moses was denied entry because he had disobeyed God. Yet, the Jews honoured him by making him their chief prophet and also calling the first five books of the Bible, the 'Five Books of Moses'. According to Jewish tradition, there has never since been a prophet like Moses.

Ezra the Scribe

Many centuries after Moses, in the sixth century B.C.E., the people again found themselves in captivity in a foreign land, Babylon. (Jews prefer to use B.C.E., instead of B.C., meaning before the Common, or Christian, Era.) Some 70 years later, in 538 B.C.E. a new king, Cyrus, king of the Medes and Persians, gave the Israelites permission to return to their homeland. Not all of them wanted to return as they had made homes in a new land and were happy there. Those that did return were pioneers; they had to be. Their country was in ruins, their proud Temple destroyed. It appeared that their religious lives had also deteriorated. Many of their customs had been neglected, even their festivals had not been observed, and the Torah, the Five Books of Moses, could not be read for so many had forgotten the holy language of Hebrew. Could their religion and heritage be revived? One man thought it could. Just as Moses had been a saviour of his people returning from Egypt, Ezra became the saviour of a people returning from Babylon. He had been given authority over all Jewish religious matters by the Persian king. Ezra traced his descent from Moses' brother, Aaron the High Priest, and his arrival kindled a new wave of religious and national enthusiasm. His most significant reform was the establishment of a body known as 'The Men of the Great Synagogue'. This group arranged and canonized Israel's sacred writings. It also made God's word available to all the people through the institution of schools and the use of public occasions as an opportunity for adult education.

Because of Ezra's many reforms, he is often known as the 'father of modern Judaism'. The Bible became the property of the people. Up to then it was only known by the priests. Because so many had forgotten the Hebrew language, Ezra translated the Bible when passages from it were read to the men, women and children. The people of the book now studied the book of the people. These public readings reminded the people of their obligations and often the people wept as they realized they had forgotten their observances. The book of Nehemiah records that the festival of *Succot* (Tabernacles) had not been observed since the days of Joshua, a period of many centuries (Nehemiah 8:17).

One of Ezra's reforms was not welcomed by many of the people. Israelite men had married foreign women. Ezra instructed them to divorce their wives. A harsh decree, but the concern was for the spiritual future of the Israelites. Such marriages introduced idolatrous practices and values alien to the Jewish tradition. Ezra's concern was for the religious purity of his people. It was not a racial policy, as the Israelites themselves were of mixed racial background. This policy and his other reforms maintained the unity of the people. It is estimated that about 5,000 men women and children returned with Ezra. They were all determined to rebuild both their land and their religion. Ezra was their guide who began the process that transformed Judaism into the religion of an entire people, and it is this religion which we shall now study.

The Temple and the Synagogue

Mankind, from earliest times, has always been inclined to worship his gods. Very often he would build temples and offer up sacrifices to please the gods. The early Hebrews believed that their God required animal sacrifice and this became the established custom for many centuries. Already at the time of Moses, the Priests and Levites were appointed in order to be prepared for their work and service in the Temple which was to be built in Jerusalem by King Solomon many centuries later. According to the account in the Bible (1 Kings 6 & 7), this Temple was one of the most beautiful buildings in the known world. Thousands of men worked on it with cedar and cypress timber coming from Lebanon, and costly stones, to be used in the building, were quarried. It took seven and a half years of all-out effort to construct. According to Jewish tradition, as the Temple symbolized peace, tools of iron, the metal used in warfare, were not to be used in its construction. At the dedication ceremony the wise Solomon prayed to God, 'Behold, heaven and the highest heaven cannot contain You, how much less this House which I have built!' (1 Kings 8:27). This Temple, together with the rest of the country, was destroyed by the Babylonian king, Nebuchadnezzar, in 586 B.C.E. and the people were taken into captivity.

When the captives returned to Israel in 538 B.C.E. they decided to rebuild the Temple, and within a year the foundations of a new one had been completed. The work then came to a sudden halt. We are not sure of the reason, but perhaps it was because the money had not yet been given to ensure its completion. This was eventually provided by king Darius (521–486 B.C.E.). It was fully 18 years before the people, inspired by the prophets Haggai and Zechariah, went back to work. In all, it took 23 years to finish and yet the new structure was far less impressive than the old. It was dedicated at a ceremony in 515 B.C.E. King Herod, some 430 years later, undertook some major alterations on the Temple, making it more splendid than the Temple of Solomon. Indeed, this Temple is often known as Herod's Temple. This too was destroyed by the Romans in 70 C.E. How did the Jewish people react? One Talmudic teacher said, 'Since the destruction, there has never been a perfectly clear sky.' Others agreed with another rabbi who felt that with the Temple destroyed, 'an iron wall was removed from between Israel and their Father in heaven.' It is true that the actual services in both Temples were very impressive. Many of the ceremonies had been immensely colourful. Indeed, Jews came to the Temple on the Festivals of *Succot* (Tabernacles), *Shavuot* (Pentecost) and *Pesach* (Passover) not only from all over the land of Israel, but also from the communities in neighbouring countries. Yet, many felt uneasy about animal sacrifices, the main object of the services. Each day, two animals were sacrificed, morning and late afternoons. On Sabbaths and Festivals there was an additional sacrifice. Thus, around 700 animals were offered up every year on the Temple altar in Jerusalem. Ordinary Israelites disliked the practice that only priests could officiate. They felt themselves more like spectators than participants. Moreover, the priests were often ignorant, some were even corrupt, yet they held office because it was handed down, father to son. Even some of the prophets were not enthusiastic about the temple services. Had not Hosea written in God's name, 'I desire love and not sacrifice, and the knowledge of God rather than burnt offerings'? (Hos. 6:6) The people were ready for a change from the splendour of the Temple.

The Rise of the Synagogue

We do not know when the synagogue came into existence. It is not mentioned in the post-exilic books of Ezra and Nehemiah although most scholars believe it started in Babylon, sometime before the return, as a means of assembling the people, and possibly to instruct them in their religious traditions. It is certain, however, that by the time of the birth of Jesus of Nazareth, the synagogue was well-established, both in Israel and in other countries in the area. The New Testament records that Jesus worshipped in many synagogues in Galilee and Jerusalem, and the apostle Paul preached in many synagogues. According to the Talmud, 394 synagogues existed in Jerusalem alone prior to the destruction of the second Temple in 70 C.E. Whilst the Temple existed, synagogues were mainly meeting places. The word 'synagogue' comes from the Greek word for assembly. It was a place where Jews could meet to pray, study and discuss problems. Thus in addition to it being called *Beit Haknesset* (House of Assembly), it became known as *Beit Hamidrash* (House of Study), *Beit Teffila* (House of Prayer), and *Beit Ha'am* (House of the People).

The synagogue became a popular institution, for most Jews felt that it had many advantages over the Temple. Firstly, you did not need a priest to officiate. Any capable man acted as the representative of the congregation. Secondly, instead of sacrifices, prayer became the main act of worship. Thirdly, there could only be one Temple, whereas synagogues could flourish wherever there was a Jewish community. Another advantage was the informality of the services. Gone was the complex Temple ritual with the priest's ornate vestments. With the destruction of the Temple, and the expulsion from their land, the Jews could and did survive because they had their synagogues. As one Christian writer, Travers Herford, aptly put it, 'The religion of the Torah learned to do without the Temple, but it never dreamed of doing without the Synagogue.' The early Christians modelled their forms of worship on the synagogue, as did the Muslims. Both church and mosque owe their existence to the synagogue. The same Christian scholar wrote some 60 years ago, 'To have created the Synagogue is perhaps the greatest practical achievement of the Jews in all their history.' Another non-Jewish writer, Ernest Renan, declared: 'The Synagogue has been the most original and fruitful creation of the Jewish people.'

A synagogue, unlike places of worship in some other religions, is not in itself holy. Jews speak of a holy congregation, people, rather than a building. It is also important to realize that Judaism is not synagogue-centred, and whilst it has become a central place for Jews, the home is still far more important in the preservation of the Jewish religion and people. The synagogue has been more than a place of worship; during the Middle Ages, it was a hospital for the sick, and a boarding house for Jewish travellers.

The rise of the synagogue could be described as a revolution. It created a democratic institution whereby ordinary people could pray directly to God without the assistance of the priestly class and without animal sacrifice. Today, nearly 2,000 years later, the synagogue continues to serve as a house of prayer, study and meeting.

The Holy Ark open, showing the Torah Scrolls.

Synagogues can be large, or small, buildings. Most are purpose built, whilst a few are converted churches, halls or even schools. They come in many different designs, traditional or modern. The Hadassah synagogue in Jerusalem, for instance, looks extremely futuristic.

In Britain, most synagogues are named after a locality, for example, Birmingham Hebrew Congregation or St John's Wood Synagogue. Reform synagogues usually include the word 'Reform' in their title. A few prefer the word 'New', although this is also used by some Orthodox synagogues. Liberal synagogues include either 'Liberal' or 'Progressive'. In America, many non-Orthodox congregations are called 'Temples' rather than synagogues. It is also common in America for these houses of worship to be known by Hebrew names, for example Temple Beth El (House of God), Beth Shalom (House of Peace), Beth Emet (House of Truth). Sometimes it is the name of a prophet, for example, Temple Isaiah or Temple Micah. There are not many synagogues in Britain with only a Hebrew name. There are, however, two known as Sinai Synagogue, one orthodox, in London, the other reform, in Leeds. Most synagogues have rooms and perhaps a hall adjoining the synagogue proper. These are used for Schools of Religion for Jewish children on Sundays and often during the week after school as well. They will also be used for adult study groups and various social functions, ranging from a dance or social to a book exhibition or jumble sale.

Whatever their size, there are certain features common to all synagogues throughout the world. There is the *Ner Tamid*, the Everlasting Light, which hangs above the *Aron Hakodesh*, the Holy Ark. It represents God's eternal presence in the sanctuary. Most synagogues today have an electric light, but a few, like the West London Synagogue, have oil lamps. Within the Ark, the Torah scrolls are housed. Synagogues normally have two scrolls, and many congregations have a lot more. They are usually decorated with silver ornaments.

In every synagogue there is a raised platform, known as the *Bimah*, or *Almemar*, a word derived from Arabic. In most Orthodox synagogues it is in the centre of the building, whilst in most Reform and Liberal synagogues it is on the same platform as the Ark. Thus in the former, the officiant prays facing the Ark, whereas in the latter he is facing the congregation. The people in all synagogues are facing the Ark, that is eastwards towards Jerusalem. In many synagogues

A rabbi at the reading desk in the synagogue, in front of the Holy Ark.

there is a separate stand, the pulpit from which the rabbi delivers his sermon.

The word *Rabbi* means teacher, and for centuries his most important function was that of teaching his people. He would interpret the Torah and rabbinic writings, informing his fellow Jews what the law was and how it should be observed. In the last 200 years, the rabbi has taken on other duties, similar to those undertaken by Christian clergy. He will participate in synagogue services, normally by reading the Torah and preaching the sermon. He will officiate at marriages and funerals, and will visit the sick in hospitals, and the lonely in their homes. As spiritual leader, he will often represent his congregation at inter-faith and other non-Jewish activities. In Britain, and in some other countries, the spiritual leader may not be a rabbi but just a minister with the title 'Reverend'. Those who have studied for a longer period are ordained with the title 'Rabbi'.

The Reader of the synagogue is very often also called Reverend in British synagogues, as he is also regarded as a minister. He does not actually read the service, rather he chants it, and is known as the representative of the congregation. He, too, has undergone training in many cases, and is known as *chazan*, or cantor, and very often he has a fine singing voice which enhances the services. Larger synagogues will have both a rabbi (or minister) and cantor, whilst smaller congregations will have only one officiant. Some congregations are unable to support any paid official and they themselves will take most of the services, and therefore act as lay readers.

Orthodox and Progressive Customs

A noticeable difference between Orthodox and Progressive (Reform and Liberal) synagogues is that in the Orthodox women do not sit in the main body of the synagogue with the men, but usually in a gallery. Muslim women are also segregated from the men in the mosque, and this practice was common in the religions of the Near East. In Progressive synagogues there are mixed pews and, in many of them, women can officiate in the service. Indeed, Progressive Judaism, both in Britain and America, has ordained women as rabbis and cantors. The ordination of women is impossible within Orthodox Judaism or in the Roman Catholic Church.

The main officiant in an Orthodox synagogue is the *Chazan* (Cantor), also known as the Reader. The rabbi plays very little part in the service, other than to give the sermon and recite the prayers for the Royal Family and the State of Israel. Sometimes he may read from the Torah portion, but often either the cantor or another person will do this. In British Progressive synagogues, there are very few cantors and the service is usually conducted by the rabbi, sometimes assisted by a layperson, and the choral pieces sung by a choir, accompanied by the organ or some other musical instrument. Orthodox synagogues are not permitted any accompanied music on Sabbaths and festivals. Some argue it is because they still mourn the loss of the Temple, others say it is wrong to play instruments on the Sabbath, and others maintain that the organ is a Christian instrument, although a very similar instrument is mentioned in the Talmud, as being played in the Temple.

Another difference is that Progressive services include some prayers in English, the amount varies from synagogue to synagogue. In Orthodox synagogues, apart from the prayer for the Royal Family and the sermon, the whole service is in Hebrew. Generally speaking, Orthodox services are longer than Progressive ones.

Visiting a Synagogue

Most synagogues welcome visitors, Jewish and non-Jewish. You may come with a school or church group, or you may have been invited to a Jewish friend's *Bar Mitzvah*, or perhaps you have come on your own. Boys are expected to wear a hat or *kippa* (skull cap). Girls visiting an Orthodox synagogue, will be expected to sit upstairs, although very young girls will normally sit with their fathers. If it is a Sabbath or festival morning service, you will find the men wearing a *tallit* (prayer shawl). They will not be wearing *teffilin* (phylacerties), as they are not worn on these days. You will be given a *siddur* (prayer book), containing an English translation of all the prayers. At various stages in the service you will stand. In some Orthodox synagogues, the congregation tends to talk during the service. It may appear a lack of decorum, but they maintain they are 'at home' in the synagogue, and you are unlikely to be silent at home.

You will find that the tunes which are used vary from synagogue to synagogue and there is no such thing as Orthodox or Progressive music. Certain prayers are recited every day at every service, others are solely for Sabbaths or festivals. The siddur is used in the home as well as the synagogue. Worship is public when 10 males over the age of 13 are present; this may be in a home. With less than this number the service is private, although it may take place in the synagogue.

Festivals

'Jewish people always seem to be celebrating a festival'. Hardly a month goes by without some festival or fast being observed.

The Sabbath

Some people regard Saturday as the 'Jewish Sunday'. As the Jewish Sabbath is much older than Christianity, it would be more correct to call Sunday the 'Christian Sabbath or Sunday'. The seventh day, Sabbath, has always been a very special day amongst Jews. A Jewish legend tells of the six working days pairing off. Only the Sabbath, Saturday, was without a partner. It complained to God, who comforted it by saying, 'Fear not, the people Israel shall be your partner'. A Jewish writer, a few years ago, conscious of this story, put it this way, 'More than Israel has kept the Sabbath, the Sabbath has kept Israel.' The Jewish Sabbath has also served as the model for the Christian Sunday and the Muslim Friday. Spend a week in Jerusalem and you will find that the three communities each observe their respective Sabbath.

The Jewish Sabbath, as all Jewish festivals, begins the evening before. This is because it says in the Bible regarding the days of creation, 'It was evening, and it was morning...' (Genesis 1:5). Traditionally, the Sabbath begins at sundown. In Britain, for example, it can begin as early as 3.30 during the winter months, and although it could begin as late as 10 p.m. in the summer, it is usual to begin it no later than 8 p.m. Prior to this the family would prepare for it. Father would be home from work, mother making the meals, and the children taking a bath and putting on their best clothes. In today's society, however, it is not always possible to leave work at three in the afternoon! Progressive Jews prefer to go by the clock rather than by the sun, and they bring in the Sabbath at about 6 p.m. throughout the year. But amongst truly Orthodox Jews, they will still observe the commencement of the Sabbath at the traditional time, and will request that their children finish school early on Fridays during the winter.

A beautiful ceremony ushers in the Sabbath. It begins with the women of the house lighting two candles and reciting a Hebrew blessing, praising the Lord of the Universe who has commanded us to kindle the Sabbath lights. In an Orthodox household this will be done whilst the father and sons are in the synagogue before the meal. In Progressive homes, it is performed with the rest of the ceremony, as most Progressive synagogues hold their services at around 8 p.m., after the meal. The man of the house then recites the two blessings over the wine. This is known as *kiddush*, a word meaning holy, or sanctified. After all present have drunk the wine, he then recites an additional blessing over the two *challot*, twisted loaves of white bread, and a piece, sprinkled with salt, is given to everyone around the table. The husband blesses his wife and then his children. During the courses, Hewbrew songs are sung, and after the meal a rather lengthy grace is recited, much of it is sung by the assembled group. This whole ceremony can be found in any prayer book. The Sabbath is referred to as both a queen, and a bride. A popular hymn which begins the Friday evening service has as its refrain: 'Beloved come, the bride to meet, the presence of the Sabbath, let us greet.' The traditional greeting of the Sabbath is 'Shabbat Shalom' – a peaceful Sabbath. The next morning, the whole family will attend the synagogue, the service lasting about $1\frac{1}{4}$ hours (Progressive) to $2\frac{1}{2}$ hours (Orthodox), a little longer on special occasions. The central feature of the service in all synagogues is the reading of the Torah.

The Sabbath is a day of rest, a day of refraining from work and everyday labour. 'Work' in Jewish tradition does not mean just hard work, but also activities such as writing, cooking, carrying, and even turning on lights. It also means walking rather than travelling by car or public transport. The idea is to abstain from all potentially creative acts on the Sabbath, just as God rested on the seventh day. Progressive Judaism does not prohibit doing these things but it does urge that one should not do unnecessary work that can be done on weekdays, such as shopping or household chores.

It would be wrong, however, to think that the Sabbath is just a day of prohibitions. All religious Jews regard the Sabbath as a day of delight, a day to praise God for making a beautiful world and giving us loved ones. It is a day when the family can be together and do things together. It is a day to

77

relax from everyday work and cares. It is a day when Jews can study their heritage. It is therefore more than just a day of rest. Yet, in cases of danger and accident, even the most Orthodox Jew must break this holy day as Jewish tradition teaches that we should live by God's laws, not die by them. As one teacher put it: 'To save a life, disregard a Sabbath, that the endangered may observe many Sabbaths'. Or, as another rabbi stated, 'The Sabbath has been given to you, not you to the Sabbath'.

The Sabbath, as with all festivals, is ushered in by kindling the lights and drinking wine. It departs also with candlelight, wine and spices. The ceremony is called *Havdalah*, a word meaning division, or distinction, for it stresses the distinction between the sacred Sabbath and the secular weekdays. A special braided candle, or two candles held together to give a torch-like appearance, is used. It is normally held high in the air by the youngest child. The spices, which all can smell, represent the Sabbath itself. Just as the aroma will linger on, so the Jew hopes the special fragrance of the Sabbath will stay a little while after the Sabbath has terminated, and sweeten the days of the coming week. The candle is finally extinguished in the wine, and everyone shouts: *Shavua tov*, a good week. The Sabbath ends when three stars appear in the evening sky. This ceremony, observed in synagogue and home, tells us that the special day is no more, but one can look forward to the next Sabbath. Songs are then sung, including one about Elijah, the prophet of peace and brotherhood.

Rosh Hashanah

You might be surprised to learn Jews wish one another a 'Happy New Year' in September/October, but before you decide it is so unusual, remember: September is the beginning of the new year for schools, the Inland Revenue begins its new year in April, and cars have a new year in August. Muslims and the Chinese also have their own different new year. The Christian new year begins with Advent in November.

Another surprising feature of the Jewish new year is that it is not a very happy occasion since it is not ushered in by parties or celebrations. It is a day of judgement with long services in the synagogue. It is not a judgement of others but a self-examination of ourselves. It is a day of memorial, or remembrance, as we remember our past deeds and faults, praying that God will not remember them and will give us a happy new year. The music in the synagogue is less joyful than on Sabbaths and other festivals, and the prayers themselves often mention our sins.

Christians send Christmas cards in December, Muslims send cards for *Eid al Fitr*, and Jews send new year cards. Sometimes, when there are so many relatives and friends to send cards to, some people prefer to put in a greeting in the national Jewish newspaper, in Britain *The Jewish Chronicle*, or one of the provincial papers. The full Hebrew greeting is 'May you be inscribed and sealed for a good year', but usually it is shortened to just *Shana Tova* a good (happy) new year.

It may appear that this festival, which most Jews celebrate for two days, is a very dull and even unhappy one. This is far from true. On the eve of the holy day, kiddush is recited with the additional feature of dipping a piece of apple or bread into honey. The former represents the land's produce, whilst the latter is a symbol of the hope of a sweet year to come. The prayer is recited: 'May it be Your will, O Lord our God, and God of our fathers, to renew unto us a happy and sweet (pleasant) year'. On entering the synagogue one sees that the ark curtain, Torah mantles, even the robes of the rabbi and cantor, are decked in white, the colour of purity.

The central feature of the morning service is the blowing of the *shofar*. This instrument, a ram's horn, is the oldest Jewish musical instrument, and although centuries ago it was blown on various occasions, today it is reserved mainly for the new year service. In Orthodox synagogues, if the first day of the festival is a Sabbath, it is not blown, whereas Progressive congregations will hear the shofar on a Sabbath, especially as many only keep one day. Another name for the festival is 'The Day of Sounding' (i.e. the shofar). It is blown in remembrance of Abraham's readiness to sacrifice his son Isaac. It reminds us that God is our ruler and judge. Its notes warn us that we need to improve. The blowing of the shofar is a very dramatic part of the service. The person who blows the shofar may be the rabbi or cantor, or it may be any member of the congregation who has the ability. It may even be a young person, as long as he has the stamina to blow the required 100 notes, including the final blast, which is very long; everyone holds their breath to see how long the sound will last.

The most common name for the festival is *Rosh Hashanah*,

Head of the Year. This name, however, is neither found in the Bible nor in rabbinic writings, but as a Jewish custom observed for a long time becomes a tradition, that is why this name is the most popular. Secondly, since it celebrates the creation, the festival, according to the Jewish tradition, is the birthday of the world. A popular hymn sung on the day begins. 'Today is the birthday of the world'. Thus Jews are not just praying for themselves, but for all humanity.

Yom Kippur

The holiest day of the Jewish calendar is *Yom Kippur*, the Day of Atonement, the Sabbath of Sabbaths (although it can fall on most weekdays as well as on the Sabbath). It occurs nine days after Rosh Hashanah and is a fast day, although fasting as such is not mentioned in the Bible which states that 'you shall afflict your soul', or 'practise self-denial' (Leviticus 23:27). The early rabbis interpreted this to mean fasting. Every healthy adult Jew is obliged to fast. Pregnant women, the infirm, people who need essential medicines, and young people under the age of 13, are exempt. (These are similar to the exemptions for the Islamic fast of Ramadan). There are a number of fast days in the Jewish calendar, but Yom Kippur is by far the most important and the most observed. In order to understand that we are all dependent on God's providence, we abstain from food and drink for a period of 25 hours, after which we in the West are fortunate enough to eat heartily, whereas two thirds of the world's population will experience 'fasting' every day of their lives. Many Jews give the money they save on food during Yom Kippur to an agency helping the hungry of these countries. Fasting takes some self-discipline. Judaism does not ask that we hurt ourselves with restrictions, but ignoring the need to eat, we may be somewhat weakened physically, but we are free to pray all day, with no distractions, and thus gain spiritual strength.

After a good meal on the eve of Yom Kippur, the family will attend the first service, known as *Kol Nidre* (all vows). Synagogues are normally very full for this service. A unique feature is that it is the only evening of the year when the *tallit* (prayer shawl) is worn by worshippers. It is normally worn during morning service only, but Yom Kippur is regarded as one long day beginning with *Kol Nidre*. All the scrolls are taken out of the Ark whilst the moving prayer *Kol Nidre* is sung three times. As with Rosh Hashanah, the music is solemn but not sad, and the prayers are pleas for God's forgiveness for our sins. Nearly every prayer is couched in the plural, for Jews stand as a community. Yom Kippur atones only for sins of man against God. Judaism insists that if a man has not forgiven his neighbour, he cannot expect God to forgive him on this holiest day. In the days leading up to Yom Kippur, Jews are expected to seek forgiveness from relatives and friends for any wrong they have done.

The following morning many synagogues will begin the service around 7.30 a.m. and continue until dusk, around 7 p.m. The Torah will be read during both the morning and afternoon services, and a Memorial service, for departed relatives and congregants is also included. There are five services throughout Yom Kippur. The concluding service is also a very moving occasion, when towards the end in front of the open Ark, the shofar is blown once more, this time one long blast pierces the air. Yom Kippur is over. Hopefully God has forgiven our sins, we can hope for a good year to come.

Succot

A few days after Yom Kippur, Jews will again be celebrating, this time a joyful festival, called *Succot*, meaning Tabernacles. For a week some Jews will build a *succah* and at least have their meals in it and, if the weather permits, also sleep there. A succah is a type of Jewish tent, except it has no proper roof and is decorated with foliage and fruit. It is to remind us that life is only for a short time and, just as the succah is subject to rain and wind, so our lives are, alas, often shortened because of illness or fatal accidents. At one time in the land of Israel, every family would build is own succah, but as the custom became observed less, it was left to just a few families and the synagogue built one on behalf of the entire community. The commandment to build a succah is found in the Bible (Leviticus 23:42). Exact measurements will be found in the Talmud. The Bible also mentions the taking of four plants, the palm, myrtle, willow, and 'the fruit of a goodly tree', which the later rabbis defined as the *etrog*, a citron, a relative of the lemon, the same colour, but larger and far more expensive. They are waved in all directions during part of the morning service, to show that God is everywhere. The Talmud compares these plants with everyday symbols such as parts of the human body; the elements around us such as

81

A school group visiting a succah *(tabernacle) at the synagogue. The rabbi is holding the four* species *which are used during Succot services.*

fire and water; the different types of people in the world. All are different, yet all can come together in unity.

Succot lasts for eight days, although Orthodox Jews outside Israel observe nine days. On the last day it is in many respects a new festival with a new name, *Simchat Torah*. The name is not Biblical and all the rituals are only a few hundred years old. The eve of the festival is the only evening of the year when the Torah is read. Both at this service and the following morning service all the Torah Scrolls are taken from the Ark for seven processions, or circuits, around the synagogue. The children follow, often carrying flags or miniature scrolls. After each circuit, those carrying the scrolls dance and other congregants sing and clap hands. Samuel Pepys describes, in his famous diary written some 300 years ago, how he visited a London synagogue on this festival and, poor man, he didn't know what to make of it. He wrote: 'But Lord! to see the disorder, laughing, sporting, and no attention, but confusion in all their service... and indeed I never did see so much, or could have imagine there had been any religion in the whole world so absurdly performed as this.' But, for Jews, this is the day to celebrate. Everybody, including the children, is 'called up' to the reading of the Torah. (In Orthodox Synagogues only the men are involved.) Two leading members of the community are elected 'bride-grooms' and as at a wedding, or party, food and drink is provided. After all, you can't be expected to dance and sing on an empty stomach!

All these festivals fall in September (*Tishri*), beginning with the more solemn high holy days and concluding with the joyful days of Succot and Simchat Torah.

Chanukah

According to the early rabbis, *Chanukah* was not a military but a spiritual victory, winning the right of every person to follow their own religion. The Talmud also mentions aspects of the story and includes an incident not found anywhere else. It tells that when Judah and his followers entered the Temple after it had been defiled by the soldiers for the past three years, they wished to rededicate it, thus the name Chanukah which means dedication, was later given to the festival. The seven-branched *Menorah* had to be rekindled but they found sufficient oil for only a day. It would take a further week before new olive oil could be prepared. But a miracle occurred and the oil intended for just the one day lasted eight. A new festival was declared, a festival of lights; a *Menorah*, or *Chanukiyah*, was to be kindled in every Jewish home and synagogue for eight nights and special prayers recited and songs sung.

An important feature of many Jewish festivals is the special food eaten, and Chanukah is no exception. Food cooked in oil is the order of the day. In Israel, doughnuts are popular, elsewhere families enjoy 'Jewish chips', or potato pancakes, known as *latkes* in Yiddish, and *levivot* in Hebrew.

A special game of the festival is spin the *dreidle*. Also known in Hebrew as *sevivon*, it is a put-in-and-take-out spinning top having a Hebrew letter on each side. Where it lands determines whether you put in more 'valuables', such as sweets, or nuts, or take from the kitty; indeed, you may even be fortunate enough to break the bank. Children enjoy this game throughout the festival. In recent times it has become the custom to give presents and to hold parties. Many synagogues put on parties for the children and they, in turn, provide the entertainment in the form of pantomimes, such a 'Aladdin and his Magic Menorah' or 'Peter Pan in Latkeland'.

All in all, both adults and children enjoy themselves during these happy festivals.

Purim

Purim, like Chanukah, is about the deliverance of the Jews. The whole story can be found in the Bible in the Book of Esther. In seeking a new queen, the Persian king, Ahasuerus, chose a girl called Esther who, unknown to him, was Jewish. The king's chief minister, Haman, disliked the Jews, and decided he would kill them all. He cast lots (*purim*) and the day selected for the massacre was the 13th day of the 12th month, which is Adar. However, the Jews were saved because of intervention by Esther who was greatly inspired and encouraged by her cousin, Mordecai. In grateful thanks for their deliverance, it was ordained that Purim should be a new joyful festival to be celebrated by every future generation of Jews.

Should you pass a synagogue during the reading of Esther, you may be forgiven for thinking that you are at a football match, since, at regular intervals, you will hear hissing, stamping and even the sound of football rattles. This is because whenever the villain's name, Haman, is mentioned, the children make as much noise as possible in order to blot out his name. In some countries, they even make a dummy to represent him, and ritually burn it (like Guy Fawkes). It is rare to find a Jewish person drunk, even though Judaism encourages the drinking of wine for certain ceremonies. At Purim, however, it is nearly an obligation to get drunk, for it is said in the Talmud that we should drink enough wine so as not to distinguish between 'blessed be Mordecai' (the hero) and 'cursed be Haman' (the villain). A few Jews try to carry out this command seriously, but most remain sober.

Children have fancy dress parties at Purim, and also put on plays, often written by themselves. It is also a custom to exchange presents and give to the poor, and for the past 800 years, a special biscuit has been enjoyed called *hamantashen*, a word of German origin. It is three-cornered in shape, some say to represent Haman's hat, others say it was the shape of his ears. They are filled with poppy-seed, and whilst you can buy them from a Jewish baker, many families make their own.

Pesach

Perhaps the most popular and best known festival is *Pesach*, or Passover. This week-long celebration marks the birthday of the Jewish people. Celebrated in the spring, it commemorates the exodus from Egypt to the promised land of Israel, when the Hebrews were delivered from slavery to freedom (Exodus 12–14). There are, of course, services held in the synagogue, but the most important feature is the ceremonial meal at home known as the *Seder* (order). There are up to 14 parts for the ceremony. It is not a service and so a prayer book is not used, but participants read passages and sing songs from a book known as *haggadah* (story). It is very much a family get-together, very much like Christmas Day lunch. Often, friends will also be invited, but Jewish tradition insists that no one is alone for the event which takes place during the first evening of the festival. Most Jews hold another seder on the second evening too. It may be again in their own home, in a friend's or relative's home, or even in the synagogue hall where perhaps some 150 people are assembled. In Israel, on the *kibbutzim*, the communal settlements, all the members assemble in the dining room, sometimes as many as 800. Over the centuries, different groups have produced their own haggadah, and it has been estimated that there have been some 3,000 versions including many with beautiful illustrations and others especially for children.

The youngest child present asks four questions, beginning with 'How is this night different from all other nights?' There will be a special dish with some unusual items on it and no bread or rolls on the table; everyone present will drink, not one but four cups of wine. The answers to the child's questions take up the whole seder, and often the real or whole answer is not known. As a symbol for these uncertainties, a fifth cup is filled, left undrunk, called Elijah's Cup. Throughout the whole festival of Pesach, Jews will not eat bread, or to be more precise, leavened bread (bread containing yeast). They certainly do eat unleavened bread, called *matzot*. Today, it is factory-produced, normally square in shape. Since it is made without yeast it does not look like ordinary bread. Three *matzot* will be on the seder table, and near the beginning of the ceremony, the middle one is broken into two, one piece being hidden. After the meal, the children will play 'hide and seek' by attempting to find it, the winner being rewarded with a small gift.

On the seder dish there are several items of food. A roasted or hard-boiled egg is a reminder of the festival sacrifice brought to the Temple in Jerusalem. (Hard-boiled eggs will also be eaten prior to the meal proper. They will be cut up in salt water, which represents the tears shed by the Hebrew slaves in Egypt.) A roasted shankbone, is symbolic of the paschal offering brought to the Temple. *Charoset* is a mixture made from chopped apples and nuts, wine and cinnamon, which represents the mortar that the Hebrews used to make bricks. *Maror* are bitter herbs in memory of the bitter times experienced during the many years of slavery. Usually a horseradish root is used. Another type of herb that goes bitter, such as cucumber, is also required, as is a vegetable symbolic of spring, such as parsley or watercress.

During the readings from the *haggadah*, one will hear of famous rabbis, the ten plagues, and sing special songs and psalms. One name that will be missing but would be expected to have a central place, as he was the man responsible for the exodus is that of Moses. Jewish tradition insists that God himself redeemed his people and although Moses was the leader, praise is due only to God.

Shavuot

Fifty days after Pesach Jews celebrate another festival, *Shavuot*. The Greek name is Pentecost which means 'fifty'; its English name is the Festival of Weeks. Whereas Pesach is the birthday of the Jewish people, Shavuot is the birthday of the Jewish religion. Judaism teaches that the Torah was given on Shavuot. Here the Torah means the Ten Commandments. Like Pesach and Succot, Shavuot is a pilgrim festival, or foot festival. It means that in ancient times the people would make a pilgrimage to the Temple in Jerusalem, usually by foot. There they would offer their produce to the priests and sing psalms and say prayers. Shavuot, unlike the other two pilgrim festivals, only last a day, although Orthodox Jews outside Israel have added an extra day, as they have done with Pesach, Succot and Rosh Hashanah. It is a Jewish custom to stay up all night on Shavuot. During this time the Torah is studied. Today, only the very pious manage to last the whole night. To keep people awake coffee is drunk at intervals, and it is the custom to eat dairy produce. The most popular food is cheesecake. Honeycake is also traditional as the Torah is compared to sweetness. During the synagogue morning service the Ten Commandments are read and also the Book of Ruth. It is said that King David was born and died on Shavuot; Ruth was his great-grandmother. There is an additional reading in many synagogues of a poem written some 100 years ago. Part of it reads:

> Could we with ink the ocean fill,
> Were every blade of grass a quill;
> Were the world of parchment made,
> And every man a scribe by trade;
> To write the love of God above
> Would drain the ocean dry;
> Nor would the Scroll contain the whole,
> Though stretched from sky to sky.

The Scriptures

Islam's greatest prophet, Muhammad, called both Jews and Christians 'people of the Book'. By this, of course, he meant the Bible. As far as Jews are concerned, it would be more correct to call them 'people of the Books', as more than one book is considered sacred.

Both Jews and Christians regard the Bible as holy literature. For the Christian it includes both the Old and New Testaments. For the Jew only the Old Testament is holy scripture or, in Hebrew, *Tanach*.

The first five books, often called the Five Books of Moses, are the *Torah*. Some Christians in the past have wrongly translated this word as law. The *Torah* contains laws, but a more accurate translation would be teaching, or instruction. It is also known as the *Pentateuch* meaning five. From a Jewish point of view, this section is regarded as the most important part of the Hebrew Bible.

The second section, *Nev'im* (prophets) comprises the books concerning the many prophets of Israel. The third section, *Ketuvim* (writings) contains eleven books of miscellaneous character, such as Psalms, Proverbs and Chronicles. (*Tanach* therefore, stands for the three sections of the Old Testament: Torah, Nev'im and Ketuvim.)

There are some Orthodox Jews (and Christians) who maintain that the Bible is the direct word of God, whilst other Progressive Jews feel that it was written by many people over a long period of time, and although there were inspired by God, they had limitations as human beings, so that while much of what they had written still has meaning for us today, some of their teachings conflict with modern ideas and therefore should be modified. All Jews agree, however, that the Bible has shaped Jewish life, and still has an important message for both Jews and non-Jews.

Jewish tradition teaches that Moses, in fact, was given two Torahs, the Bible, known as the 'Written Torah', and the Rabbinic writings, called the 'Oral Torah' as it was handed down by word of mouth. Eventually it was collected and

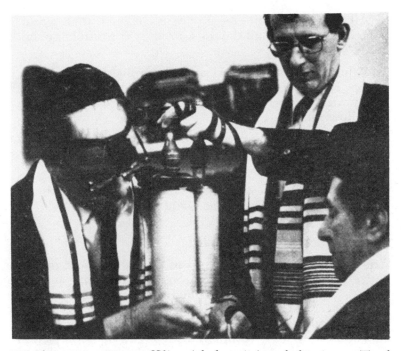

Worshippers wearing teffilin *(phylacteries) and dressing a Torah Scroll during weekday morning service.*

edited, in about 200 C.E., by a rabbi known as Judah 'the Prince'. He divided his book into six sections or 'orders', and these were further sub-divided into 63 tractates. His work was called *Mishnah*, meaning 'teaching by repeating'. Within this great work, can be found laws and regulations concerning prayer, festivals, marriage and divorce, civil and criminal law, purity, as well as a whole section concerning the temple ritual. It is possible to buy the whole Mishnah in one volume in English and for this we have to thank a Christian clergyman who undertook this mammoth task.

Perhaps the most popular and widely known of all the tractates is *Pirke Avot*, the Ethics of the Fathers. Originally it consisted of five chapters, although an extra chapter was added when it was included in the prayerbook. Unlike the other tractates, which deals mainly with legal rulings, *Avot* is concerned with ethical behaviour and includes the sayings and teachings of some 60 rabbis, covering a period of 500 years. The following are just a few of their sayings:

89

'All is foreseen but free choice is granted. The world is judged with mercy and all is measured by the number of good deeds.'

'Who is wise? He who learns from every man. Who is strong? He who controls his passions. Who is rich? He who is happy with his portion. Who is honourable? He who honours his fellow men.'

'There are three crowns: the crown of the Torah, the crown of priesthood, and the crown of royalty; but the crown of a good name excels them all.'

'Rejoice not when your enemy falls, and when he stumbles do not allow your heart to be glad.'

The Talmud and the Midrash

After the death of Judah, many of the rabbis went over the entire text of the Mishnah, discussing, debating and even voting. They were like a parliament recording all views, even the most trivial, and enabling everyone who wished to speak the opportunity to do so. Their views and teachings became an addition to the Mishnah, called *Gemara* (completion). Much of it was written in Aramaic, the language that the Jews, and many non-Jews, spoke at the time of Jesus. When combined with the Mishnah, the book became known as the *Talmud*, which means 'study'. There are, in fact, two Talmuds, The Jerusalem (or Palestinian), and the Babylonian, the latter is the superior one.

The early rabbis would often give sermons in the synagogues commenting on the biblical texts. Often they would put over an important teaching by using parables. These were collected and form the *Midrash*, which we often translate as 'search', i.e. for meaning. The following are some sayings from the Rabbinic literature of the Talmud and Midrash:

'In finances, be strict with yourself, generous with others.'

'There are three kinds of companions: Some are like food, indispensable; some like medicine, good occasionally; and some like poison, unnecessary at any time.'

'Why was man created a solitary human being, without a companion? So that it might not be said that some races are better than others.'

90

'If two men claim your help, and one is your enemy, help him first.'

'A man is forbidden to eat anything until he has fed his beast.'

'Greatness seeks out the man who runs away from greatness.'

'You have entered the city; abide by its customs.'

'Truth is heavy; therefore few wear it.'

Religious Practices and Customs

Birth

Jewish tradition teaches that three are responsible for creating a baby: father, mother and God. Every birth is greeted with great joy. If it is a girl, the father is 'called up' to the Torah on the next Sabbath and his daughter is given a name. If the child is a boy, on the eighth day the baby is circumcised. If the eighth day is a Sabbath, or Day of Atonement, the circumcision still takes place. Only the illness of the baby can postpone it. For Jews, circumcision is a *brit*, a covenant, commanded by God, as stated in the Bible when Abraham was the first Jew to practise it. Thus, it is not done for health reasons, but is a religious obligation and is carried out even by non-religious Jews. Of course, many non-Jews practise circumcision, notably Muslims. In fact, one in seven of the world's males are circumcised. Amongst the Jewish community the rite is carried out by a specially qualified man called a *mohel*, who need not be a doctor nor a rabbi, but is obviously skilled and pious. At the circumcision the child is given a Hebrew name which will be used on every religious occasion in the future. If a boy, the name will be followed by *ben* (son) and then his father's name. If a girl, *bat* (daughter). Amongst most western Jews, it is not the custom to name a child after a living relative. Some will have names that are already Hebrew, names such as Michael, David, Ruth. Others may have names like Maurice, and their Hebrew name may be Moshe (Moses). Yet others will have Yiddish names. Amongst Orthodox Jews, if the first born is a boy, a ceremony of redemption takes place on the 31st day after birth.

Bar Mitzvah

When a Jewish boy reaches the age of 13 years and one day (for girls it is one year earlier) he is, from a Jewish legal point

A Bar Mitzvah boy reading his portion from the Torah Scroll.

of view, a fully-fledged member of the religious community, and is called a *Bar Mitzvah*, a son of the Commandment, whereas a girls is called *Bat Mitzvah*, a daughter of the Commandment. With prior preparation he reads a portion from the Torah scroll during a Sabbath, or Monday or Thursday morning service. If he is Orthodox, he will also put on his *teffilin* (phylacteries) for the first time. These are two small leather boxes containing biblical verses. One is placed on the forehead, whilst the other is put on the upper arm, opposite the heart. It is placed on the left arm unless the person is left-handed. They are not, however, worn on Sabbaths or festivals. In some synagogues, the boy will also conduct the whole service and even address the congregation.

In most Progressive synagogues, there is a similar ceremony for a Bat Mitzvah. Those Orthodox synagogues that permit Bat Mitzvah hold a ceremony on Sunday afternoons when the girl, or girls, will read a few passages from the Bible and prayer-book. They will not read from the Torah scroll.

In order to be a Bar Mitzvah one does not need a ceremony, the status is automatically attained by reaching the age of 13. From then on young men can be 'called up' to the Torah and be counted in the *minyan*, the quorum of 10 males needed for public worship. It is usual for some form of party to follow the ceremony, sometimes on the Sunday. It should be a modest affair, but some families today have large parties, more like weddings. Others decide to save the money for a visit to Israel. Indeed, in recent years, it has been the practice for many families to hold the ceremony in Jerusalem at the Western Wall. Often, a number of boys share the occasion. In some Progressive synagogues, a further ceremony takes place when the boy or girl reaches the age of 16. It is sometimes called *Kabbalat Mitzvah* (acceptance of the commandment) or simply Confirmation, but not to be confused with Confirmation as practised in many churches. Very often this will be a mass celebration, similar to Bar Mitzvah, with a whole class of youngsters participating.

Marriage

The Talmud states that without a wife a man is incomplete, advising men first to study, then to marry, but if it is not possible to live without a wife to reverse the order. Most marriages take place in a synagogue but they can take place elsewhere. Marriages cannot be performed on Sabbaths or

Festivals, and there are other times in the Jewish year when marriages, at least in Orthodox synagogues, cannot take place. According to Jewish law, and also English law, only Jews may be married in a synagogue, thus it is not possible for, say, a Jew and a Christian to marry with a Jewish ceremony. At one time it was possible for a Jewish man to marry more than one woman, but, as one rabbi in the Talmud put it, 'one wife is enough for any man'. To hold a Jewish wedding, in addition to the bride and groom, you need: a canopy under which they will be married, called a *chupa*, a cup of wine from which the couple will drink on two occasions, and a plain wedding ring which will initially be placed on the forefinger of the bride's right hand, whilst making the declaration in Hebrew, 'Behold, you are consecrated unto me by this ring according to the law of Moses and Israel'. The ring then can be placed on the usual marriage finger. This part is the most important, from a Jewish point of view, and makes the couple man and wife. They will be presented with a marriage certificate, known as a *ketubah*. In addition to the couple, two witnesses will sign it. At most weddings, a printed certificate is used. At some weddings in America and Israel, handwritten documents are used, often beautifully illustrated. At the end of the ceremony, the groom will step on and break a small glass. No one knows the real reason for this ritual. Some say it is to ward off evil spirits, others maintain that marriage will not bring only joy, but sadness will be part of life as well, and this must be accepted. It is also a reminder that the Temple is in ruins and has not been restored.

Traditionally, Judaism sanctions sex only with marriage. It has also looked upon the sexual relationship as good and beautiful; in the words of a rabbi living in the Middle Ages 'The act of sexual union is holy and pure... the Lord created all things in accordance with His wisdom and whatever He created cannot possibly be shameful or ugly... when a man is in union with his wife in a spirit of holiness and purity, the Divine Presence is with them.'

The majority of Jews no longer favour arranged marriages. Even when they existed it was said 'a youth need not obey his parents if they urge him to marry not the girl he loves, but another with money', and that you should 'wait until your daughter reaches her majority and can express her consent before you give her in betrothal'.

Divorce

Judaism realizes that one thing is worse than being alone, and that is being with the wrong person. Some couples fall in love and then out of love. Neither should be captive, they should be given the opportunity of trying again if their relationship has no chance of being repaired. Thus, Judaism has always allowed divorce, although, according to the Talmud, 'if a man divorces the wife of his youth, the very altar (of God) weeps'. At one time it was possible to divorce a wife merely if she spoiled a man's food, or was unable to provide him with any children. Although only a man could initiate divorce, a woman could not be divorced except by her own consent. In Orthodox Judaism, the woman still does not have the power to divorce her husband, and in many cases this puts the woman in a most difficult and unhappy position. It is not possible for Orthodox rabbis to change the law, but Progressive Judaism has made a number of changes with regard to marriage and divorce. According to Jewish law, a document of divorce, known as a *get*, is written out. Once all the formalities have been completed, both parties are free to remarry.

Death

Jews hope that they will live to the biblical expectation of 80 years (Psalm 90:10). Often, on a senior citizen's birthday, he is wished 'until 120', the age of Moses when he died. Jewish tradition requires that burial takes place as soon as possible after death, usually within 24 hours. Orthodox Judaism does not permit cremation, although Progressive Judaism sanctions it. The larger synagogues have their own cemeteries, whilst the smaller ones have a portion of a council cemetery. You will not find ornate coffins at Jewish funerals. In the Talmud it was decreed that the dead should be buried in simple linen and plain coffins so that the poor would not be embarrassed by high cost. For similar reasons, flowers are not encouraged at funerals. If people cannot be equal during their lives, at least we owe them equality when they die. At death, rich and poor are equal and so it should appear at their funeral. It is a great honour to be obliged to accompany the dead to their final resting place, and also to help bury them.

There are many regulations regarding mourning, many of which are no longer observed by a growing number of Jews.

These include the cutting of a garment (e.g. a tie) by the next of kin; the covering of mirrors in the home; sitting on low stools for a week; abstaining from shaving or cutting the hair. This week of mourning is known as *shiva*. Many maintain that mourners need a week when relatives and friends can visit them and bring them comfort. Others feel that grief is a personal affair, and some people prefer to be on their own, or back at work. In the home, a special candle is lit in memory of the departed. For the next eleven months, many Jews will not participate in any entertainment such as going to a dance or a cinema. During this period they will recite the so-called mourner's prayer, the *kaddish*, whenever they visit the synagogue. At a funeral, or house of mourning, the mourners are often greeted with the words 'I wish you long life'. In some families in Britain, only the men attend a funeral. Death, according to Jewish tradition, is not the end, only the body has died; the soul, the spirit of man, returns to God his Maker.

Eating Kosher

There are many foods we really enjoy and others which we don't. Indeed, some foods may make us ill if we are allergic to them. Doctors often advise us to cut out, or at least cut down, on 'fatty' foods. Health food shops are now very common in every high street, so we are certainly more conscious than ever about our diet. The Bible, too, records certain dietary rules, animals, fish and birds that should not be eaten by the Jewish people (Lev. 11). No reasons are given but it does not mean that these forbidden foods are in any way unclean, although there are some who maintain that many of these foods can be injurious to health. Jews call these regulations the Dietary Laws, or in Hebrew *kashrut*. The things we can eat are *kosher* or *kasher* meaning 'fit', and those we cannot eat are *teraifa*, meaning 'torn'. Other religions also have dietary laws. The Muslim also abstains from eating pig; the Hindu refrains from eating beef; the Mormon will not drink tea or coffee. A Jew is allowed to eat any animal which chews the cud and has cloven hooves. He, therefore, can eat the cow or sheep, but not the pig or hare. With regard to fish, he may eat anything which has fins and scales, such as cod, haddock and trout. He is forbidden to eat shellfish, octopus, eel and whale. As far as birds are concerned, he is permitted to eat all birds which are not birds of prey, such as the eagle, with the exception of the swan, stork and partridge.

Although Jews are allowed to eat certain animals, such as the cow, it must be ritually killed a certain way. Only a trained person, known as a *shochet*, is allowed to slaughter the animal with a smooth and very sharp blade, free from notches. The shochet makes a rapid forward and backward stroke in the windpipe and gullet of the animal, or bird, which produces immediate unconsciousness. All this is done to ensure that pain is reduced to the absolute minimum. From time to time, some non-Jews criticize this method for they feel it is rather primitive. There are other non-Jews who agree with Jews that this method is indeed one of the most humane ways of killing for food. An expert once said that if he were to choose the way he died, he would prefer this way to any other! This method also allows the blood to drain, because it is forbidden for Jews to eat blood (Leviticus 7:26). In order that all the blood is removed, either the Jewish butcher, or housewife, will soak the meat in salted water for at least an hour. There are no special rules regarding fish.

Another important factor of kashrut is that a Jew may not mix meat and milk dishes. For example, he cannot have a beef sandwich that has been spread with butter. In a Jewish restaurant only black coffee, or lemon tea, is served after a meat meal. For many Jews, separate crockery and cutlery must be used depending on whether the meal is meat or non-meat. The interval one must wait before having a milk dish varies between communities. Jews from Eastern Europe wait six hours; German and West European Jews wait three (this is the main custom amongst British Jews); Dutch Jews consider 72 minutes to be sufficient.

Not all Jews keep kashrut. Some may refrain from eating forbidden foods, but purchase their meat from a non-Jewish butcher, or supermarket. Others may observe it in the home but not when on holiday, or when eating out. A few may find it totally irrelevant. Some may keep it because the Torah commands it. Others keep it because of historical associations, family tradition, or because it is a good self-discipline and makes them more aware of their religion. We can do no better than to sum up in the words of Moses Maimonides, the great philosopher and physician of the 12th century, when he wrote: 'The dietary laws train us to master our appetites and not to consider eating and drinking the end of man's existence.'

The Home Symbol

Before you even enter a Jewish home, you become aware that it is one for on the front door there will be a *mezuzah*. This is a small, hand written, parchment scroll, enclosed in a wooden or plastic case, which is attached to the doorpost. Its use is commanded in the Bible (Deuteronomy 6:9). A scribe writes the *shema* prayer in the same way as he would write a Torah scroll. The container is attached to the upper half of the doorpost, in a slanting position, just above eye-level, on the right hand side of the entrance. Many Jews fix them on their doors in the house, with the exception of the toilet. Some Orthodox Jews, on entering or leaving the front door, touch the mezuzah with their finger tips and then lightly kiss their fingers, showing respect for God's word which it contains. However, there is nothing magical about the mezuzah, and it is forbidden to regard it as a good luck charm. It just reminds the Jew of God's presence and of his loving care.

The shema is one of the most important prayers in Judaism. It is recited during the morning and evening services, before going to sleep at night, and as a confession on one's death bed. It has often been called the watchword of Israel since it is not really a prayer, but a declaration of the unity of God.

Judaism Today

We have already mentioned Orthodox and Progressive Jews. We have seen how their services differ and how they regard the Torah. A few Jews are ultra-Orthodox. They are known as *chassidim*, the pious ones. They originally came from Eastern Europe, in particular Poland. Most of the men have long beards, and all males will shave their hair but have long sidecurls. The women also shave their hair and wear either a wig or scarf. Amongst themselves they will speak Yiddish and the men and boys will spend much of the day in prayer and study of the Torah. They will have very little contact with non-Jews, indeed very little contact with other Jews either. Unlike other Jews who you will find in many cities and towns of Britain, this group will only be found in parts of North London (Stamford Hill), Manchester, and Gateshead in the North-East. You will also see them if you ever visit Jerusalem; they have their own quarter and often go to pray at the Western Wall.

Many Jews today would call themselves Zionists. This means they have a special love and concern for the land of Israel and its people. They work hard to raise money and gifts to send to institutions and individuals. They will make many visits to Israel, and perhaps one or more of their children will go and live there. Not all Zionists are religious, sometimes their only attachment to the Jewish community is through their Zionism.

There are also Jews who could be termed secularists or assimilationists. They have little or no contact or interest in Judaism or the Jewish people. They may even change their name if they think it sounds too Jewish! They just happen to be born Jews and there the interest and loyalty ends.

The Chosen People?

It has often been said that Jews consider themselves to be the Chosen People. An American author chose as a title for a book nearly 50 years ago: *How odd of God to choose the Jews.*

Some time later, someone replied, 'It's not so odd. The Jews chose God'. Judaism teaches that we can only be chosen if we desire it. One English Jew remarked that we are more of a choosing people than a chosen people. Many people, including Jews, have misunderstood the whole concept. It does not mean that God in choosing to love the Jewish people loves the rest of humanity less. God does not have favourites, nor are the Jews in any way superior to any other group. It does not mean that the Jews were to dominate the world or enjoy a special position of power among the other nations. But it does mean being chosen to perform a special task or mission in the world. It means being a good example to others; teaching and holding a light to the nations by following the Torah. It means often standing alone in a frequently hostile and intolerant world, remaining faithful and being prepared to stand up and be counted in spite of suffering and persecution. In the words of a British rabbi nearly 80 years ago, 'It is in no arrogant temper that we claim to be the chosen people. We thereby affirm, not that we are better than others, but that we ought to be better.'

The Devil and Sin

Nearly all religions teach about evil and the Evil One. In Hebrew he is called Satan, and by this name he is also known by Christians and Muslims. In Judaism, Satan is not a rival of God, but is subject to him and strictly controlled by him. Judaism teaches that every person has two inclinations – *yetzer hara*, the inclination to do evil, and *yetzer tov*, the good inclination. It is possible, according to Judaism, for man to have dominion over his *yetzer hara*. There is a delightful story of a rabbi living in Russia a century ago. It was the middle of winter, very cold, with thick snow on the ground. It was early morning and time for the rabbi to go to synagogue. His yetzer tov beckoned him, 'Arise and go to praise your Maker!' The yetzer hara urged him to remain in bed, 'You are frail', it said. 'If you leave the warmth of your home you are certain to catch a cold, and at your age it could kill you. What good then would you be to God?' The rabbi replied, 'I am touched by your concern for my health. I, too, an concerned with yours. I suggest *you* stay in the warm bed whilst I will attend synagogue prayers!'

The early rabbis felt that the yetzer hara was even necessary, as without it no man would build a house, take a wife, have a family, and engage in work. It was also argued that although God had created the yetzer hara, he had also created its antidote, the Torah. *All people sin*. The Jew has the opportunity to repent at any time. As a community the Jews have Yom Kippur to atone for their sins. Sin in Hebrew means 'missing the mark'. If we realize that we are off course, with God's help we can redirect ourselves if we are sincere in our prayers and in our actions.

The Messiah and Life after Death

A basic teaching of Judaism is that at some time in the future all nations will live together in peace, and wars will be a thing of the past. Some teachers taught that a person sent by God would usher in this new age. He was to be called the Messiah, a man anointed by God for this purpose. There have been many through the ages who have proclaimed themselves to be this Messiah, or others claimed it for them. Amongst these hundreds of would-be Messiahs, three became well-known, indeed, one internationally known with millions of followers to this day. This man lived some 2,000 years ago in Israel which was then under the control of the Romans who renamed the country Palestine. His name was Jeshua, a form of Joshuah, which in Greek is Jesus. His first disciples were all Jews, and some of them wrote about the life and death of their leader; these books, later became the New Testament. His followers regarded him not only as a rabbi or teacher, but also as the long-awaited Messiah. For most Jews, however, he was not accepted in this role, for the Messiah would bring peace. Many Gentiles, when they heard the message, gladly followed and since they were Greek speaking, they called him *Christos*, later shortened to Christ, also meaning 'anointed'. They became known as Christians and although, at first their religion was considered part of Judaism, they soon became part of a new religion which was destined to have much influence over millions of people in many countries throughout the world.

A century later, also in Israel, another man claimed that he was the Messiah and was known as Bar Kochbah, meaning 'son of a star'. One of the greatest rabbis of the time, Akibah recognized him in this role, and encouraged him to rebel against the Romans. However, the battle was not won, despite his great strength and courage. He died in battle and dismayed Jews renamed him 'son of a lie'.

Only 300 years ago another Jew proclaimed himself the Messiah, this time in Turkey. He was Shabbetai Zevi (1626–76). There were many who believed in him, and even sold their property and all they had in order to follow him back to the land of Israel. The Sultan arrested him and he was given the choice of converting to Islam or being put to death. He chose the former and his movement came to an end except for a few faithful followers who continued to proclaim his messiahship.

Some Jews have stressed the coming of the Messianic age rather than the coming of a personal Messiah. Such a view is shared by many Jews today. The Jewish religion is not affected by belief or disbelief in a Messiah. Although Judaism can function without the belief in a personal Messiah, it cannot function without the belief in the age of the Messiah. No Jew who cherishes the spirit of Judaism will surrender belief in the Messianic Age when all men will find their brotherhood in the Fatherhood of the One God. Thus, peace, justice and freedom will prevail throughout the world.

What of the world to come? Is there a life after death? According to Judaism, the soul, which comes from God, is eternal. There is some sort of after-life but we have not been given many details and should leave it to God in His wisdom rather than try to work out some kind of picture. True, both Bible and Talmud speak of a heaven and, in a few places only, a hell. This is symbolic language and they should not be taken as literal places. A Jewish story tells of a visitor who came to Paradise and found it entirely populated by groups of old men, all bent over in study of the Torah. Surprised, he questioned the heavenly guide who told him, 'You have the mistaken idea that the men are in heaven. Actually, heaven is in the men,' A final point, for the past 2,000 years Judaism has taught that the righteous of all nations have a share in the world to come. Whatever heaven is like, you can be sure it will contain people of all faiths and even those who have no religious faith but have lovingly observed the God-given commandment to love you neighbour as yourself.

BUDDHISM

ANIL D. GOONEWARDENE

Introduction

The teaching of a Buddha is called the *Dhamma* (*Dharma*). Buddhism is therefore the teaching of a Buddha and the practice of that teaching. After Enlightenment, a Buddha begins to teach the Dhamma. It is known to the people for a long time but they understand and practise it less and less over the years, and it then dies out after a long time. Later another Buddha attains Enlightenment and begins to teach. The Dhamma is a natural law which continues to exist as a law of nature.

Buddhism helps people to understand and come to terms with life and death, and to overcome unhappiness. Buddhists believe that the purpose of life is achieved through the study and practice of the Dhamma and obtaining the fruits of that practice to attain *Nibbana* (*Nirvana*). *Mahayana* emphasizes the attaining of Buddhahood and helping others to attain the same goal. Nibbana is explained in brief as the complete ending of greed, hatred and ignorance, and therefore of rebirth and the continuity of life.

There has been some discussion in the west as to whether Buddhism is a philosophy or a religion. The Buddhist teaching has a vast and complex philosophy. It also includes guidance on religious practice for the devotee to progress as a Buddhist. Buddhism comes within the dictionary meanings of religion, and, like all religions, explains the meaning of life and gives guidance on how one should live one's life. Buddhism is not a 'revealed' religion and does not teach of a God as the creator of the world.

Buddhism has always been a subject of intellectual and academic study. The Buddhist universities of India such as Nalanda and Valabhi attracted students from all over Asia. Today universities such as Otani in Japan and Mahachula-

104

longkorn in Thailand are equally famous as centres for the study of Buddhism.

The Buddha himself said that for a devotee intellectual study by itself was insufficient. There must be the practice, too, of the teaching. In fact some of the concepts in Buddhism cannot be intellectually understood. They have to be realized by mindfulness and meditation while practising the ethical guidelines laid down.

> Not insulting, not harming, restraint according to the fundamental moral code, moderation in food, secluded abode, intent on higher consciousness, this is the Teaching of the Buddhas.
>
> The Dhammapada, v. 185

Buddhism spread out of India and has been accepted by the peoples of other countries. The core of its teaching is common to all the traditions. Its flexibility and tolerance enabled it to evolve so as to fit into different cultures.

The ethical and moral guidelines in Buddhism lead to the achievement of harmony and peace both for the individual and for society. The teaching relating to mental culture guides the devotee to realizing the truth. The living being is considered to be a microcosm of the universe.

> Within this body, six feet high, endowed with perception and consciousness is contained the world, the origin of the world and the end of the world, and the path leading to the end of the world.

Gotama Buddha did not ask the people to accept his teachings simply because it was the word of a Buddha. He invited them to understand and practise the teaching and realize the truth for themselves.

Being a Buddhist

There is generally no initiation ceremony to become a Buddhist. Sometimes there may be a Refuge ceremony where a person undertakes a commitment to the Three Refuges, and Tibetan Buddhism has initiation vows and ceremonies for those proceeding on the Buddhist path.

In essence it can be said that a Buddhist is one who:

1. Takes the Buddha, Dhamma, and Sangha as guides to life and thought, and

105

2. Makes an effort to live according to the Buddha's teaching.

The teaching is expressed in the simplest form as:

Not to do any evil
To cultivate good
To purify one's mind.

The Dhammapada, v. 183

N.B. The two languages most important to the Buddhist texts are Pali and Sanskrit. When a technical word is first used both versions of the word are given and thereafter the Pali term is used for convenience, unless the Sanskrit term is more appropriate to the context. In this book, for example, Bodhisattva (Sanskrit) is used in the context of Mahayana Buddhism but Bodhisatta (Pali) is used in the Theravada context.

The Buddha, Arahats and Bodhisattvas

The Buddha

The term Buddha is derived from 'budh', to understand or be awakened, and is the title given to an Enlightened being. Theravada recognizes two kinds of Buddhas, Pacceka Buddhas who understand the truth but do not teach it and Samma Sambuddhas who understand the truth and go on to teach it. Theravada considers the Buddha to be an extraordinary human being with mental powers far beyond those of an ordinary human being, and refers to 27 named Buddhas before Gotama Buddha (Gautama or Sakyamuni Buddha) who was the last of the line of Buddhas. There were Buddhas before him and there are Buddhas to come.

The historical Buddha is recognized in the Mahayana and is called Sakyamuni. The Mahayana extended the idea of the Buddha to a transcendental being who is ever present, and who can appear in the world as a Buddha or in another form in order to help people to progress on the spiritual path. Gautama or Sakyamuni Buddha is taken to be a manifestation of this transcendental Buddha. The Mahayana also developed the idea of several heavenly Buddhas such as Amida, Bhaisajyaguru and Vairocana. The Mahayana normally refers to six Buddhas but Buddhas beyond that are known. According to Vajrayana Sakyamuni Buddha was one of over a thousand Buddhas of this time period. Mahayana further developed the idea of *Tri-kaya*, the three bodies or aspects of the Buddha:

1. *Nirmanakaya* – the earthly manifestation of the universal transcendent, 2. *Sambhogakaya* – manifested for the benefit of Bodhisattvas, visible to them, and adopted by the Buddha to teach them, and 3. *Dharmakaya* – the truth or knowledge body, an expression meaning reality.

Arahats

The aim of practice in early Buddhism and in Theravada is to become an *Arahat*, a being who has attained Enlightenment and Nibbana and will not be reborn.

> For him who has completed the journey (Samsara, cycle of life), for him who is sorrowless (completely eradicated ill will and attachment to sense desires) for him who from everything is wholly free, for him who has destroyed all ties, the fever (of passion) exists not.
>
> The Dhammapada, v. 90

An Arahat continues to live because the *Kammic* forces which caused him to be born still operate. He is not free from physical suffering, but his actions do not have Kammic effects any more.

> Calm is his mind, calm is his speech, calm is his actions, who rightly knowing, is wholly freed, perfectly peaceful and equipoised.
>
> The Dhammapada, v. 96

The Arahat lives out his life peacefully and having developed the qualities of lovingkindness and compassion continues to teach others formally and by example.

Bodhisattvas

Each Buddha goes through many human and non-human lives in preparation and development towards becoming a Buddha. In these lives he is known as a *Bodhisatta* (*Bodhisattva*), one intent on wisdom and Enlightenment. In Theravada a Bodhisatta is an individual working towards Enlightenment and becoming a Buddha, Gotama Buddha in his previous lives, which are recounted in the Jataka Stories, is referred to as a Bodhisatta. The Buddha to come, Maitreya Buddha, is now living as Bodhisatta in a heavenly world until the time when he will be born in the human world to attain Enlightenment.

The Bodhisatta in the Theravada teaching practises ten virtues or perfections in order to progress towards Enlightenment. They are generosity, morality, renunciation, wisdom, energy, patience, truthfulness, determination, lovingkindness and equanimity. The Jataka Stories relate how Gotama Buddha perfected these qualities as a Bodhisatta in his

108

previous lives. He even sacrificed his life several times for the benefit of other beings.

The Mahayana emphasized the idea that a Buddhist should aspire to become a Buddha and the important aspect of this path was to help others on the same path. This was the development of the idea of the Bodhisattva as one who is a future Buddha and who is motivated primarily by the wish to help others to progress on the Buddhist path. The Mahayana is sometimes called Bodhisattvayana because of the importance it gave to this idea.

In some traditions the person may take the Bodhisattva vow to follow this path which has two aspects: to benefit others now and to attain Enlightenment in order to benefit others in the future.

The first step in the Mahayana path is to generate *Bodhichitta* (Buddha mind). This is a strong wish to attain Enlightenment for the benefit of all beings and to help them to progress on the Buddhist path. This mental attitude does not arise naturally and has to be achieved by ethical practice, devotion, meditation and an understanding of the suffering of all beings and need for Buddhas and their teaching. The foundation of Bodhichitta is a great compassion for all beings. It is understood that each person has Buddha nature or the potential for Enlightenment.

Having achieved this the Bodhisattva then resolves to practise the six *Paramitas* or perfections which form the path to Buddhahood. These are:

1. Generosity (*Dana*) – giving material things, money, service of all kinds, teaching the Dhamma, helping others;
2. Moral discipline (*Sila*) – living according to the ethical rules, restraining one's senses and evil passions;
3. Patience (*Kshanti*) – overcoming anger, ill-will, and hatred, maintaining an inner peace and tranquillity, not retaliating;
4. Energy (*Viriya*) – abandoning laziness and postponement, being energetic, not being weak or discouraged;
5. Meditation (*Dhyana*) – developing mindfulness, concentration and insight;
6. Wisdom (*Prajna*) – understanding what is virtuous, and realizing emptiness and the truth.

Four perfections were added later, namely skilful means (*Upaya*), resolution (*Pranidhana*), strength (*Bala*), and knowledge (*Jnana*).

The Bodhisattva path has ten stages. The six perfections

109

correspond to the first six stages of the Bodhisattva path. At the sixth stage the person is an Arahat (Theravada) as well as a Bodhisattva (Mahayana). There are four more stages in the path namely, going beyond rebirth, becoming certain to attain Buddhahood, expanding his teaching ability, and, lastly, acquiring all the powers and characteristics of a Buddha and being consecrated by the Buddhas. The being is now just one step away from becoming a Buddha.

The Mahayana knows of many Bodhisattvas; Maitreya (Theravada says that he will be the next Buddha and according to Mahayana on becoming a Buddha he will send a spiritual manifestation of himself to be the next Buddha on earth), Avalokitesvara (Kuan-Yin in China and Kwannon in Japan), Manjushri, and Samantabhadra are well known.

The Life of Gotama Buddha

A look at the account of Gotama Buddha's life is an essential element in the study of Buddhism. The story of his life is interesting and important not simply in relation to the historical events and details but because various Buddhist ideas and concepts are woven into his life story. During the course of his teaching Gotama Buddha related the stories of his previous lives. These appear in the texts and are known as the Jataka Stories. It is during these lives that the Bodhisatta developed the mental qualities which enabled him to attain Enlightenment as a Buddha. The Jataka Stories are often used for teaching the Dhamma and are also acted out as plays.

Vessantara Jataka

This is the story of the last human life of the Bodhisatta, the one previous to the life in which he became the Buddha. The Bodhisatta was born as Prince Vessantara, the son of King Sandumaha who ruled the kingdom of Jayatura. When the prince came of age his father delegated many official duties to him. The prince was generous and charitable and helped the people of the kingdom a great deal. The people came to love him and his fame spread to other lands.

The ruler of a neighbouring kingdom jealous of the prince's fame, decided to do some harm to the prince. That king sent some men dressed as holy men having instructed them to ask for the royal elephant as a gift. Because of his generosity the prince gave the elephant to them.

King Sandumaha's ministers were furious and asked that the prince be punished by being exiled to the forest. The king agreed and with great sorrow made the order. The Bodhisatta's wife Princess Mantridevi insisted on accompanying him together with their two small children, Krishnajina, a daughter, and Jalia, a son.

While the family were living in the forest a wicked man

called Jujaka came to their home. 'I have heard that you have developed the qualities of generosity and non-attachment to a very high degree. So then let me have your two children to attend on my wife who is old and infirm,' said Jujaka. The parents were astonished. But since the Bodhisatta had perfected the qualities of generosity and non-attachment he could not refuse the request and allowed Jujaka to take the children away with him. He had also developed the qualities of lovingkindness and compassion. He loved his children and cared deeply about their welfare. Knowing that his father would pay the man a large sum of money and get the children back and look after them, as Jujaka was leaving with the children the Bodhisatta asked him to go and see his father King Sandumaha.

The chief of the deities was Sakra. He understood that Prince Vessantara was just one human life away from becoming a Buddha. He wanted to test this. So he came to the prince in the form of a holy man and said, 'I would like you to give me your wife as a gift.' Both the prince and the princess were shocked. Again the prince found that he could not refuse the request. Sakra was filled with admiration and respect. Disclosing his identity he said, 'I am Sakra the chief of the deities. I do not wish to take your wife away and was only testing the extent to which you have developed the qualities of generosity and non-attachment. As for your children, your father has recovered them and will bring them to you soon.'

Sakra then returned to his heavenly home. The family were reunited when the king arrived with the children. They all went back to live in the palace. When the king's ministers and the people heard the story their admiration and love for the prince was even greater than before.

After Prince Vessantara passed away he was born as a deity in a heavenly world to await the time when he will be born in the human world for a last lifetime during which he will attain Enlightenment as Gotama Buddha.

Having related the story the Buddha explained the importance of the qualities of generosity and non-attachment. He identified the persons associated with him in his present life with the characters in the story saying, 'Princess Mantridevi was Princess Yasodhara, Princess Krishnajina was Ven. Uppalavanna, Prince Jalia was Ven. Rahula, and I was Prince Vessantara.'

Birth and Early Life

Different dates, e.g. 623, 624, 566, 563 B.C.E. are given for the birth of the Buddha. This is due to inaccuracies of dating and the conversion of the lunar calendar used during that time to the present calendar. It is sufficient to say that he lived in the 6th century B.C.E.. He was born in Lumbini Park at Kapilavastu on the Indian borders of present Nepal on the day of the full moon in May (Vesak). His father was King Suddhodana of the Sakya clan and his mother was Queen Maha Maya. She passed away a few days later and the baby was looked after by her sister Queen Maha Pajapati Gotami.

A scholarly ascetic named Asita who had been the teacher to the king visited the palace to see the baby. He realized with his intuitive vision that the child would become a Buddha and announced this to the king.

A few days later at a special ceremony the child was named Siddhattha (Siddhartha). His family name was Gotama (Gautama). The naming ceremony was an auspicious celebration. According to custom several holy men were invited, amongst whom there were eight who were particularly distinguished. On looking at the child seven of them said that the child would become a great emperor or a Buddha. The youngest of them, Kondanna, said, 'In time he will see four special signs. As a result he will renounce the world and eventually attain Enlightenment, and become a Buddha.'

Siddhattha showed a talent for learning. His teachers were impressed with the ease with which he mastered languages, arts, science, mathematics and the Vedas. He was also good at sports such as wrestling and archery.

In order to promote agriculture there was a celebration known as the ploughing festival. The king and all the people took part in the festivities. Young Siddhattha was taken to see the celebrations. His attendants left him under a tree and went forward to get a better look at the proceedings. On returning they found him seated cross-legged meditating. He had not been taught meditation. The king and others paid their respects to him, as they understood that this was a skill he had brought from a previous life and that he was a very extraordinary baby.

Even at an early age he had great compassion for living beings. Once he was playing in the forest with Devadatta, his cousin. Devadatta shot a swan with his bow and arrow. The bird fell wounded and Siddhattha ran to the bird and

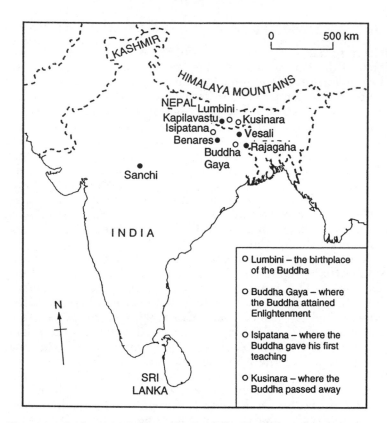

Four sacred places in India and Nepal for Buddhist pilgrimage

attended to it. Devadatta claimed the bird on the grounds that he had shot it but Siddhattha claimed the bird because he had saved his life. They took the dispute to a council of wise men who decided that the bird belonged to Siddhattha, the person who saved his life. This story reflects the Buddhist attitude of compassion and respect for life.

The king wanted Siddhattha to follow him on the throne. So because of the prophecies made by the holy men he arranged for young Siddhattha to lead a secluded life without seeing signs of unhappiness such as illness, old age and death. At the age of sixteen he was married to his beautiful cousin Princess Yasodhara. They led a luxurious life wanting for nothing in the way of palaces, clothes, attendants, entertainers

114

and food. However amidst all this comfort Siddhattha was not entirely happy and often reflected on the real value of these comforts.

Four Sights

Once when young Siddhattha was feeling bored inside the palace he asked Channa, his charioteer, to take him for a ride in the countryside. On the way they saw an old man bent in two and walking with difficulty with the help of a walking stick. Siddhattha had not seen such a man before and inquired from Channa who that might be. 'That is an old man who has lived many years. His body is worn out and he is very frail. All of us grow old like that,' Channa replied. On another trip they saw a man ill, lying on the ground groaning with pain. Siddhattha asked Channa who that was and Channa replied, 'That man is ill with some disease. We all fall ill with various diseases. We cannot prevent that.' On a third journey they saw a funeral procession. The corpse was being carried for cremation. Again Siddhattha inquired of Channa what the matter was 'That man has lived his life. His body has become old, the breathing and the heart has stopped so he has died. What remains is the corpse, the old dead body. This is being taken for cremation.'

Siddhattha was greatly disturbed by Channa's explanations. He understood that actual life was not full of the luxuries to which he was accustomed, that the pleasures he enjoyed were superficial and that old age, illness and death were the lot of all living beings.

On a fourth trip they encountered a holy man dressed very simply in a robe and carrying an alms bowl together with his few other possessions. Again Siddhattha inquired of Channa who that might be. 'He is a man who has given up worldly life because he was not satisfied with such a life. He has no home and has few possessions. He travels from place to place leading a life of great simplicity and discipline. By means of leading a good life and mental development he strives to understand and realize the meaning of life, and how to transcend its imperfections. As he goes from village to village he teaches the people what he has realized.' It suddenly struck Siddhattha that this was the way to find an answer to the imperfections of life.

115

Renunciation

Now Siddhattha decided, at the age of 29, to renounce his luxurious way of life and set out in search for the meaning of life. At that time Princess Yasodhara gave birth to a son. When informed of this, in addition to his joy, he felt that the baby was an impediment to his wish to break away from family life. Despite his love for his family he decided to proceed with his plan because of his compassion for humankind. Taking a farewell look at his sleeping wife and baby, at midnight Siddhattha rode away from the palace on his horse Kanthaka accompanied by the faithful Channa.

When they came to a river called Anoma, Siddhattha cut off his long hair exchanged his fine clothes for a simple robe, took up the alms bowl and walked into the forest. He sent a message through Channa to his family in the palace that he was setting off to find out the meaning of life and that when he realized this he would return to teach them and other people. When Princess Yasodhara heard the news, though saddened, she understood the reasons for his leaving. She too gave up a luxurious way of life, wore simple robes and led a very simple life in the palace.

Enlightenment

Siddhattha went to several holy men who taught spiritual progress and meditation. Two of this early teachers were Alara Kalama and Udakka Ramaputta. We need to remember that in his previous lives he had perfected many qualities of mental development and he was now progressing from that position. Once again he was an excellent pupil and very quickly grasped all that he was taught. He felt however that there was more to be realized.

There was a group of five ascetics whose leader was Kondanna, the holy man who had prophesied that Siddhattha would become a Buddha. He joined this group. They lived a very hard life eating very little, wearing rags, living in the forest without cover and meditating for long periods. The idea was that austerity and self-mortification would make them progress spiritually. Siddhattha found that he was not progressing spiritually now mainly because he was growing weaker and weaker physically.

He had not been happy with the luxurious life in the palace. He now felt that this austere style of life was not

116

conducive to his spiritual development either. He decided that the answer was a middle way between a luxurious life and an austere life. Later, on attaining enlightenment, he said:

There are these two extremes which should be avoided:

1. Indulgence in sensual pleasures – this is base, vulgar, worldly, ignoble and profitless, and
2. Addiction to self-mortification – this is painful, ignoble and profitless.

Dhammacakkappavattana Sutta

He began to take sufficient food and look after himself physically. The five ascetics left him, thinking that he did not have the stamina for spiritual progress.

He now began to practise meditation by himself. Finally seated in the lotus posture under a Bodhi tree on the bank of the Neranjara river he commenced his final meditation as a Bodhisatta. He moved through various meditative states, remembered his former births, realized the way of appearance and disappearance of beings and considered the nature of mental defilements. Finally he attained Enlightenment at the age of 35 on the day of the full moon in the month of May (*Vesak*) in Buddha Gaya and became Gotama Buddha.

Some of his first words, explaining craving, life and the end of rebirth, were:

Through many a birth I wandered in Samsara (existence)
Seeking, but not finding, the builder of this house (body)
Sorrowful, is repeated birth
O craving, you are seen. You shall build no house (body) again
All your passions are broken. Your ignorance is shattered
The mind attains Nibbana
Achieved, is the end of craving.

The Dhammapada, v. 153. 154

Teaching Life

Gotama Buddha spent seven weeks near the Bodhi tree under which he attained Enlightenment. He often looked at the tree with gratitude for having given him shelter during his meditation. Two merchants called Tapassu and Bhallika offered food to the Buddha who told them of his experience, and they became his first disciples.

The first formal teaching was to the five ascetics with

117

whom he had led an austere life, and whose senior was Kondanna. This was on the day of the full moon in July at the Deer Park in Isipatana, Benares. The teaching is called the *Dhammacakkappavattana Sutta* (the Teaching Setting in Motion the Wheel of Truth), and explained the Four Noble Truths and the Noble Eightfold Path. Soon after he gave them another teaching, the *Anattalakkhana Sutta*, about the Three Signs of Being namely Impermanence, Dukkha and No-self. The five understood the teaching and were ordained as the first members of the Sangha.

The Buddha wandered from place to place in that part of India teaching the Dhamma. Kings, nobles, men and women came to listen to him, accepted the teaching and became lay disciples. Some men requested and were ordained into the Sangha. When the Order reached 60 in number the Buddha encouraged them to go forth and teach. He accepted persons from all backgrounds, rich and poor, and with no caste distinctions as lay disciples and members of the Sangha.

The Buddha's Homecoming

About seven years after leaving home the Buddha returned to Kapilavasthu the capital city of his father's kingdom. On hearing the Dhamma his father and stepmother together with many others became his followers. He met his former wife Princess Yasodhara who had been living the life of an ascetic in the palace. Later he was to explain that she had been his wife in former births also. She sent their son Rahula, now aged seven, instructing him to ask for his inheritance from the father. The Buddha thought, 'I shall give him far greater wealth than a kingdom,' and asked a senior monk to ordain the boy. When King Suddhodana heard of this he spoke to the Buddha and obtained a promise that children would not be ordained without the consent of their parents. The Buddha took an interest in Ven. Rahula's spiritual progress and gave him special teachings on honesty and truthfulness.

Teaching Continues

The Buddha had special concern for the care of the sick. A monk called Putigatta Tissa Thera had a skin ailment. His condition was so unpleasant that some monks carried him out of the monastery. When the Buddha heard of this he, with the assistance of some monks, bathed the patient and made him comfortable saying, 'Whoever attends on the sick attends on me.'

Some of the teaching was very down to earth. King Pasenadi of Kosala liked food and used to eat enormous quantities of rice and curries. After such a meal he came one morning to the Buddha and could hardly keep his eyes open. The king complained that he felt like this after meals. 'Your trouble is eating too much,' the Buddha said, 'It is wise to observe moderation in food, because that way lies contentment. A person who is abstemious in eating will grow old slowly and will not have a lot of physical trouble and discomfort.'

The Buddha ordained several relatives such as his stepbrother Nanda and his cousins Devadatta and Ananda. Venerable Devadatta, whom we met in the story of the wounded bird, created various difficulties for the Buddha. Once he led a break-away group of monks but later on realized the errors of his ways.

When the Buddha was 55 years old he felt the need for a personal attendant. Ven. Ananda was chosen for the task and he attended on the Buddha with great devotion. Because of his position Ven. Ananda was privileged to hear much of the teaching and it was he who recited the Dhamma at the Second Council.

Women

The position of women socially and in religion at that time was somewhat low. When some women led by Queen Maha Pajapati Gotami and Princess Yasodhara wanted to be ordained as nuns the Buddha at first refused, since he did not wish to create difficulties for the Order of Sangha. It was Ven. Ananda who persuaded the Buddha to ordain women:

'Are women, Sir, capable of realizing the highest fruits of the teaching (Nibbana)?'

'Yes, they are capable, Ananda.'

'Then, Sir, since Queen Maha Pajapati Gotami looked after you so well when you were small and your mother had passed away, why not ordain her?' The Buddha said, 'If she accepts the extra rules let her be ordained' and he formulated extra rules to protect the Order of Nuns.

Vinaya Pitaka, Cullavagga

Practical Teaching

The Buddha insisted that he was a human being but one Enlightened and therefore with extraordinary powers, and not a deity or a God. He asked the people not to worship him but to practise his teaching. A monk Ven. Vakkali by name was in the habit of coming to the Buddha and gazing at him day after day. When the Buddha asked him why he did this Ven. Vakkali replied, 'I gaze at you because you are so smart in appearance.' Then the Buddha said, 'Ven. Vakkali, what is the use of gazing all the time at my body which is something transient and impermanent? If you really want to see me, look at my teaching' (Samyutta Nikaya).

The Buddha taught village folk, learned people and monks. He adapted the teaching to suit the audience. For instance, to the lay people he might teach about ethical matters connected to their daily lives while to the senior monks and nuns he might talk about complex philosophical matters. Each talk was a fine example of a logical exposition of a subject with illustrations and examples so that the talk could be easily understood. He asked people not to accept the teaching simply because it came from him but to consider and practise it in order to see its value.

Sometimes the Buddha set a person a task to perform so that the person would realize some aspect of the Dhamma. The story of Kisa Gotami is an excellent example. Kisa Gotami was a young woman from a wealthy family married to a successful merchant. A son was born to her. She was overjoyed and cared for him with great love. When he was about one year old he died suddenly and the mother was overcome with grief. She refused to accept that the son was dead and went from person to person asking whether they knew of a medicine which would bring her son back to life. Finally a wise person asked her to go to the Buddha for help. She then went to the Buddha who was staying at Jetavana monastery and related her story. The Buddha understood that no explanation of death being universal and irrevocable would be understood by her in her frame of mind and decided to teach this to her in an indirect way. 'I know of a medicine for your son,' the Buddha said, 'Go and get some mustard seeds from a house in which no one has died.' So Kisa Gotami went from house to house, carrying the body of the little son. When she explained her quest for the mustard seeds and asked whether anyone had died in that house the answer was

120

always the same, 'We are sorry but one of our family died sometime ago.' Kisa Gotami realized that in each family in each house someone had died.

She returned to the Buddha and said, 'It is impossible to obtain mustard seeds from a house in which no one has died for in each family someone has died recently. Death seems to be common to all beings.'

'That is the lesson I wanted to teach you,' the Buddha said, 'Death is common to all living beings. All things are impermanent.' He gave her a talk on the Dhamma and granted her request to be admitted to the Order of Nuns. One day much later it was her turn to light the lamp in the meeting hall. Observing the movement of the flame, and taking that as a subject of meditation she thought, 'Even so is it with living creatures, they rise and pass away and on attaining Nibbana they are no more.'

The Buddha understanding her thoughts, made an image of himself to appear before her, and giving another talk on the Dhamma, said,

> Rather than live a hundred years,
> And not attain Nibbana
> Better is the life of a single day,
> For him who has seen Nibbana.'
>
> The Dhammapada, v. 114

Passing Away

Gotama Buddha had now reached the age of 80 years, having taught the Dhamma for the last 45 of those years. He fell ill and realized that his life on earth would soon come to an end. He summoned Ven. Ananda and said, 'What does the Sangha need from me? The Dhamma I have taught is clear. There is no secret part of it distinct from what I have explained. I have not kept a closed fist on anything. Now I am old, Ananda, I am past 80 years ...

So, Ananda, let each of you be an island, be a refuge to yourself. Let the Dhamma be your refuge. Seek no other refuge.' (Maha Parinibbana Sutta).

He recovered from that illness and continued his walk with his followers arriving at a town called Kusinara. He lay down on a couch prepared for him. Then addressing Ven. Ananda and the gathered Sangha he said, 'When I am gone do not think that you have no teacher. The Dhamma that I have taught will be your teacher.' ...

121

His last words were 'Subject to decay are all component things. Strive on with diligence' (Maha Parinibbana Sutta).

He then passed away attaining *Parinibbana*. At this moment one of the monks gathered there, Ven. Anuruddha, recited these words:

'When he who from all craving want was free,
Who to Nibbana's tranquil state had reached,
When the great sage finished his span of life,
No grasping struggle vexed that steadfast heart.

All resolute and with unshaken mind,
He calmly triumphed over pain of death,
Even as bright flame dies away, so was
The last emancipation of his heart.'

Maha Parinibbana Sutta

Temple, Thailand

History and Development

Geographical Development

India

In the present Buddha cycle Buddhism arose in North India where Gotama Buddha lived and began to teach the Dhamma about the 6th century B.C.E.. At the time of his Parinibbana, or passing away, Buddhism was well established in the north-eastern part of India. Emperor Asoka (3rd century B.C.E.) united the northern part of the sub-continent into a great empire. He became a Buddhist and an ardent supporter of Buddhism, using the State machinery to encourage the spread of Buddhism. He initiated the holding of the Third Council to rehearse the scriptures. After the Council missions were sent to Kashmir and other areas in the North West, to Syria, Greece and Egypt in the West, to Sri Lanka in South and to countries such as Burma and Thailand in the South East Asia. About the 1st century C.E. the Kushan Emperor Kanishka sent Buddhist missions to Central Asia, China and Mongolia.

Buddhism flourished in India until about the 7th century C.E. and then there was a decline. This was due to a reduction in the vigour of the Sangha, dwindling lay support, the spread of Jainism, and the emergence of devotional and philosophically coherent forms of Hinduism which gradually absorbed the followers of Buddhism. The Buddhist university monasteries such as Nalanda, Valabhi and Taxila continued their religious and scholastic activities. The Muslim invasions and the resultant spread of Islam about the 11th century ended the leading position of Buddhism in the cultural life stream of India, although it did continue its influence in some parts of India and in the neighbouring northern kingdoms such as Bhutan and Ladakh.

Since about 1850 C.E. there has been a revival of Buddhism in India in line with renewed Buddhist activity in Asia. Some important features of this revival have been the conference in Adyar, Madras in 1891 to agree on fundamental Buddhist beliefs common to different schools and traditions, archaeological discoveries, restoration of Buddhist shrines, the adoption of Buddhist symbols as national symbols and numbers of Indians led by Dr. Ambedkar and others embracing Buddhism in increasing numbers.

South and South East Asia

The ancient chronicle of Sri Lanka, the Mahavansa, relates that Gotama Buddha predicted the Dhamma becoming established in Sri Lanka. The same chronicle relates how the son and daughter of Emperor Asoka, Ven. Mahinda and Ven. Sanghamitta, both of whom had entered the Order of the Sangha, brought Buddhism to Sri Lanka about 250 B.C.E. during the reign of King Devanampiyatissa of Sri Lanka. The country has been a stronghold of Buddhism since then and it was in Sri Lanka that the Teachings were written down for the first time about 25 B.C.E.. The monks and nuns of Sri Lanka played an important role in the spread of Buddhism in Asia and the rest of the world. Since 1850 the Buddhist resurgence has seen the Buddhist-Christian debates culminating in the Panadura debate of 1873 C.E., the work of Anagarika Dharmapala and The Maha Bodhi Society which he established, the establishing of Buddhist schools and universities, the inauguration of the World Fellowship of Buddhists in 1950 and increased activity in Buddhist archaeological work.

Similarly in other South Asian countries, such as Burma, Cambodia, Indonesia, Laos, Thailand and Vietnam, Buddhism has played an important role in the religious and cultural development of those societies. The Burmese Buddhist Sangha are known for developing and teaching special meditation techniques. Thailand, where Buddhism has received strong and continuing State support, has been a centre for the development of the teaching and practice of the Dhamma. Buddhism is a State institution in Thailand with a Sangharajah (Head of the Sangha), often a member of the royal family, managing Buddhist affairs. The senior member of the Sangha holds the office of Supreme Patriarch and even the Prime Minister greets the Supreme Patriarch with a prostration. In keeping with the custom for a young man to spend some time as a Buddhist monk, the king himself was ordained as a monk for some time.

Nepal, Bhutan and Ladakh

Gotama Buddha's birthplace was in Lumbini Park, Kapila-vasthu in present-day Nepal. Buddhism became established in Nepal and continues there influenced to some extent by Hinduism. Bhutan and Ladakh are Buddhist countries.

China

Buddhism came to China first overland from North India along the Silk Route and later from the South Asian countries across the seas. Official histories of China record the presence of Buddhism there in the 1st century C.E. China saw a remarkable expansion and development of Buddhism. In some Chinese kingdoms Buddhism was accepted as the State religion. Commencing in 200 C.E., the Sanskrit texts were translated into Chinese over the next 1000 years. New traditions developed and new texts were written. Nuns from Sri Lanka journeyed by sea to China in the 5th century to establish an Order of Nuns there. In the same century an invading Chinese army defeated Kucha in Central Asia and, on the express instructions of the Chinese Emperor, captured the famous scholar monk Ven. Kumarajiva and carried him back to China to organize Buddhist work including translations there. Monks from Southern Asian countries went to China to teach. Chinese pilgrims including Fa-hsien in the 5th century and Hsiian-tsang and I-tsing in the 7th century spent many years on study pilgrimages in South Asian countries. There was a close and dynamic exchange of Buddhist teaching, learning, scholarship and practice between China on the one hand and countries such as India and Sri Lanka until about the 12th century C.E., Buddhism in China was influenced by Confucianism and Taoism. The Ming dynasty, from about 1368 C.E., saw the gradual decline of the position of Buddhism though it continued to influence the cultural stream. Since about 1980 there has been a resurgence of Buddhism in China. An increasing number of temples are active today including Fayuan Si which houses the Beijing Buddhist Academy. There is a Buddhist Association of China officially recognized by the State.

Korea and Japan

Buddhism was introduced to Korea in the 4th century from

China. It became established quickly and was accepted as the State religion by the 7th century. Buddhism has maintained its dominant influence in Korean culture and today Korea has a flourishing Sangha of monks and nuns.

It was from Korea that Buddhism was introduced to Japan in the 6th century C.E.. It was immediately accepted in royal circles and was given enthusiastic support by Prince Shotoku who, as regent, ruled Japan from 592 to 622 C.E.. It was Chinese Buddhism which had the main influence on the development of Buddhism in Japan. Many Japanese monks went to study in China and returned with Chinese texts. There was some influence from the indigenous Shintoism which continues as a separate religion today, but Buddhism, made up of different traditions, remains the main religion in Japan. Several universities such as Otani and Koyasan specialize in Buddhist studies and scholarship.

Tibet, Mongolia and Central Asia

Buddhism was first introduced to Tibet in the 7th century C.E. but did not become widely established. Later in the 11th century C.E. it was introduced again and then became firmly established. Tibetan Buddhists were very active in translation and literary work, scholarship, building and maintaining temples and monasteries, and in the study and practice of Buddhism.

One of the missions sent by King Kanishka in the 1st century C.E. was to Mongolia. Buddhism became established there and has remained the main religion. There has been a resurgence of Buddhism in recent years. There were several Buddhist kingdoms in Central Asia and recent archaeological findings indicate the importance of Buddhism in this area in the past.

There is no country in Asia which has not been influenced at one time or another by Buddhism. For more than 2,500 years Buddhism has been the primary inspiration behind Asian civilization and the source of its greatest cultural achievements. The spread of Buddhism has always been peaceful, more an acceptance of the teaching than a propagation.

United Kingdom

In the United Kingdom from about 1826 there was an

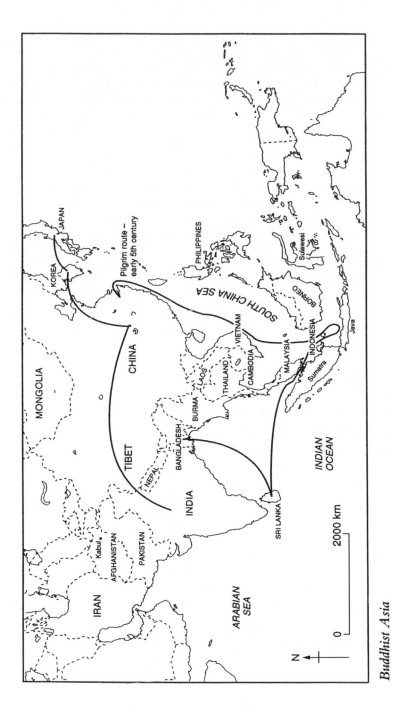

Buddhist Asia

increasing number of English translations of Buddhist texts by various scholars and a growing scholarly interest in Buddhism. The formation of the Pali Text Society in 1881, and the teaching of Pali, Sanskrit and Buddhism in some universities fostered this interest. The first English person to be ordained a Buddhist monk was Gordon Douglas who was ordained in Sri Lanka in 1899 as Bhikkhu Asoka. In 1898 Allan Bennett left London to study Buddhism in Sri Lanka. He then travelled to Burma in 1901 and was ordained soon after as Ven. Ananda Metteyya. He led a Buddhist mission to the country of his birth in 1908, and in that year, was the first Buddhist monk to teach the Dhamma in the United Kingdom. The Buddhist Society was established in its present form in 1926 by Christmas Humphreys. As a consequence of a mission from Sri Lanka, led by Anagarika Dharmapala, the London Buddhist Vihara, was established in 1926. From about that time Buddhism has been accepted as a religion by an increasing number of people in the UK. Since 1960 Buddhism has come to the UK from various Asian countries and there has been an ever-increasing interest, study and practice of Buddhism. The Buddhist Society Directory lists over 250 Buddhist temples, monasteries and groups.

Continental Europe

In Germany Buddhist studies began about 1850 and many texts were translated into German. In the present century some German nationals such as Ven. Nyanatiloka and Ven. Nynaponika ordained as monks in Sri Lanka, established monasteries, translated texts, and published much Buddhist material in English in Sri Lanka. They also influenced the development of Buddhism in Germany, where new temples have been established recently. There has been a similar development of Buddhism in France and much scholarly work has been done in the universities.

In countries such as Denmark, Netherlands and Sweden, too, there was at first an interest in Buddhism in academic circles. In recent times some people have become interested in Buddhism as a religion. In Italy Buddhism has been taught in the universities including the Roman Catholic Gregorian University, and now there are some temples in Italy.

In some parts of Russia and the adjoining countries, Buddhism has been established as a religion from the earliest times. There has also been much academic work in the universities and also archaeological work. In the 1990s Buddhist temples have been re-established in Leningrad and Moscow, and the Buddhist Religious Board co-ordinates the Buddhist activities in the country.

The European Buddhist Union was formed some years ago to provide a forum for the discussion of Buddhist activities in Europe.

The Americas

Interest in Buddhism was kindled in the United States when Professor Rhys Davids lectured there in 1881 and when Anagarika Dharmapala spoke at the Parliament of World Religions in 1893 in Chicago. About the same time Japanese people finding new homes on the western coast brought Buddhism to their new country. Oriental Studies Faculties in universities such as Yale and Harvard have contributed to the development of Buddhism by scholarship, translations and publications. In the present century various forms of Buddhism have come to the USA where one sees representatives of all the schools and traditions and also some new movements. The position in Canada is similar. In South America, again, Japanese finding new homes brought Buddhism with them, and new traditions have come in recent times.

Australia and New Zealand

People from China and Sri Lanka who came to live in Australia brought Buddhism with them in the 19th century. In recent years Buddhist temples and groups have been set up amidst an increasing interest in Buddhism as a subject of study and of practice as a religion.

Buddhist Councils

Introduction

Councils were held from time to time to discuss the Teachings and practices and are a feature of the development of Buddhism in southern Asia. Their composition and nature varied. Sometimes only ordained members of the Sangha took part while at other times lay Buddhists also were involved. Councils were held for various purposes, for instance, to recite, rehearse and authenticate the Teaching, settle disputes, write the Teaching, reorganize the Sangha, to unify the *Sasana* (the Buddhist community and teaching), and to preserve the teaching.

First Council

Even during the Buddha's lifetime there were differences of opinion among some members of the Sangha on matters of discipline. A few days after the Buddha's passing away a monk called Ven. Subhadda was heard to say that now that the teacher was no more they could do as they wished. On hearing about this Ven. Maha Kassapa, the senior monk, and the other senior monks decided to call a Council to protect the Sasana by determining and authenticating the teaching.

The First Council was held at Rajagaha, the capital of Magadha, under the patronage of King Ajatasattu about three months after the Buddha's passing away. Ven. Maha Kassapa presided and the *Vinaya* (rules of monastic discipline) and the Dhamma were rehearsed at this Council. Ven. Upali dealt with the Vinaya and Ven. Ananda dealt with the Dhamma. In the presence of the senior monks who were members of the Council these two monks recited and explained their respective parts of the teaching. They were questioned systematically by Ven. Maha Kassapa and the other members of the Council. After much discussion the Council arrived at a final definitive version of the Vinaya and the Dhamma.

Second Council

About one hundred years later there were some differences of opinion among the Sangha about certain aspects of the teaching, specifically relating to the interpretation of some monastic rules and the proper spiritual status of the Buddha. A Second Council was called to meet at Vesali during the reign of King Kalasoka. Ven. Sabbakami the most senior monk presided. The Vinaya and the Dhamma were recited, rehearsed and authenticated. The Sangha were united at this time and the Vinaya and the Dhamma agreed at this Second Council form the foundation of the teaching in all the schools and traditions of Buddhism. There were divisions in the Sangha later.

Third Council

In the 3rd century B.C.E. some undesirable elements had entered the Sangha and were disturbing the unity, peace and status of the Buddhist community with their improper views and unorthodox lifestyles. A Third Council was called by Emperor Asoka of India to purify the Sangha and reaffirm the texts. It was held at Pataliputra (Patna) and the senior monk Ven. Moggaliputta Tissa presided. The undesirable elements of the Sangha were excluded and various matters of conflict sorted out. The Vinaya and the Dhamma were rehearsed and the *Abhidhamma* (higher philosophy) added to the texts as the third part.

Fourth Councils

A Fourth Council was held at Aluvihara in Sri Lanka about 25 B.C.E. Ven. Rakkita Mahathera presided. Now for the first time the teaching was written down in Pali as the *Vinaya Pitaka* (rules of monastic discipline), *Sutta Pitaka* (the Dhamma) and the *Abhidhamma Pitaka* (higher philosophy), in three sections known as the *Tripitaka* (three baskets) and collectively as the Pali Canon.

About the 1st century C.E. during the reign of Emperor Kanishka in north-west India another Council (Fourth Council in the Mahayana tradition) was called to resolve some differences of opinion and to commit the teaching to writing. This Council was presided by Ven. Vasumitra. The teaching was now written down in Sanskrit in three sections namely *Vinaya Vaibhasa* (rules of monastic discipline), *Upadesa Vaibhasa* (Dhamma) and *Abhidhamma Vaibhasa* (higher philosophy), showing the same divisions as the Pali Canon, and came to be known as the Sanskrit Canon.

Other Councils

In the 5th century C.E. a Fifth Council was held in Sri Lanka to reform the Sangha and to settle some disputes between different schools of Buddhism. This Council came down in favour of the Theravada school as a result of which other traditions declined and ceased to exist in Sri Lanka. A Sixth Council was held in Burma in 1871 to rehearse the Pali Canon and to inscribe it on marble slabs. Finally in 1954 there was a Seventh Council in Burma to study the Tripitaka.

131

Schools and Traditions

Introduction

Sometime after the Second Council held about 100 years after the passing away of the Buddha there was a division in the Sangha between the *Sthaviras* or Elders, who in time formed the Sthaviravadin school, and the other monks known as the *Mahasanghas* (the greater community), who in time formed the Mahasanghika school. The main points of difference were the Sthaviravadin's refusal to agree to any change in the rules of monastic discipline and the Mahasanghika's views that gave a reduced status to the arahat (one who had attained Nibbana) and promoted the Buddha to a super-human transcendental status.

In the development of Buddhism over the years several schools and traditions arose. Most of them ceased to exist being absorbed by others and today we have three main schools of Buddhism namely the Theravada, the Mahayana and Vajrayana (which is sometimes taken to be a tradition within the Mahayana). Within each school there are different traditions.

Theravada School

After the Third Council, at the time of Emperor Asoka, missions were sent to various parts of South Asia taking the teaching as finalized at that Council to different countries. This teaching, sometimes referred to as early Buddhism, was that of the Sthaviravadin school. It was this teaching, brought to Sri Lanka by Ven. Mahinda and Ven. Sanghamitta, which was written down in Pali in Sri Lanka about 25 B.C.E. as the Pali Canon. Teachings of other traditions reached the South Asian countries but did not become established there. The school of Buddhism in the South Asian countries, such as Burma, Cambodia, Sri Lanka and Thailand, based on the Pali Canon is known as the Theravada school and sometimes as 'southern Buddhism'.

Mahayana School

In the first century B.C.E. the important schools of Buddhism in India were the Mahasanghika and Sarvastivada Schools. The language of these schools was Sanskrit. About this time there were new developments within the existing schools. New interpretations of Buddhist ideas were developed in India in a religious environment which included Brahminism and later Hinduism. These new developments went to form the Mahayana (Great vehicle or career) Teachings.

The special characteristics of the new Mahayana School were the emphasis on the Bodhisattva ideal, the aim of each person to become a Buddha, the promotion of the Buddha to a super-human transcendental status, and an elaborate and complex philosophy. Because of the importance given to the Bodhisattva ideal Mahayana was also referred to as Bodhisattvayana (Bodhisattva path or career). New Sutras (texts) were composed similar in form to the existing ones but expounding the new ideas. The older non-Mahayana traditions of Buddhism in India at that time were collectively referred to as the *Sravakayana* (path or career of the disciples).

The Mahayanists, because of their aim to become a Buddha and to work for the happiness and welfare of all beings, considered their teachings to be superior to that of the Sravakas whose aim was to attain Nibbana, and referred derogatorily to the Sravakayana teaching as *Hinayana* (lesser vehicle or career). Ven. Professor Walpola Rahula explains that it is incorrect to refer to the Theravada as Hinayana, since the Theravada teaching was formulated and finalized before, and quite independently from, these developments in India.

The growth of the Mahayana was gradual and was not accompanied by violent disagreements. The Mahayana was an extension of the Sravakayana teaching. They were more than anything else differences of outlook and attitude, rather than institutional differences. Chinese Buddhist monks such as Hsuan-Tsang and I-tsing who travelled in India in the 7th century C.E. write that both Mahayana and Sravakayana monks lived in the same monasteries. Those who accepted the Mahayana teachings were Mahayanists and the others were Sravakayanists.

The main characteristics of the developed Mahayana were:

1. The Bodhisattva ideal and path,
2. Aim to become a Buddha,
3. Trikaya concept,
4. Compassion and wisdom,
5. Devotion,
6. Importance of lay persons,

7. New ideas in philosophy,
8. Relationship of Nirvana to Samsara, and
9. Special Sutras.

John Snelling: *The Buddhist Handbook*, 1987, p. 98

The doctrines of the different schools of Buddhism at this time fell into four schools of philosophy:

(a) *Vaibasika* (Sarvastivada School) – Upheld realism and accepted the existence of phenomenal objects on direct perception.
(b) *Sautrantika* – Examples are adequate proof for a thesis and that external objects are only mere appearances and their existence has to be proved by inference. Also that subtle forms of matter were transferred from existence to existence until they ceased to exist on attainment of Nibbana.
(c) *Madhyamika* – Held that reality was void or emptiness. Life of the world was the same as Nibbana and the bliss of Nibbana was available to everyone.
(d) Reality was void or emptiness which was without origin, decay or destruction and hence beyond description. This reality was pure consciousness.

Dr Ananda Guruge:
Buddhism: The Religion and its Culture, 1984, p. 59

In China it was the Mahayana which became established. Different traditions developed, each having its own monasteries and teaching facilities. Each tradition was based on one or more of the Mahayana Sutras. Similarly the Mahayana became established in Korea and Japan. The main Chinese traditions influenced the development of corresponding traditions in Japan. In addition there were new traditions in Japan. The main traditions in Japan today are:

1. *Jodo Shin* – New Pure land practising devotion to Amida Buddha.
2. *Nichiren* – Practising devotion to the founder Nichiren and to the truth as revealed in The Lotus Sutra.
3. *Zen* – Emphasizing meditation.
4. *Tendai* – Practising devotion and meditation.
5. *Shingon* – Tantric.

Vajrayana School

About the 7th century C.E. there were new developments from within the Mahayana. This was the growth of Buddhist Tantra activated by the mutual influence of Mahayana and Hinduism. It drew on the Mahayana Madhyamika philosophy and incorporated Hindu yoga practices involving working with subtle mental processes. Buddhist Tantra or *Tantrayana* (Tantra path) is also referred to as *Mantrayana* (Mantra path) or *Vajrayana* (Thunderbolt or Diamond path). The aim of Vajrayana is the same as that in Mahayana, that is to attain Buddhahood, but the tantric practices showed a quick way to achieve this end. New tantric sutras were written expounding these new ideas.

The teachings of the different schools of Buddhism go to form Tibetan Buddhism which includes:

(a) *Sravakayana* – A path that serves for achieving liberation from cyclic existence for its own sake.
(b) *Mahayana* – A path seeking the rank of Buddhahood for the sake of others.
(c) *Tantrayana* – A quickened path to Buddhahood involving complex tantric practices and meditations.

The different traditions of Buddhism in Tibet are as follows:

(a) Kadam
(b) Kagyu
(c) Nyingma
(d) Gelug

New Developments in the West

There are new developments in the West which may in the fullness of time become new traditions.

Common Features

Though there are different schools and traditions the fundamental parts of the Vinaya and Dhamma go back to the Second Council before there was any division in the Sangha. This central part of the teaching is therefore common to all the schools' traditions. Different traditions give varying emphasis to different aspects of the teaching and practices. There are also additional teachings specific to

135

Rock Temple, Sri Lanka

particular traditions. The *Abhidhamma* (higher systematic philosophy) has developed independently within the different schools and traditions, though even here we see many common features.

A conference was arranged by Col. H. S. Olcott in Adyar, India in 1891 and a document entitled 'The Buddhist Catechism' was published setting out the fundamental Buddhist teachings. This document was agreed, accepted and signed by representative members of the Sangha in Burma, Sri Lanka, Japan, and Chittagong (in Bangladesh), and its contents, apart from the date of the Buddha, were accepted by Mongolian Buddhists. About 1945 Christmas Humphreys at The Buddhist Society in London drafted 'Twelve Principles of Buddhism'. These were accepted as correct by representative Buddhists in Burma, China, Japan, Sri Lanka and Thailand. Professor Hajime Nakamura, who was the Professor of Indian philosophy in the 1950s in the University of Tokyo, Japan, in the chapter entitled 'Unity and Diversity in Buddhism' in the *Path of Buddhism* (ed. Professor Kenneth W. Morgan, New York, 1956) discusses these matters in great detail. Finally we need to remember the words in The Lotus Sutra, 'There is only one yana – Buddhayana', the path of the Buddha:

Buddhas by their tactful powers
Separately preach the three vehicles;
But there is only One Buddha-vehicle

The Lotus Sutra,
Kosei, Tokyo, 1975, Ch. VII

Buddhist Scriptures/Texts

Oral Tradition

The Buddha's teaching was oral. He taught for 45 years, adapting the teaching to suit the group he was addressing, and there is duplication in the texts. The language he used is understood to be Magadhi.

The Sangha memorized the teachings and there were group recitations at festivals and special occasions. The teachings were rehearsed and authenticated at the First Council and were handed down from generation to generation accurately by means of these group recitations.

The oral tradition continues today. The Sangha chant selected texts at ceremonies and sometimes the lay people join in. The chanting is considered to be a sacred act, in addition to reminding and teaching the Dhamma. Buddhists feel that the chanting calms the mind, gives protection from evil, produces a sense of mental well-being and promotes health and prosperity.

Pali Canon

The teaching was written down first at the Fourth Council in Sri Lanka about 25 B.C.E. in Pali. The writing was in three sections, *Vinaya Pitaka*, *Sutta Pitaka* and *Abhidhamma Pitaka*, following the division at the Councils, and is called the *Tipitaka* (three baskets).

The Vinaya Pitaka consists of the 227 rules of conduct and discipline applicable to the monastic life of the monks and nuns. It is divided into three parts and, in addition to the rules, gives accounts of the circumstances under which a rule was promulgated and exceptions to the rule.

The Sutta Pitaka consists of the main teaching or Dhamma. It is divided into five *Nikayas* or collections. These are the long teachings (*Digha Nikaya*), medium length teachings (*Majjhima Nikaya*), groups of shorter teachings according to common topics (*Samyutta Nikaya*), a collection arranged according to subjects discussed (*Anguttara Nikaya*) and a collection of a variety of shorter texts in verse and prose.

The Abhidhamma Pitaka consists of seven books called the higher or further teaching. This is a philosophical analysis and systematization of the teaching and seems to be the scholarly activity of the monks.

The writing was on strips of dried palm leaves cut into rectangles and etched with a metal stylus and rubbed over with carbon ink. A thread was passed through the pages to keep them in order and elaborately painted wooden covers fixed at the ends. This is done even today and is considered to be a meritorious activity.

The Pali Canon has been recited, checked and agreed at the Councils. The whole of it has been translated into English. The Pali Canon was put on to a single CD-Rom disk which is published by the American Academy of Religion and Scholar's Press in Atlanta, USA.

Sanskrit Canon

The Buddha advised the monks to teach in the different languages of the people. The oral teaching continued in India in forms of oral Sanskrit. At the Fourth Council in India the teaching was written down in Sanskrit and was known as the Sanskrit Canon. There were different versions of the Sanskrit Canon, all similar in form and content. Both the Pali and the Sanskrit Canons can be traced to the common original teaching of the Buddha.

The Sanskrit Tripitaka, or Canon, displayed the same three divisions as the Pali Canon, namely:

1. *Vinaya Vaibasha* – monastic rules
2. *Sutra Vaibasha* – the Dhamma, the five Agamas corresponded to the five Nikayas of the Pali Canon, and
3. *Abhidhamma Vaibasha* – the scholarly philosophical analysis which differed from the corresponding section of the Pali Canon.

The Sanskrit Canon does not exist in a complete form in India, but does exist in translation in Chinese, Japanese and Tibetan. Sections of it have been unearthed by archaeologists in Central Asia.

Mahayana and Tantric Texts

With the growth of the Mahayana, new Sutras were written. The teaching in the Sanskrit Canon was incorporated into the Mahayana teaching. The new Sutras were based on the existing texts but new material was added to incorporate the Mahayana ideas.

Of the many new Sutras written, nine are considered particularly important. Four of the most popular and important are:

1. *Prajnaparamita Sutras* (wisdom, perfection Sutra) which set out the teachings of Emptiness.
2. *Saddharma Pundarika Sutra* (Lotus Sutra) which sets out the teaching, explains the one-ness of the teachings and praises the Bodhisattva. *Mahayana* considered this to be the supreme teaching, and it is considered the most important Sutra in China and Japan.
3. *Vimalakirtinirdesa Sutra*, which explains that a lay person can become a Bodhisattva.
4. *Sukhavati Sutra* teaches that Buddha Amida's land was open to all believers.

With the growth of Tantric Buddhism, new Tantric texts came into being dealing with the new ideas. They deal with:

(a) *Kriya tantra* – ceremonies and rites,
(b) *Carya tantra* – practical rites,
(c) *Yoga tantra* – practice of yoga,
(d) *Anuttarayoga tantra* – higher mysticism.

Tantric Buddhism and now Tibetan Buddhism (Vajrayana school) emphasize personal teaching and these texts are difficult to read and understand since they need to be complemented by oral teaching.

Examples of tantric texts are:

1. *Hevajra Tantra*,
2. *Guhya samaja tantra* (Union of the triple body of the Buddha) and
3. *Kalacakra tantra* (Wheel of Time).

Chinese, Korean and Japanese Texts

Buddhism came to China in the 1st century C.E.. The development of Buddhism in China and the recording of the teaching as the Chinese Canon is one of the great achievements of human civilization.

The Sanskrit texts of different traditions were taken to China and the translation of the texts into Chinese went on from 200 C.E. to about 1200 C.E.. At first non-Chinese, and later Chinese monks, working individually and in teams, carried on the translation work. State translation projects were established. Original Chinese Sutras were added.

The Chinese Tripitaka, or Canon, was compiled and followed the same pattern. There was the Vinaya, Sutra and Abhidhamma Pitakas, and it included the original Chinese Sutras. About the 8th century the Chinese invented wood block printing to make multiple copies of the Sutras. The oldest printed book in existence is the Diamond Sutra dated 868 C.E.. The vast Chinese Canon is in the process of being translated into English. The Chinese Tripitaka was translated into Korean about the 10th century C.E. and later the Korean Tripitaka was printed. The Chinese Tripitaka was brought to Japan and copied. Sutra copying became an important religious activity in Japan. It was published in the 17th century C.E..

The Chinese Tripitaka and the Pali Tripitaka have been translated into Japanese this century.

Tibetan and Mongolian Canon

The Sanskrit texts were translated into Tibetan and were edited in the 14th century in 333 volumes. The Tibetan literature is in two parts:

1. *Kanjur* (Translation of the Word of the Buddha) includes the Vinaya, Sutra and Abhidhamma and also the Tantric texts.
2. *Tanjur* (Translation of Commentaries) consists of commentaries on the main texts, hymns and also writings on medicine, grammar and so on.

The first printed edition was published in Beijing in 1410 C.E.. Only a small portion of the Tibetan Canon has been translated into English. The Tibetan Tripitaka was translated into Mongolian in the 18th Century C.E..

Commentaries

In addition, as a result of Buddhist study and scholarship,

there is a vast amount of commentarial matter published over 2,500 years by Asian scholars in the different countries. A notable work is the *Visuddhi Magga* by Ven. Buddhaghosa on mental training. There have also been original works in English such as Sir Edwin Arnold's *The Light of Asia*.

Teachings

'Buddhism not being a revealed religion ... is based wholly on human experience. The follower of the Buddha is exhorted to believe nothing until he has experienced it and found it to be true.'

The teachings '... are not presented to the would-be Buddhist as articles of faith in which he must believe in order to be saved. They are the result of one man's (the Buddha's) search for truth and freedom, and they have been found valid by many millions who followed after him; but each individual ... must reason out each step for himself, and must in time come to experience the truth, not by hearsay but by direct knowledge during his own lifetime.'

Ven. Saddhatissa, *The Buddha's Way*, p. 37

Four Noble Truths

The first teaching *Dhammacakkappavattana Sutta* by Gotama Buddha sets out the Four Noble Truths: *Dukkha*; *Samudaya*, the origin of Dukkha; *Nirodha*, the cessation of Dukkha; *Magga*, the path leading to the cessation of Dukkha.

1. Dukkha

Dukkha is often translated by suffering. This is only one of its meanings and is misleading in that it has led people to believe that Buddhism is melancholy and pessimistic in outlook. The Buddha asked his followers to be joyful and happy because he, the teacher, had found the remedy for the illness.

Birth is suffering, ageing is suffering, sickness is suffering, death is suffering, association with the unpleasant is suffering, separation from the pleasant is suffering, not to get what one deserves is suffering.

Dukkha also implies imperfection, impermanence, un-satisfactoriness and insubstantiality, and it is this wider meaning which is relevant here. All beings are subject to birth, ageing, sickness and death (note the four sights seen by Prince Siddhattha). All beings have a certain amount of happiness but this is impermanent. 'Ordinarily the enjoyment of sensual pleasures is the highest and only happiness to an average person ... According to the Buddha, non-attachment or the transcending of material pleasures is a greater bliss' (Ven. Narada, *The Buddha and his Teaching*, p. 321).

There are three aspects of *Dukkha*:

(a) ordinary suffering – physical and mental suffering, birth, old age, sickness, grief and so on.
(b) change – the impermanence of life, sensual pleasures and happy physical and mental states change and come to an end. (Of course, unhappiness, too, will come to an end and this helps a Buddhist to see life in a detached manner.)
(c) conditioned states – a living being is composed of ever-changing physical and mental energies and these are constantly changing and impermanent.

2. Samudaya, the origin of Dukkha

It is this craving which provides rebecoming (rebirth) accompanied by passionate greed and finding fresh delight... craving for pleasure, craving for existence and craving for non-existence.

Because of ignorance, the consciousness shows us a stable world of identifiable things. Perception of these through the senses creates an emotional reaction which sets up the craving. This craving, greed, desire or thirst is a powerful mental force which is the immediate and principal cause of Dukkha. It is an incessant process. As soon as one desire is satisfied, craving for something else begins. Four ingredients provide fuel for craving and rebirth, namely ordinary material food, contact of the same organs with the external world, consciousness and mental volition.

3. Nirodha, the cessation of Dukkha

It is the complete cessation of that very craving, giving it up, relinquishing it, liberating oneself from it and detaching oneself from it.

144

If craving causes Dukkha and Dukkha must be eliminated, then if craving or greed is transcended there will be no Dukkha. This will be Nibbana, the complete ending of greed or craving, hatred and ignorance, and therefore of rebecoming or rebirth.

4. *Magga, the Noble Eightfold Path*

'... namely right understanding, right thoughts, right speech, right actions, right livelihood, right effort, right mindfulness, right concentration.'

The Noble Eightfold Path is known as the Middle Way between indulgence in sensual pleasures and addiction to self-mortification. It is the Fourth Noble Truth which makes Buddhism a religion, a way of life to be pursued diligently. The Buddha criticized those who merely studied texts, and emphasized that practice, which is to live as a lay Buddhist or ordained Buddhist according to the Teaching was even more important. Mere knowledge without practice does not take the Buddhist very far on his journey and the practice must be with the background of the Dhamma, or Teaching, so that he understands the reason, purpose and aim of the practice.

The Noble Eightfold Path

The Wheel is the symbol of the Dhamma and is shown with eight spokes which represent the Noble Eightfold Path.

The Noble Eightfold Path can be depicted diagrammatically as:

1. *Right Understanding or Views*
2. *Right Thoughts or Intentions*

3. *Right Speech*
4. *Right Actions*
5. *Right Livelihood*

6. *Right Effort*
7. *Right Mindfulness*
8. *Right Concentration*

I. *Morality,* or Love or True respect for oneself and others (Sīla)

II. *Mental Development,* or Mental discipline or Meditation (Samādhi)

III. *Wisdom* (Pannā)

1. Right understanding (Samma ditthi)

Understanding the various aspects of the teaching involves questioning one's view, arriving at a correct understanding of reality and developing wisdom.

2. Right thoughts (Samma sankappa)

Eliminating unwholesome thoughts and developing wholesome thoughts, overcoming greed, hatred and ignorance and developing unselfishness, lovingkindness, generosity and compassion.

3. Right speech (Samma vaca)

Refraining from telling lies, defamatory, harsh, rude and impolite talk, idle gossip and chatter and talk which may cause hatred, enmity and disharmony.

4. Right actions (Samma kammanta)

Avoiding acts which go against the *Dhamma*, specifically the Five Precepts. Means pursuing good actions, peaceful conduct and helping others.

5. Right livelihood (Samma ajiva)

Making a living in a way that does not cause harm to other living beings. Five kinds of trade are expressly prohibited, namely dealing in arms or weapons, human beings, flesh, intoxicating drinks and substances and poison.

6. Right effort (Samma vayama)

Developing insight, intuition and will-power and making an effort to develop mental states conducive to progress as a Buddhist.

7. Right mindfulness (Samma sati)

Extending one's awareness so that all actions, thoughts and speech are performed with full concentration. Being mindful of the body, feelings, thoughts and mind objects.

8. Right concentration (Samma samadhi)

Developing the mind by mindfulness and meditation to achieve higher states of awareness of insight, and realization of the truth.

This applies to the Sangha and to lay people. The order of development is morality, mental development and wisdom – the threefold discipline common to all the traditions. These factors are equally important and interconnected and must be practised simultaneously and the practice developed in a circular way. This will depend on the inclination, capacity and stage of development of the individual. However, in the end they form one Path and this is open equally to men and women, for the Buddha did not distinguish between them in their intellectual and spiritual potential.

A similar division of the path is given in Tibetan Buddhism. The path to liberation from *Samsara* (the cycle of rebirth) are the three higher trainings:

1. Higher moral discipline – a determination to avoid faults.
2. Higher concentration – concentration practised with the aim of renunciation.
3. Higher wisdom – the realization of emptiness.

The Three Signs of Being

1. Impermanence (Anicca)

The Buddha realized and taught that nothing in this world is permanent. Everything, all mental and physical states are changing and are in a state of constant flux or change. This is the law of the universe. Nothing whatever of our ordinary physical, mental or emotional world ever stays the same for two consecutive moments. World systems are impermanent. Even a specific Buddha and his teaching is impermanent in that the Buddha's life comes to an end and the teaching dies out, and later a new Buddha is born, attains Enlightenment and teaches the Dhamma. The permanency and stability which appears is because the mind does not notice the change because it is happening so quickly.

All things have four stages of existence. They arise, gain strength, fade and cease to be. Physicists tell us that even atoms consist of ever-changing and moving particles. Medical doctors tell us that the cells in the human body are being constantly regenerated.

2. Dukkha

Dukkha is the First Noble Truth and is considered as the second sign of being. It has a wide variety of meanings. This poem by Anagarika Sugatananda, who was Francis Story, an English Anagarika who lived in Sri Lanka, shows the range of meanings of Dukkha.
Dukkha is:

> Disturbance, irritation, dejection worry,
> despair; fear, dread, anguish, anxiety; vulnerability,
> injury, inability, inferiority; sickness,
> ageing, decay of body and faculties, senility;
>
> Pain/pleasure; excitement/boredom;
> deprivation/excess; desire/frustration, suppression;
> longing/aimlessness; hope/hopelessness;
> effort, activity, striving/repression;
> loss, want, insufficiency/satiety;
> love/lovelessness, friendlessness;
> dislike, aversion/attraction; parenthood/childlessness;
> submission/rebellion; decision/indecisiveness, vacillation,
> uncertainty.

3. Selflessness (Anatta)

In another teaching given to the group of five holy men at Benares, the Buddha taught that living beings do not have a soul or self in the sense of a permanent, unchanging spiritual entity created by God or having a divine source. Buddhism explains that a living being consists of mind, heart and matter which are constantly changing. The living being is a grouping of constantly changing physical and mental forces which can be analysed into five aggregates or energies or *khandas* (*skandhas*). These are:

1. Matter
2. Feelings
3. Awareness
4. Thoughts
5. Consciousness

and form the body and the mind.

> The body is not self. Feelings are not self. In like manner, awareness, thoughts and consciousness are not self. These must be understood in their true nature as being not I . . . not myself.
>
> Anattalakkhana Sutta.

These forces are kept together by greed and selfishness generated by ignorance. Through practising the Noble Eightfold Path and attaining Nibbana the process comes to an end.

The doctrine of selflessness is not negative. It is reality, absolute truth. Of course, in relation to our own daily activities Buddhism recognizes that there is a person in the conventional sense since this is necessary to understand our position in society.

Kamma (Karma)

Buddhism sets out five laws, namely the physical, biological, moral, supramundane and mental laws. These are natural laws which operate in relation to all events and activities in the world. The moral law or the law of Kamma explains a person's status and condition in life and how he can improve this. Kamma is the action and the consequence is known as the *Vipaka*. Kamma is often used to mean both the action and consequence.

149

The Buddha said:

'We are the heirs of our own actions.'
'All human beings have actions (Kamma) as their own ...
it is Kamma that differentiates beings into low and high
states.'

Cullakammavibhanga Sutta

Mind foreruns all conditions ... if one speaks or acts with
a wicked mind, because of that, pain pursues him ... if
one speaks or acts with pure mind, because of that
happiness follows him ...

The Dhammapada, v. 1. 2

The law of Kamma is that good or skilful actions have good
consequences, and bad or unskilful actions have bad
consequences. An action is good, bad or neutral depending
on the intention that motivates it.

Kamma applies only to intentional actions and the action
may be physical, verbal or mental. Unintentional actions do
not constitute Kamma and every intentional action constitu-
tes Kamma, except in the case of a Buddha, Arahat or
Bodhisatta.

Kamma includes both past, whether in this life or in
previous births, and present intentional actions. These govern
a person's present condition and will contribute to the pattern
of life in the future. This is not a rule of predestination as a
person can improve his future Kamma by good, skilful and
meritorious actions.

The law of Kamma explains a person's condition and
circumstances in life. Every action leaves an imprint on the
mind and this gives rise to a consequence. The main causes of
Kamma are ignorance and craving, greed or mental thirst.
The Kamma force is a part of the consciousness of a person
and the unexhausted force transmitted from one life to
another.

Good and skilful Kamma are given as:

1. Generosity – in money, service and time
2. Morality – observing the ethical rules, being the Five
   Precepts for lay persons
3. Meditation – mental culture
4. Reverence – respect for people
5. Service – doing work beneficial to the community
6. Transference of merit – to others
7. Rejoicing in others' merit

8. Hearing the Teaching – Dhamma
9. Expounding the Teaching
10. Understanding the Teaching correctly.

The benefits include wealth, good health, happiness, good fortune, wisdom, confidence in the Dhamma, confidence in the ability to cope with day to day life, and birth in fortunate circumstances.

In the general Mahayana view there are two types of good Kamma – that conducive to merit and that conducive to liberation. The former only yields mundane forms of happiness, the latter is related to an aspiration for Enlightenment.

Bad or unskilful actions are classified as follows:

(a) Those caused by deeds:
   1. Killing or harming living beings
   2. Stealing or taking what is not rightfully given
   3. Misuse of the senses, including sexual misconduct.
(b) Those caused by words:
   4. Lying
   5. Slander
   6. Harsh speech
   7. Frivolous talk.
(c) Those caused by the mind:
   8. Greed, craving
   9. Ill-will
   10. Incorrect understanding of reality.

The consequences include poverty, ill-health, unhappiness, misfortune, foolishness, doubts about the practice of the Dhamma, inability to cope with day to day life, and birth in unfortunate circumstances.

The Kammic consequences may be immediate or later, in this life or another life. Some Kamma influences the conditions of rebirth. Kamma may increase, decrease or neutralize the effect of other Kamma and the Kammic consequences have different strengths according to the nature of the action.

Ven. Moggallana, one of Buddha's senior disciples, was clubbed to death by a band of robbers because of bad Kamma. On the other hand, Angulimala, a highway robber and murderer, on hearing the Dhamma from the Buddha, became a monk and with the help of good Kamma attained Nibbana.

The law of Kamma places the responsibility for his or her life on the individual:

By oneself is evil done
By oneself is one defiled
By oneself is no evil done
By oneself is one purified
Both purity and defilement depends on oneself
No-one purifies another.

The Dhammapada v. 165

Rebirth or Rebecoming

After enlightenment, some of Gotama Buddha's first words were:

Through many a birth I wandered in samsara (existence)
. . .
Sorrowful is repeated birth . . .

The Dhammapada v. 153, 154

Rebirth or rebecoming is a fundamental element of Buddhist Teaching. The living being is a grouping of constantly changing physical and mental forces or energies. There is a continuous flow of consciousness without any interruption. Each thought moment is not absolutely the same as its predecessor, nor entirely different.

The Buddhist view and understanding of life is that it is a stream of energy continuing through many deaths and rebirths until its momentum is ended by the realization of Nibbana. This cycle is called Samsara. There is movement up into happy states and movement down into unhappy states dependent on the forces of the Kamma.

His Holiness the present XIV Dalai Lama explains Samsara or the Round of Rebirths as cyclic existence which '. . . is the contaminated mental and physical aggregates appropriated through contaminated actions and afflictions.' He refers to the six main minds (eye, ear, nose, tongue, body and mental consciousness) and says that afflictions are peripheral mental factors such as desire, hatred, pride, wrong view and so forth caused by attachment to oneself and resulting in the cycle of rebirths or cyclic existence. (*The Buddhism of Tibet*, p. 25).

There are different explanations of rebirth, or rebecoming. One explanation is that after a being's physical or biological life ends, the life forces continue in another biological entity.

152

At death the mind leaves the present body and goes to the next life, which is determined by the imprints placed on the mind by previous actions, or Kamma. The continuing mental thirst or craving grasps at a new biological base and there is rebirth. Viewed this way the human body is a biological vehicle which provides temporary accommodation to the life forces.

A second explanation is that since the mental and physical energies are changing from moment to moment, there is death and rebirth from moment to moment. The being at any given moment is not the being at the previous moment nor the being that will be in the moment to come. The feeling of continuity is a mental illusion.

A third explanation is connected to the arising of 'I', the ego or self. When the impression of 'I' arises due to desire or aversion to some physical or mental object, there is birth. This self continues so long as that desire or aversion continues, and dies with the end of that desire or aversion. Birth is therefore mental birth at the arising of the 'I' or self, life is so long as that lasts, and death is when it ends. In a single day or hour there can be several lifetimes.

A fourth explanation is that there is continuity of life rather than what can be called death or rebirth. A being is a continuous stream of energies. Death and rebirth are therefore merely changes in direction in the continuity of life which ends with Nibbana.

Rebirth can be in different planes or spheres of existence. One explanation is according to physical spheres. There are three main spheres of existence.

1. Sentient sphere (*Kamaloka*) where there is an emphasis on the sensual attractions.
2. Form sphere (*Rupaloka*) where the beings have renounced sense desires and delight in meditation and high mental states.
3. Formless sphere (*Arupaloka*) where the beings do not have physical form or bodies.

The sentient sphere is divided into unhappy spheres and happy spheres. The unhappy spheres include hell, the animal kingdom, ghosts or spirits. The happy states include the human sphere and spheres of devas, deities and gods.

The human sphere is considered to be the most fortunate because it is a mixture of happiness and unhappiness, and consists of lifetimes neither too short nor too long, both of which features are most conducive to mental and spiritual development along the Buddhist path. A human being is considered to be very lucky to be born as such since he or she can understand and practise the Dhamma and so progress towards Nibbana.

A second explanation of the spheres of existence is that the different spheres are purely mental states. They refer to the mental attitude of the being at a given time. If he is afraid and angry, he is in hell; if he cannot understand things, he is like an animal; if restless, a spirit, and if bent on sensual pleasure, a human being, and so on. A mind bored with sensual pleasure and wishing to live a pure life indicates the mentality of the form sphere, and a mind which considers the material body an impediment and prefers to exist in a purely mental form is the mind living in the formless sphere.

Tibetan Buddhism has similar classifications and explanations. Cyclic existence is divided into three:

1. Desire realm
2. Form realm
3. Formless realm.

Six different types of sentient beings migrate in cyclic existence – gods, demi-gods, human beings, hungry ghosts, animals and those living in hell (*The Buddhism of Tibet*, p. 24).

The Japanese Tendai school sets forth a world system of ten realms:

(a) Saintly realms
    1. Buddhas
    2. Bodhisattvas
    3. Pratyeka Buddhas
    4. Sravakas (disciples)
(b) Ordinary realms
    5. Heavenly beings
    6. Asuras (fighting spirits)
    7. Humans
    8. Pretas (departed beings)
    9. Animals
    10. Depraved beings

Professor Junjiro Takakusu
The Essentials of Buddhist Philosophy,
Honolulu, 1956, p. 137–139.

Dependent Origination

The more technical formulation and explanation of rebirth or rebecoming is given in the Twelve Links in the Chain of Dependent Origination or Conditioned Co-arising, represented in Tibetan Buddhism as the 'Wheel of Becoming'. The Pali expression is Paticcasamuppāda, Paticca meaning dependent upon and samuppāda meaning arising or origination. It consists of the twelve interdependent causes and effects, and is a statement of the process of birth and death and the causes of rebirth, dukkha and death.

Dependent origination is the doctrine of the conditionality of all physical and psychical phenomena. It shows the conditioned and dependent nature of the stream of life. Together with Anattā, the doctrine of selflessness or impersonality, it forms the basis of the Buddhist explanation of life and the continuity of life. The doctrine of selflessness or Anattā proceeds to analyse the meaning of life while the doctrine of Dependent Origination proceeds to synthesize the various elements of life and to demonstrate that they are conditionally related to one another.

This doctrine of Dependent Origination is very complex. Ven. Nyanatiloka says, 'Though this subject has been very frequently treated by Western authors, by far the most of them have completely misunderstood the true meaning and purpose of the doctrine of Dependent Origination, and even the 12 terms themselves have often been rendered wrongly. (*Buddhist Dictionary* p. 128.)

The doctrine may be stated as follows:

1. Ignorance of the truth of suffering, its cause, end, and the way to end it, is the chief cause that sets the wheel of life in motion.
2. Conditioned by Ignorance Intentional Activities arise.
3. Conditioned by Intentional Activities re-linking Consciousness arises.
4. Conditioned by re-linking Consciousness Mind and Matter arise.
5. Conditioned by Mind and Matter the Sixfold (sense) base arises.
6. Conditioned by the Sixfold base Contact arises.
7. Conditioned by Contact Feeling arises.
8. Conditioned by Feeling Craving arises.
9. Conditioned by Craving Grasping arises.
10. Conditioned by Grasping Becoming arises.

11. Conditioned by Becoming Birth arises.
12. Conditioned by Birth, Ageing, Death, Sorrow, Lamentation, Pain, Grief and Despair arise.

Thus does the entire aggregation of Dukkha arise.

Ven. Dr. Hammalawa Saddatissa
The Buddha's Way, 1971, p. 115

This explains how the sense of self arises, continues and ends. When these factors are considered from the point of view of termination or cessation, starting with ignorance, rather than arising, we have an account of the ending of the process. A friend from Amarāvati Buddhist Centre adds, 'That is, with the ending of ignorance there is no longer identification with the five Khandas. Because of this, there are no ego drives (gratification, defence, guilt) to affect consciousness. One no longer feels separate from the world, but a part of it; the senses are not driven by greed, hatred or delusion and so the mental aims and purposes are free from egotism. This is the end of suffering.'

The first two factors relate to the past, the middle eight to the present, and the last two to the future. Intentional activities and becoming, or actions, are regarded as kamma. Ignorance, craving or mental thirst, and grasping or clinging are regarded as passions or defilements. The others are regarded as effects. Ignorance, intentional activities, craving, grasping and kamma are the five causes of the past which condition the five effects of consciousness, mind and matter, the sixfold sense base, contact and feeling, of the present. Similarly the five corresponding causes of the present condition the five corresponding effects of the future.

When the twelfth link is reached unless the person has attained Nibbana there is rebirth and the process is repeated and so on. Hence the process is referred to as the cyclic existence.

The following diagram shows the relationship of dependence between three successive lives.

The doctrine of Dependent Origination in its serial order can be considered a detailed analysis of the second of the Four Noble Truths the arising of Dukkha, and in its reverse order a similar analysis of the third of the Four Noble Truths, the cessation of Dukkha.

Past	1. Ignorance 2. Intentional activities	Kamma process 5 causes: 1, 2, 8, 9, 10
Present	3. Consciousness 4. Mind and Matter 5. Sixfold base 6. Contact 7. Feeling	Rebirth process 5 results: 3–7
	8. Craving 9. Grasping 10. Becoming	Kamma process 5 causes: 1, 2, 8, 9, 10
Future	11. Rebirth 12. Old age and death	Rebirth process 5 results: 3–7

Ven. Nyanatiloka, *Buddhist Dictionary*, p. 129

Some Mahayana Teachings

The *Mahayana* developed the idea of Emptiness (*Sunyata*). It is an extension of the idea of no-self. It includes the idea that since there is no self there can be nothing that belongs to a self and this is a means to counter the bonds of attachment. This idea of emptiness is extended to cover all things, ideas and conceptions. This is an awareness that nothing is self-existent, nothing has an existence of its own.

> ... form is emptiness and the very emptiness is form. Emptiness does not differ from form, form does not differ from emptiness. Whatever is form, that is emptiness. Whatever is emptiness, that is form. The same is true of feelings, perceptions, impulses and consciousness.
> The Heart Sutra.

The ideas of Wisdom and Compassion were developed. Progress in Wisdom involved increasing understanding of reality. Compassion (*Karuna*) was developed in line with the Bodhisattva idea of helping all beings to progress on the Buddhist path.

There was a growth in the meaning and practice of faith and devotion. With the recognition of the Buddhas such as Amida and heavenly Boddhisattvas the idea developed that people could worship them and they would help people on the Buddhist path.

157

Theravada emphasized the position of the Sangha as living a life which had greater spiritual potential. Now the Mahayana recognized the potential of the lay person for spiritual progress. The *Vimalakirti Niridesa Sutra* gives an account of a householder Bodhisattva, Vimalakirti, who had a profound knowledge of the Dhamma.

Mahayana developed the idea of Nibbana from the original Theravada idea that it was ending of greed, hatred and ignorance and therefore rebirth. A new idea of Nibbana was developed that it was Samsara, the cycle of life.

Some Vajrayana teachings

Vajrayana Buddhism includes the *Sravakayana* (similar to Theravada), Mahayana and Tantrayana. It is the latter which is special to Vajrayana. It incorporated some of the yoga practices and meditations, and it is understood that by these practices it is possible to progress extremely rapidly on the Buddhist path. A special feature was the oral personal teaching where the pupil progressed gradually from stage to stage and the progress was monitored by the teacher or guru.

Some practices involve concentration on channels of blood or energies in the body. These currents of energy cause the mind to be attracted by external objects so the person reverses these currents in order to control and develop the mind.

There are special initiation ceremonies where a special relationship is established with a deity. Sometimes there are public events like the Kalacakra initiations given by His Holiness the Dalai Lama, involving the receiving of blessings and establishing a relationship to a Tantra.

There is much sexual symbolism. The masculine denotes the active force of skilful means and the feminine the passive quality of wisdom. Their union results in Enlightenment.

The Tibetan teaching emphasizes that this life is very precious because people have an opportunity for spiritual development to free themselves and others from suffering. By prayers to the Buddhas and Bodhisattvas, and practices such as offerings people can try to provide the basis for good conditions in the future.

There is an exhortation to develop *bodhichitta* and enter into the Bodhisattva way of life. Liberation is explained as the mental peace achieved through the abandonment of ignorance. It urges the person to work towards overcoming greed, hatred and ignorance.

Ethics and Morality

The foundation of a good Buddhist life is morality (*Sila*). This includes the right speech, action and livelihood elements of the Noble Eightfold Path, and is the part of the path which should be developed first and then increased in quality when the balance of the Path is developed. It involves lovingkindness and compassion to oneself and other beings, not causing disharmony in the society and living a life which contributes to the harmony and well-being in the community.

Generosity or giving (*dana*) is an important aspect of a moral life. When Buddhism is taught to young children in Buddhist communities, it is generosity which is taught first. It is the giving of money, food, clothes, time, work and so on for the benefit of others. It includes alms given to the Sangha, helping the poor, donations to temples and spending money to publish books on Buddhism. In addition to making merit, or good Kamma, it has the effect of reducing selfishness and decreasing the sense of self for the giver.

The Five Precepts form the basis of the ethical action.

> Whosoever in this world destroys life, tells lies, takes what is not given, misuses the senses and is addicted to intoxicating drinks, such one interferes with his own progress in this very world.
>
> The Dhammapada, v. 246. 247

The Five Precepts are normally set out in the negative but include positive action. They are, not to:

1. Harm other beings – includes all living beings, and not only killing but harming them in any way directly or indirectly. It means to work for the benefit of all beings.
2. Take what is not given – includes stealing misappropriation and greedy accumulation of wealth. It means to be content with what one has.
3. Misuse the senses – includes improper sexual activity and an unwise gratification of all the senses. Means to be moderate and refined in sensual activities.

159

4. Speak in a way harmful to others – includes lying, harsh speech, abusive language and gossiping, and in an oral, written or pictorial form. Means not to cause disharmony by speech.
5. Take drugs or intoxicants which cloud the mind – includes not only alcohol but drugs and other substances (unless given as medicine). Means to maintain an alert mind capable of mindfulness.

Mahayana has the ten non-virtuous actions and Vajrayana the training in higher ethics which cover the same ground:
(a) Three physical:
    1. Killing 2.Stealing 3. Sexual misconduct
(b) Four verbal:
    4. Lying 5. Divisive speech 6. Harshness 7. Idle gossip
(c) Three mental:
    8. Covetousness 9. Malice 10. Wrong views
               Sutra of the Forty Two Chapters.

Note that these are the same ten factors which cause bad Kamma according to Theravada explanations. Of course, they would cause bad Kamma in Mahayana and Vajrayana, too.

A set of ten precepts is kept by novice monks and by nuns. They are the first five plus, not to:

6. Eat after noon
7. Indulge in dancing and entertainments
8. Wear perfumes and cosmetics
9. Use luxurious seats and beds
10. Deal with gold or money.

In the *Mangala Sutta* the Buddha explains the Blessings of Life as:

1. Not to associate with the foolish, but to associate with the wise, and to honour those worthy of honour.
2. Reside in a suitable locality, to have performed meritorious actions, to set oneself the right course.
3. Much learning, skilled livelihood, disciplined and of pleasant speech.
4. Support one's parents, cherish wife and children, engage in peaceful occupations.
5. Generosity, good conduct.

6. Avoid unskilful actions and intoxicating drinks.
7. Reverence, humility, contentment, gratitude.
8. Patience, obedience, religious discussion.
9. Self-control, chastity, understanding the Dhamma, realizing Nibbana.
10. Having a steady mind.

In the *Karaniya Metta Sutta* the Buddha first sets out the required standard of moral conduct:

> Make the right effort, be skilled in living, honest, obedient, gentle, humble, contented, with few requirements for life and few responsibilities, of simple livelihood, control the senses, be prudent, courteous, not seek constant company, and not do wrong things.

He then explains the method of practising lovingkindness and compassion for all beings:

> Not to deceive or despise another, not to wish harm to another, to have compassion for all beings like a mother to an only child, develop mindfulness, avoid wrong views, be virtuous, endowed with insight and to discard sensual pleasures.

Conditions of prosperity in this life are set out as persistent effort, protecting one's earnings, good friendships and balanced livelihood. Confidence in the Buddha, virtue, chastity and wisdom contribute to prosperity in future lives (*Vyagghapajja Sutta*).

Five kinds of trades are prohibited, namely, dealing in arms and weapons, human beings, meat and fish, intoxicating substances and poison.

The *Parabhava Sutta* sets out the conditions which lead to a person's downfall:

> Keeping the company of bad people, being fond of sleep, not supporting one's parents, deceiving a holy man, being selfish, being conceited and looking down on others, being a drunkard and a gambler, sexual misconduct, hatred towards others, taking life, stealing, not paying back debts, telling lies, harming relatives ...

In India during Buddha's time the highest caste were the Brahmins. A person was a Brahmin by birth. Other castes had a lower status and an outcast was at the bottom. The Buddha explained that a person should be judged not by birth but by his actions:

161

Not by birth is one an outcast,
Not by birth is one a Brahmin.
By deed one becomes an outcast,
By deed one becomes a Brahmin.

Vasala Sutta

The essentials of Theravada morality continued in the Mahayana and Vajrayana when the Bodhisattva ideal was developed. The morality or *sila* of early Buddhism was concentrated on the Bodhisattva practice, hence we see that the Bodhisattva path included generosity, morality, patience, energy, meditation and wisdom. This was the ethical ideal formulated by the Mahayana for the Bodhisattva, who could be an ordained or a lay person. Mahayanists emphasized compassion (*karuna*) and illustrated it by stating 'the Bodhisattva loves all beings as a mother loves her children'.

Buddhist Community

Buddhists seem to emphasize different inclinations in their practice, some scholarly, some devotional, some contemplative and others ascetic. In the order of development morality, concentration and wisdom are taken to be the three stages of the path to Nibbana.

Theravada recognizes four stages of sainthood: the stream winner (*sotopanna*) who will be reborn a maximum of seven times in the human realm, the once-returner (*sakadagami*) who will be reborn only once more in the human realm, the never returner (*anagami*) and the arahat.

Sangha

The Sangha at first meant monks (*bhikkhus*), nuns (*bhikkhunis*), lay men and lay women. Today it refers to the order of monks and nuns founded by Gotama Buddha. The Sangha are the third element of the Triple Gem and continue in direct unbroken line from the Buddha.

In Theravada countries, China and Korea, the Sangha consists of monks and nuns. They live in temples or monasteries and do not marry. In Japan, in addition to monks and nuns, there are priests who are in charge of temples and lead a family life.

In Tibet monks and nuns live in monasteries and do not marry, but some part-time monks have families and live in a monastery only part of the year. There are also lamas or teachers, often taken to be a reincarnation of an earlier lama. Tibet has the offices of the religious and political heads of state vested in the office of His Holiness, The Dalai Lama. The Dalai Lama is considered to be a reincarnation of the previous holder of the office and also the reincarnation of Bodhisattva Avalokatisvera. In Nepal there are tantric priests and scholar priests who have families and follow professions.

The Order of Nuns also dates from the time of the Buddha. In the Theravada countries the order has broken down due to technicalities regarding ordination and the present nuns are Ten Precept nuns who live according to the Vinaya. In Japan and Tibet also the nuns are not fully ordained. Korea, however, has a flourishing Order of Nuns. Some discussion has taken place about establishing a fully ordained line of nuns in the Theravada countries.

Many westerners have gone to the East and become ordained, and there have been ordinations in the West. In addition to full ordinations, steps less than a full ordination have been devised in the West.

Entry into the order is by ordination, an elaborate religious and social ceremony. First there is the novice ordination where the young person undertakes the ten precepts. After the age of 20 and a long period of study there is the higher ordination. On ordination a person cuts off social and family ties and takes up life in a monastery, often taking a new Buddhist name. Ordination is generally considered to be for life, but the member may leave the order. In some Theravada countries such as Burma and Thailand young men take the novice ordination for some time, weeks or months, and live in a temple to learn the Dhamma. In Thailand, men sometimes take novice ordination several times in their lives.

Monks and nuns do not own things apart from a few personal possessions such as robes and alms bowls. They shave their heads or have very short hair. Different coloured robes are worn – orange (Theravada), grey (Korea), black (Japan) and deep red (Tibetan).

The Vinaya, or rules of discipline, govern the training, conduct and organization of the Sangha. These are adhered to strictly in Theravada but in some Mahayana traditions they are regarded not so much as definitive rules, but as guidelines. They cover matters such as ordination, training, duties of teachers and novices, ways of dealing with differences of opinion and breach of the rules, lodgings, food, ceremonies and so on. A comprehensive guide of between 223 and 250 rules depending on the tradition.

There is no central authority for the Sangha. However, in each country the Sangha has sub–orders, each headed by a senior monk. In addition, each temple has a senior monk or abbot. In Thailand, the Sangha is organized as a national institution and the king appoints a *Sangha-raja* as head of the Sangha.

The members of the Sangha lead a strict life of study, devotion, meditation, practising and teaching the Dhamma and attending to the religious needs of the lay people. Some live in temples in villages and towns. In addition to their personal practice, they have a close relationship to the lay people. They teach the Dhamma, advise devotees, organize the Buddhist festivals and celebrations, visit people at home on request and those in hospitals and prisons, organize meditation classes, give talks in schools and colleges, take part in public religious and social conferences.

The lay persons like to listen to the monks chanting the texts (*Pirit*) in the form of blessings. A *Pirit* thread is often held by the monks and lay persons during the chanting to illustrate a communal activity and afterwards an orange thread of three strands (representing the Buddha, Dhamma and Sangha) is tied around the wrist of each devotee as a blessing and protection. In Tibet the monks perform elaborate religious plays at certain festivals.

In the Theravada countries the Sangha eat one main meal a day before midday. They depend on alms given by devotees. They may go on an alms round to collect alms, though the practice is growing of the devotees bringing the alms to the temple. In western countries the monks often may have to cook their own food since there are not many devotees to provide alms on a regular basis.

Some monks are members of meditation orders. These forest-dwelling monks live an ascetic life away from the people, in forests or small islands. They concentrate on meditation. They receive alms from the people in the same way and organize some meditation classes.

Certain traditions, such as the Zen in Japan, concentrate on meditation and ordinary daily tasks are done as meditations. In other traditions the Sangha perform duties similar to the Theravada Sangha. In the Vajrayana tradition, life in the monastery includes chanting, worship and elaborate meditations and rituals.

In the Theravada countries the village or town temple is the religious, social and cultural focus of the life of the people. The monks have classes in school subjects for young children and their advice is often sought by the people about various matters. Often the temple has a library and a hall for gatherings.

In all the different traditions, monks participate in blessing ceremonies at times of birth, illness and death.

Lay Buddhists

Lay persons form the vast majority of Buddhists. In Theravada the ordained Sangha have a special place in that they practise the Dhamma on a full-time basis though it is understood that lay persons can also progress very far on the path. In the Mahayana the distinction is less marked. Similarly in some western movements.

In all traditions the lay persons are considered important in that they give material support to temples and by their daily work provide the economic foundation for the teaching and practice of Buddhism.

The Buddha showed much regard for social relationships. On seeing a young man called Sigala worshipping the six geographical directions the Buddha asked him why he was doing that. Sigala replied that his father had advised him to worship the six directions. The Buddha replied, 'Your father's advice is excellent, but the six directions he had in mind are parents, teachers, wife and children, friends, employees and religious persons. They are worthy of honour and respect and should therefore be worshipped by performing one's duties towards them' (Sigalovada Sutta).

Parents and children

A child should support elderly parents, perform duties for them, maintain family traditions, be worthy of parents and perform the necessary funeral rights. A parent should guide children in conduct, persuade them to lead good lives, see to their education, advise them on marriage and hand over any inheritance to them.

Teachers and children

A pupil should respect and attend on the teacher, pay attention to the teaching, do the work set by the teacher and receive the teaching respectfully. A teacher should teach suitable subjects, ensure that the pupils understand, instruct them in arts and sciences, give good references and help pupils in later life.

Husband and wife

A husband should honour his wife, love her and be faithful to her, delegate domestic matters to her and provide security and comfort. A wife should perform her duties well, be hospitable to relatives, love and be faithful to her husband, manage the household and be skilled in her duties.

166

Friends, relatives and neighbours

One should be generous, courteous, helpful, impartial, sincere, loyal and not forsake them in time of difficulty and need.

Employers and employees

Employers should assign work according to ability, pay adequate wages and look after the employees, who, in turn, should be loyal to the employer and perform their duties well.

Religious persons

The lay persons should look after the material needs of religious persons and learn from them. Religious persons should set a good example and teach the religion.

In all traditions the lay persons are expected to support the temples and provide for the needs of monks. Some of the western movements make a charge for the teaching and classes, and engage in some business activities in order to finance themselves, due to the lack of a body of lay supporters.

Birth and growing up

It is common for the mother and father to visit a temple before a baby is born to receive blessings from the Sangha. Soon after birth the baby is often taken to the temple again to receive blessings. In some traditions the baby is ceremonially placed in a cradle and given gifts. When the baby is about a month old the head may be shaved and sacred threads tied around the wrists. Often a special ceremony is arranged and the monks are given a meal after which they chant blessings. In Burma and Thailand a time spent in a monastery as a novice monk on temporary ordination is seen as 'growing up'. In Japan the coming of age is sometimes celebrated at a temple with a special ceremony.

Marriage

Marriage is generally considered to be a secular affair, and the couple may visit a temple before or after the wedding to receive blessings from the monks. In Japan sometimes the couple may have a Buddhist wedding ceremony. A priest officiates and the proceedings include homage to the Buddha, receiving holy water, drinking holy wine, exchanging wedding rings and accepting a rosary.

Today in all countries, legal registration of a marriage is the norm and Buddhists should comply with the law of the land. Even without registration, where a man and woman are living together with a long-term serious commitment to Buddhist family life, they will be considered to be married.

In the *Rukkhadhamma Jataka* the Buddha explained the importance of the family relationship and urged people to maintain family ties together with the honour and dignity of the family as a social unit. A family will include two-parent and one-parent families, and also groups of people living in communities. Buddhists and Buddhist families in the West try to lead a good Buddhist life, following the teaching and observing the customs and practices, though their activities will differ from those living in the Buddhist societies of, say, Sri Lanka or Thailand.

Death or Passing Away

Death or passing away has a special significance in Buddhist terms because of the idea of rebirth. The physical body comes to an end, but the mind or mental energy leaves the present body and, with some change, goes to the next life in another body.

It is important that the person dies with a calm and peaceful mind, because that state of mind influences the next birth. So monks or relatives recite or read the Buddhist texts to remind the person of the teaching.

The funeral service is not a sad, sombre affair. The monks conduct the service, pointing out the person's good qualities and chanting selected texts dealing with the impermanence of life. In the Pure Land tradition, the ceremony is considered to be an ordination ceremony to prepare the person to meet the Eternal Buddha. It is normal to cremate the body.

The family and friends arrange memorial services in the temple or at home shortly afterwards. The monks conduct the service. After a meal, or alms, one of them gives a Dhamma talk and there is a simple 'transference of merit' ceremony when water is poured from a jug into a receptacle until it overflows. It is understood that the departed person, now living another life somewhere, benefits from this merit.

Often the family arrange annual 'alms givings'. Family and friends make gifts of money, books and other things required by a temple in memory of the departed. Sometimes books are published and distributed.

In some Japanese traditions the family keep memorial tablets at the shrine at home. These are made of wood, marble or china and have the names of departed relatives written on them. In Japan, *Obon* is a special festival to remember the departed relatives.

Worship, Devotion and Meditation

Worship and Devotion

Worship and devotion is an important aspect of Buddhist practice. It keeps the devotee in regular contact with the teaching and provides a Buddhist background to daily life. It is understood that intellectual understanding of the Dhamma is not enough but that there must be practice in the form of worship, devotion and meditation for the devotee to progress on the path.

In Theravada Buddhism, the Buddha is considered to be an extraordinary human being who attained Enlightenment but who has passed away. The worship is not a communication with the Buddha but a meaningful act to pay homage to a great teacher, a meditation on the teaching and an effort to remember and live according to his teaching. Gotama Buddha said:

> Whoever, a monk, nun or lay person, lives in accordance with the teaching, conducts himself or herself dutifully and acts correctly, he or she respects, honours and worships and venerates the Buddha with the highest kind of worship.

Maha Parinibbana Sutta

Worship is performed facing a Buddha image. The Buddha is shown in a seated (cross-legged, known as the lotus position), lying down, standing or walking position. The images are of varying sizes and reflect the Buddhist qualities of harmony, compassion, wisdom and tranquillity. In temples, beside the image there is often a cask containing some relics.

A Buddha image is generally kept at home in a high, respectful, prominent position. Some homes have a shrine room or a corner of a room arranged as a shrine. Some families conduct a short private service at home daily, on days

170

of the full moon, or special days. The service is similar to, but perhaps shorter than, the one at a temple.

Temples and monasteries arrange devotional activities daily, on special days, or days of the full moon. On special occasions such as an alms giving ceremony, too, there will be a service. The service takes place in the shrine room of the temple and is normally conducted by a monk. People dress modestly when going to the temple and take their shoes off at the entrance as a mark of respect. The devotees are expected to conduct themselves in a calm manner.

The devotees bow or prostrate themselves, keeping the palms of the hands together respectfully, before the Buddha image. Offerings of food, flowers light and incense are made. After paying homage to the Buddha the devotee recites, or if a monk is conducting the service, follows the monk in reciting the Three Refuges:

> I take Refuge in the Buddha
> I take Refuge in the Dhamma
> I take Refuge in the Sangha.

This is recited thrice, then the Five Precepts and words in praise of the Buddha, Dhamma and Sangha. The monks then chant a Buddhist text such as the *Karaniya Metta Sutta* on lovingkindness. This may be followed by a period of meditation or a talk on the Dhamma.

The Mahayana developed the idea of a permanent spiritual Buddha. Also heavenly Buddhas such as Amida and Maha-vairochana, and Bodhisattas like Avalokatisvera, Manjushri and Tara. Images of these Buddhas and Bodhisattas as well as images of Sakyamuni Buddha are used in Mahayana worship. The images represent living deities so the Mahayana worship is then a communication with these beings who are then able to respond.

In Japan, Buddhist homes generally have a shrine called a *Butsudan*. Images of Sakyamuni Buddha, other Buddhas and Bodhisattas are kept here, as are ancestral mortuary tables and some Sutra texts. The family worship here, sometimes daily. Each temple has a resident priest who conducts daily services. On days of festivals and celebrations special programmes are arranged.

The Pure Land (*Jodo*) Buddhists concentrate their worship on Amida Buddha. They repeat the formula 'Namu Amida Batsu' meaning 'Hail to Amida Buddha'. This concentrates the mind, overcomes the distractions and creates a communication between the devotee and Amida Buddha. Devotion focused on Bhaisajya-guru Buddha and Bodhisattva Avalokatisvera (*Kwanon*) is also popular. The Nichiren Buddhists revere the Lotus Sutra and chant 'Namu Myoho Renge Kyo (I seek refuge in the Lotus Sutra)' and long passages of the Sutra in their worship. They understand this to purify the mind, protect and benefit the devotee and develop the Bodhisattva perfections. The Lotus Sutra is also chanted by other traditions. Chapter 25 is a popular chant and ends with these words:

> Bodhisattva Avalokatisvera, pure and holy,
> In pain, distress, death, calamity,
> Able to be a sure reliance
> Perfect in all merit,
> With compassionate eyes beholding all,
> Boundless ocean of blessings!
> Prostrate let us revere him.

A Tendai worship may include offering incense and candles, chanting mantras, prayers for the happiness of all beings, chanting the Heart Sutra, repeating the Three Refuges, praising Amida Buddha, chanting Dharanis, taking refuge in Saicho and the Three Prostrations.

In Tibetan Buddhism the devotees worship at home, morning and evening, at shrines decorated with images, offerings of flowers, perpetually burning lamps and scented or pure water. There is daily worship in the temples and special devotions on days of the full moon and holy days. Lamps burn before the images of Buddhas and Bodhisattvas. There are seven kinds of offerings – water, for drinking and for washing, flowers, incense, light, perfume and food. Full-length prostrations are the norm, and the monks lead the service with Sutra reading and chanting.

The recitation of mantras is done by monks and lay persons. A mantra is a word or series of words through which spiritual power is exercised and is repeated for spiritual progress. Mantras are prescribed for good memory, avoiding misfortune and helping concentration. The mantra relating to Bodhisattva Avalokatisvera 'On Mani Padme Hum (Hail the Jewel in the Lotus)' is a common chant.

A prayer wheel is used for repeating mantras. Mantras are written down, consecrated by rituals performed by monks and lamas, and placed inside the prayer wheel. Turning the prayer wheel mindfully has the same effect as reciting the mantra. Sometimes the devotee recites the mantra while turning the prayer wheel.

Religious dances or plays are a feature of Tibetan Buddhism. These are performed by monks wearing masks and elaborate costumes which have religious meanings. Many of these dances or plays act out sacred historical stories and take place at special festivals.

Meditation

After starting the practice of morality, the devotee then develops mental development. This comprises the Right Effort, Mindfulness and Concentration of the Noble Eight-fold Path. A devotee intent on serious practice of Buddhism is not content with mere intellectual understanding of the teaching and will wish to experience and realize the teaching. This can only be done by mindfulness and meditation which goes beyond intellectual analysis and understanding.

Bhavana, the Pali word for developing the mind is translated as meditation but has a much wider meaning than spending some time in formal concentration.

Mindfulness means extending awareness so that all actions, thoughts and words are performed with increasing concentration and consciousness. It applies to bodily actions, feelings, mental states and activities and to the teaching. Meditation involves the formal training of the mind, concentration and the development of insight. It is generally accepted that some personal guidance is needed in meditation. The aim is to purify the mind and to develop awareness, energy and tranquillity leading to realizing the truth or Nibbana.

> Indeed from meditation wisdom arises
> Without meditation, wisdom wanes ...
>
> The Dhammapada, v. 282

There are two kinds of meditation in Buddhism. The first is *Samatha* meditation, to concentrate the mind on one object to the exclusion of everything else so that the mind becomes calm, tranquil and concentrated. There are various subjects of meditation, such as fire, dead bodies, the Buddha, loving-kindness and so on. The meditator finds that the calmness achieved carries over to daily activities and gains more confidence in dealing with day to day things. With practice there is an elevation of consciousness and he achieves higher

173

mystic states (*jhanas*). This type of meditation does not lead to insight into Nibbana.

Gotama Buddha discovered the second type of meditation, *Vipassana*, which gives an insight or realization into the nature of things and to Nibbana. This involves an increasing mindfulness, observation, attention and analytical realization. The meditator experiences and realizes various insights which cannot be understood intellectually. It is the Vipassana meditation which is essentially Buddhist meditation.

The Buddha said:

> 'Two things are conducive to knowledge: tranquillity and insight. When tranquillity is developed, mind is developed. When insight is developed, right understanding is developed.'

Anguttara Nikaya

In the Pali canon the important text dealing with meditation is the *Satipatthana Sutta*. Satipatthana may be interpreted as The Foundation of Mindfulness. The Buddha said: 'This is the unique way for the purification of beings, for the destruction of suffering, for the attainment of wisdom, and for the realization of Nibbana – namely the Four Foundations of Mindfulness. They are:

1. Contemplation of the body
2. Contemplation of feelings
3. Contemplation of mind
4. Contemplation of mind objects (Dhammas, Thoughts).

The section on the contemplation of the body begins with instructions on the mindfulness of in-and-out breathing (*anapana sati*). It goes on to deal with bodily postures, bodily movements, the repulsiveness of the biological body, the analysis of the material body and contemplation of death specifically related to corpses in various stages of decay. Contemplation of the feelings involves considering the arising and perishing nature of pleasant, painful and neutral feelings. Contemplation of the mind involves noticing when the mind in influenced by lust, hatred and ignorance, and noticing states of mind such as distraction, elevation and concentration, and impermanence.

Contemplation of Dhammas or mind objects includes meditation on the Five Hindrances, Five Aggregates, the six sense-bases, Factors of Enlightenment and the Four Noble Truths. The Five Hindrances are sensual desires, ill-will, sloth

174

and torpor, restlessness and worry, and doubts. The Factors of Enlightenment are mindfulness, investigation of reality, energy, joy, tranquillity, concentration and equanimity.

The Buddhist teaching recognizes six different kinds of temperament: lustful, hateful, ignorant, devout, intellectual and discursive. A meditation teacher recognizes the temperament of the devotee and prescribes a suitable subject for meditation. For the breathing meditation the cross-legged sitting position is prescribed. The meditator may sit, stand, walk or lie down for the other forms of meditation. On starting Vipassana meditation soon the devotee begins to see himself, others and things around him in a new light.

In Japan the different traditions emphasize different kinds of meditation. The Tendai meditation involves contemplation on subjects like emptiness, impermanence, compassion and the Four Noble Truths, which are closely connected to the teaching. Devotees in Shingon meditate on the Five Vows: to save all beings, bring together wisdom and love, learn the Dhammas, serve all Buddhas, and to attain the highest Enlightenment and meditate on these vows. They also use breathing exercises and meditate on the body, speech and mind. In the Pure Land tradition the devotees develop calm and tranquillity by bowing to Amida Buddha, chanting words of praise and developing a wish to be reborn in his Pure Land. They contemplate upon a visualized image of Amida Buddha and other complex meditations leading to insight.

The Zen tradition concentrates on meditation or *zazen*. The practices include both the Samatha type meditation to develop calmness and tranquillity, and Vipassana type meditation to develop insight similar to the Foundation of Mindfulness practice. Zen relates meditation to all activities and work, and aims to identify the meditator with the highest reality. Zen uses *Koans*, which are riddles with no intellectual meaning. This breaks the thought pattern and the meditator realizes emptiness.

Tibetan Buddhism recognizes that meditation must be preceded by morality and concentration. The devotees practise calm abiding (Samatha) meditation and insight (Vipassana) meditation. Five faults are recognized: laziness, forgetfulness, lethargy and excitement, non-application of antidotes and over-application. The antidotes to the faults are faith, aspiration, effort, physical and mental pliancy, mindfulness, awareness application and non-application of the antidotes.

Buddhists worshipping at the Bodhi Tree in Anuradhapura, Sri Lanka

Tantric meditation

Tantric meditation is a feature of Tibetan Buddhism. It involves the awareness of the fundamental reality of phenomena. The lama or guru chooses a mantra, a tutelary deity and a *mandala* for the devotee. The devotee does breathing exercises and practises meditation focused on his tutelary deity and mantra.

At the supreme Tantra stage the devotee at first by actions such as homage to the Triple Gem and the spiritual master, taking the Bodhisatta vows, dedication of offerings to deities, recitation of prayers and mantras and so on – meditates that he and his tutelary deity are spiritualized and transformed into a higher state. At the second stage, the devotee concentrates on the channels of spiritual energy and the creative powers in the body to purify the body and perfect the mind to realize Absolute Reality. Yoga practice is carried on to harness the natural spiritual powers within the devotee.

In Tibet and Japan the mandala is used as an aid to meditation. Some have Buddhas and Bodhisattvas and show heavenly lands. Others are diagrammatic. The devotee at first meditates on the pictures or diagram and then concentrates on the higher meanings of the mandala.

Pilgrimage, Festivals and Celebrations

Pilgrimage

In Buddhist countries going on pilgrimage is considered a devotional activity. The devotees visit places of importance in Buddhist history, special shrines, temples and monasteries, in some of which Buddhist relics have been enshrined. They like to recall past events and to pay homage to these places which are visible evidence of Buddhist life. People from western countries also go on pilgrimage to Buddhist sites in Asia.

In Asian countries the pilgrims may be individuals, small family groups or bigger groups. Sometimes groups of devotees arrange a coach, take foodstuffs and go on a pilgrimage of several days, visiting several temples and shrines. Some of the temples have simple accommodation and cooking facilities for use by pilgrims.

Shortly before he passed away Gotama Buddha spoke to Ven. Ananda of four places made sacred by his association which devotees should visit with reverence. They are:

1. Lumbini in the Nepal, the birthplace of the Buddha,
2. Buddha Gaya where he attained Enlightenment,
3. Isipatana near Benares where he gave the first teaching and
4. Kusinara where he passed away.

'And they Ananda,' the Buddha went on, 'who shall die with a believing heart while on pilgrimage shall be reborn in heavenly states' (Mahaparinibbana Sutta).

There are temples and shrines at these places and at Buddha Gaya there stands a Bodhi tree descended from the one under which Gotama Buddha attained Enlightenment.

In Sri Lanka a Bodhi tree which has grown from a sapling of the original tree grows in the ancient capital Anuradhapura. In the temple of the Tooth in Kandy, Sri Lanka, there is enshrined a tooth of Gotama Buddha. On the top of Sri Pada, a mountain in Sri Lanka, there is a footprint considered to be that of the Buddha who came there to teach. Two other temples, the ones at Kelaniya and Nagadipa, also mark places in Sri Lanka visited by the Buddha. Apart from these temples there are many others of great importance visited by pilgrims.

Two strands of the Buddha's hair are enshrined in the Shwe Dagon Pagoda in Rangoon, Burma, and the site is considered to be one visited by the Buddha. The Temple of the Emerald Buddha in Bangkok and Phra Pathom Chedi in Nakhon Pathon are popular with pilgrims in Thailand. So also are the remains of Borobudur temple in Indonesia.

In Japan, many pilgrims visit the temples on Mount Hiei and the temples around Kyoto. The Asakinsa Kwanon (Sensoji) temple in Tokyo is a great attraction today. In Shikoku Island there is a special pilgrim route with numerous temples and shrines. In Tibet the pilgrims visit the important monasteries and especially the Potala Palace, the home of the Dalai Lama.

Festivals and Celebrations

Participation in festivals and celebrations is considered an important part of Buddhist practice by devotees. In addition to the religious background, some festivals have social and cultural features. They are forms of Buddhist community activities enjoyed by the devotees, young and old.

Some festivals, like those marking the birth, Enlightenment and passing away of the Gotama Buddha are common to all traditions. At the same time we see variations in the nature, form and dates of festivals from tradition to tradition and country to country. Some festivals are specific to a particular tradition, some are national, some local. There are numerous festivals so it is possible to mention only the more important ones.

South Asia

In the Theravada countries the festivals are generally on the days of the full moon. The more devout Buddhists visit the temple on the days of the new moon and half moon also. Some formally take the Ten Precepts and spend the whole day at the temple. A special programme is arranged of a service, formal taking of the Precepts, talks on the Dhamma, offering alms (the midday meal) to the monks, chanting, meditation and discussions on the Dhamma. Many devotees

179

visit the temple some time during the day bringing gifts and often contributions of food. There is often a communal midday meal. A special feature of the festivals in Sri Lanka is the *perahara* or a procession of musicians, dancers, jugglers, acrobats and decorated elephants sometimes carrying Buddhist relics. This starts at the temple and winds its way through the town or village and returns to the temple. In the western countries, the festival day celebrations are similar but are generally held on a Sunday.

The New Year is celebrated about the middle of April. The houses are cleaned, the people wear new clothes, start cooking at the auspicious time, prepare special foods such as milk-rice, visit relatives and friends and entertain visitors. In Thailand the New Year, *Songkran*, festivities include a special water festival when people splash each other with water, engage in water fights in the streets and boat races. Caged birds are released and fish in tanks returned to rivers and ponds.

Gotama Buddha's birth, Enlightenment and passing away are celebrated on the day of the full moon in May, called *Vesak* or Buddha Day, perhaps the most important festival. In addition to the normal programme, the temples and houses are decorated with flags and lanterns, there are various entertainments and pageants, huge decorated paintings of scenes from the Buddha's life are built, and food and soft drinks are distributed from wayside stalls. In Thailand scented water is poured on Buddha images and the monks lead the devotees in a threefold circumambulation of the *stupa*.

In Sri Lanka, the day of the full moon in June, *Poson*, is celebrated, being the anniversary of Ven. Mahinda bringing the teaching to the island. The day of the full moon in July is celebrated as *Esala* or *Dhammacakka day* to remember the first teaching by Gotama Buddha to the five ascetics in the Deer Park in Benares. This marks the beginning of the three-month retreat, *Vassa*. The *Esala Perahara*, or procession, takes place in Kandy, Sri Lanka, in honour of Buddha's tooth relic enshrined in the temple there. In addition to relics, items of historical importance are carried in the procession which might include over 100 decorated elephants.

Katina is celebrated in October or November at the end of the three month retreat of the monks and nuns. It is a special thanksgiving ceremony when the lay persons express their warm gratitude to the Sangha. The devotees make gifts of robes, money, foodstuffs and other requirements for the temple.

Japan

In Japan the festivals are celebrated at temples by making offerings, services, prayers and reading from the Sutras and chanting to honour Sakyamuni Buddha, other Buddhas and Bodhisattvas. Devotees make it a point to visit temples and shrines.

The most important festival is *Hanamatsuri* in April to celebrate Sakyamuni Buddha's birth. Images of the infant Buddha are decorated with flowers and scented water is poured over them. The Enlightenment is celebrated in December and the Buddha's passing away (*parinirvana*) in February.

The festival of *Obon* is in July to pay respects to the ancestors. The graves are cleaned and decorated with flowers. Offerings of flowers and incense are made at the family shrines at home. The ancestors are invited to return to their families, lamps are lit to show the way and food is set out for them.

Higan is celebrated in March and September at the equinox, again to remember and honour dead friends and relatives. Graves are decorated and cleaned and ceremonies are held to give blessings to the departed ones.

In addition the different traditions in Japan have festivals to celebrate teachers especially related to the tradition.

Tibet

Tibetan Buddhists have a festival to celebrate the Buddha's birth and another to celebrate his Enlightenment and passing away (parinirvana). The first teaching is also celebrated with a special festival. The traditional celebrations include a service, worship, Sutra recitation, chanting, fasting and meditation.

The Tibetan New Year in February is celebrated in an elaborate way by the *Losar* Festival. Preceding this is the *Gutor* Festival to end the old year. Houses are cleaned and special food is cooked. Devotees visit monasteries with offerings. The monks perform various religious ceremonies aimed at driving away evil spirits. Wearing masks and exotic robes they perform dances and act out plays depicting the struggle between good and evil. The dancing is accompanied by music from horns, drums and cymbals and is a deeply moving religious experience for the audience of lay persons and Sangha.

The New Year, *Losar*, festivities include wearing new clothes, preparation of special food and drink, visiting friends and relatives, entertaining and taking part in feasts and dances. *Losar* is immediately followed by the Great Prayer Festival celebrations to ensure a prosperous coming year.

There are numerous other festivals, some celebrating Buddhist events, some to make offerings for local deities and others to remember important teachers.

In western countries the festivals are not celebrated in exactly the same way. However, the temples and monasteries in the different traditions arrange some celebrations on the important days, sometimes a full day's celebration involving a service, talks, discussion, meditation and a midday meal.

Buddhism Today

There is no country in Asia which has not been influenced at one time or another by Buddhism. For more than 2,500 years Buddhism has been the primary inspiration behind Asian civilization and the source of its greatest cultural achievements. Buddhist teaching, custom and practice played an important part not only in the private lives of the people but also in State matters. The Sangha had an important and respected position in the State and the Buddhist temples and monasteries often received State support.

The spread of Buddhism has always been peaceful, more a case of the teaching being available to the persons who came to it rather than an active propagation. Buddhism developed and existed harmoniously and without conflict with other faiths, whether they were the original faiths in a country or new faiths which arrived later.

In the two or three centuries before the present century the influence of Buddhism was somewhat reduced for various reasons, mainly political ones. But in the present century there has been a resurgence in Buddhism and continuing Buddhist activities. There has been greater communication between Buddhists of the different countries. Several international organizations such as the World Fellowship of Buddhists (founded in 1950) have been established to increase the liaison between Buddhists by arranging conferences and sponsoring co-operative activities. An increasing number of people from the West go to the Buddhist countries in Asia to study Buddhism at universities and temples, to learn and take part in meditation, and sometimes to become ordained as monks and nuns.

In the West, the original interest in Buddhism from the early 19th century was by scholars. Gradually, the translation of texts, communication with Asian Buddhists and the discussions at the Parliament of World Religions in 1893, followed by the centennial in 1993 in Chicago, and the establishing of Buddhist temples, created an interest in Buddhism as a religion. When Buddhism was brought to

A group of Buddhist pilgrims at a temple in Sri Lanka

Sri Lanka by Ven. Mahinda, after some years the king asked him whether Buddhism had become established in Sri Lanka. Ven. Mahinda replied that Buddhism will become established when the people of a country learn the Dhamma in their language and become ordained as Sangha. This has happened in Europe, the United Kingdom and the Americas so that we can say that Buddhism has become established in the West. In addition Buddhism is a subject of study and research in several universities.

An interesting feature in western countries is that all the different traditions are represented. In the Asian countries generally the temples in any one country are all of one tradition. In addition there are new movements in the West which may become new traditions in time. There are many Buddhist organizations in the UK and the Buddhist Society Directory lists over 250 of them.

From the earliest times in Asia, Buddhists have been happy to engage in dialogue with those of other religions. This continues in the present day and Buddhists take an active part in inter-faith dialogue. There is a Buddhist-Christian dialogue group which meets regularly in England. In the UK, Buddhists are represented at national level on the Religious Education Council in England and at local level in the Standing Advisory Councils on Religious Education. Buddhism is one of the faiths in which there are official syllabuses for the teaching of religious education in schools.

There has been a great interest in Buddhist meditation and the many meditation classes and groups are well attended. There have been joint meditation sessions between Christian and Buddhist monks and nuns. In addition some doctors prescribe meditation for certain patients and some hospitals arrange meditation sessions. A meditation grove has been constructed in a prison by prisoners with the advice of the Buddhist Prison Chaplaincy.

Buddhism has been and continues to be a multi-ethnic and multi-cultural faith. As Buddhism looks to the future, Buddhists will have to consider issues such as the environment, economic matters and the imbalance of wealth in the world, corporate liability, human rights and equal opportunities.

CHRISTIANITY
W. OWEN COLE

Jesus

The central character in the story of Christianity is Jesus, who lived in the Roman province of Judea, the country we now call Israel, almost 2,000 years ago. Although most people seem to have acknowledged that he was a man who went about doing good he was a controversial figure in his own lifetime and has been ever since. In the following pages you will discover why people have felt so passionately about him.

The Sources

The activities of popes, dalai lamas and other religious leaders seldom attract the attention of historians unless they make some political contribution. Thus Moses is not found in the annals of Egyptian history, or the Buddha in ancient Indian texts. Similarly, little is known about Jesus outside the New Testament, a collection of books and letters written by his followers some years after his ministry. The reliability of this information has been disputed by students of the Bible at various times since it was written by Jesus' own followers. It contains stories of Jesus performing unusual actions, healing sick people, walking on the Sea of Galilee, stilling storms and even feeding a gathering of 5,000 people, These, they argue, are incredible. No one could do such things. Reasonable people could not possibly trust documents describing such events, especially as they were written by Jesus' followers. To this challenge Christians offer a variety of replies. Some say that because Jesus was the Son of God he had all the power of the creator of the world in his hands. Could not the son of the one who created water walk on it? Others go to an opposite extreme. They accept that all such accounts are to be regarded as attempts to describe the experience of believing in Jesus and not as descriptions of events which really happened. For instance, sometimes when something good happens to us we speak of 'walking on air' or being 'ten feet tall'. In a similar way, the gospel stories try to describe the influence of Jesus; one story says he walked on the water. It is probably true to say that most Christians live uneasily between these two extremes. They want a flesh and blood character to believe in but in an age dominated by reason and scientific explanations they find it difficult to decide which incidents described in the New Testament they should regard as historical, and which they should regard as ways of describing what Jesus meant to his followers.

Almost every episode in the New Testament is significant. Only very rarely does a writer give himself the luxury of describing an incident without bringing out its importance. One of the exceptions may be Mark 14:50-51 where mention is made of a young man who was almost arrested with Jesus but who managed to escape by wriggling out of his clothes. Even this probably has significance, as being Mark's way of saying 'I was there – I was that young man!'

What is known of Jesus is confined almost exclusively to four New Testament books written by his followers. These are known as the gospels. Probably the first of these was written by St Mark, the young man already mentioned, when he was middle aged, perhaps shortly after July 64 C.E. To allay false rumours that the Roman emperor Nero had set fire to part of his capital city, the emperor had arrested, and killed as scapegoats, many Christians. It is likely that by this time Mark was living in Rome as the companion of Simon Peter, that Peter was one of those executed during the reign of terror, and that Mark, a survivor, was encouraged to write down the story of Jesus as Peter had told it.

For many centuries it was believed that St Matthew's Gospel was the first to be written, and some people still hold to this view. Clearly it was written in an attempt to convince Jews that Jesus was the Messiah. It makes considerable use of the Jewish Bible, relating many of its verses to incidents in the life of Jesus and following them with the assertion that 'this was to fulfil the scripture'.

On the other hand, St Luke seems to have written his gospels for everyone, both Jews and Gentiles. He was probably converted to Christianity by Paul. Eventually he reached Rome in his company and there probably wrote the Acts of the Apostles to fill in gaps in the community's knowledge of their famous teachers, Peter and Paul, and to argue with opponents of Christianity that they were good citizens, not irresponsible trouble-makers. After the success of this book he may have been induced to write his gospel, amplifying the gospel of Mark, which he used as a source, and presenting his account in an elegant style of Greek, superior to Mark's, which educated members of Roman society might be persuaded to read.

These three gospels are all very similar, possibly because most of the material of Mark's gospel is found in all of them. Therefore, they are often called the synoptic gospels. Very different is the gospel according to St John, as the writer is clearly more concerned to bring out the universal significance of Jesus than to describe his ministry in Palestine. Even when he describes an incident in Jesus' life it fades into the background as the writer brings out the meaning.

Though it is most clearly the case with John's gospel, it is true that none of the four provides the biography of Jesus. It was never the intention of the writers to give a full account of Jesus' life from cradle to resurrection because this was not what mattered. They wanted to say that Jesus was a real historical character, someone who had really lived, not a figment of the imagination, but they also wanted to say what his living meant to them, and people like them who believed that he still lived. When they said that he calmed a storm on the Sea of Galilee what they wanted to imply was that he could calm the fears of Christians facing torture and death at the hands of the emperor, Nero. When Christians gathered together to share a meal like the last supper Jesus had shared with his disciples – even using the same words he had used – they were claiming that he was with them just as he had been on the night of his arrest.

The portrait of Jesus that can be pieced together from the four gospels, and some understanding of the Judaism of his time, is that he was a teacher of the Torah whose interpretation of scripture had much in common with that of the Pharisees, a radical and pious Jewish group of laymen rather than priests. In later times he would have been known as a rabbi. This title is, in fact, applied to him in the gospels, but scholars tend to think that this is an anachronism, rather like putting the word 'England' on a map of the Roman world, for the name had not yet been coined. However, Jesus

188

behaved like a rabbi. He taught and interpreted the Torah and gathered a number of disciples around him to whom he carefully explained his teaching, which they probably committed to memory. This supplies the answer to the question why Jesus never wrote a book. Rabbis did not write, they taught. They did not teach their own interpretations of the Torah, they handed on the tradition which they had received, which they claimed was the oral Torah given to Moses at Mount Sinai to explain the written Torah.

It is possible to say more than this. Jesus comes across as a compassionate and kind teacher who was a popular preacher. He was criticized for being the friend of tax collectors (Jews who were prepared to serve the oppressive colonial power, Rome) and sinners (men and women who rarely, if ever, followed the teachings of the Torah and did not live as pious, observant Jews should). He even included women among his followers. Jesus also possessed the ability to heal the sick, not by using medicines but by the power of his personality or God's gift, a skill quite common in the ancient world. (*See* Mark 3:22 where Jesus replies to his critics by asking who it is that gives them the power to cast out evil spirits, if his power is from Beelzebub, prince of demons!)

After a ministry which lasted for about three years, beginning in his home region of Galilee and ending in Jerusalem, holy city of the Jews, this Jewish teacher was arrested and put to death. Here the story might have come to an end, with Jesus receiving a few lines in contemporary Jewish writings, as in fact he does, but Jesus was not executed for his piety, or for befriending the rejected and healing some sick people. He died on a cross because, at the human level, he made claims which were a threat to the always uneasy peace which existed between the Romans and their Jewish subjects. It was also asserted that his death was an act of God whereby the Covenant made with the Jews at Mount Sinai was extended to all men and women who put their trust in him. It was said that the Jesus who had been executed was the long awaited Messiah, and the son of God; that he had risen from the dead so that all who believed in him could know him, just as fully as those who followed him during his earthly ministry in Palestine.

Jesus the Messiah

For most of the seven centuries before the lifetime of Jesus the Jewish people had been ruled by other nations. At one time their princes and rulers had been taken captive to Babylon; very old people might still have been able to remember their grandparents speaking with horror of a Greek king who desecrated the Temple by installing a statue of himself in the most holy part of it, and speaking with pride of the Jewish revolt which drove his army out of Palestine, though their victory was short-lived. With the desire for independence grew the belief that one day God would send a deliverer, perhaps another King David, for he was the greatest ruler they had ever had. Besides defeating the Philistines he had even captured Jerusalem and made it his capital city. The Jewish people gave this expected liberator the title Messiah. Originally the name simply meant anointed. It is used in the Jewish Bible of Aaron, the brother of Moses whom he anointed priest, of King David, and also of the Persian king, Cyrus, who is called, 'the Lord's anointed' (Isaiah 45:1). However, by the time of Jesus, to speak of the Messiah was to refer to the hoped for deliverer who would drive out the Romans and establish an age of justice and peace.

Jesus seems to have believed that he was the Messiah. Certainly his followers claimed this status for him. In fact one of the chief assertions of the New Testament writings is that Jesus is God's Messiah. His kinsman, John the Baptist, was not only a prophet warning the people to follow the ways of God, he was also regarded by Christians as the herald of the Messiah. In the Jewish Bible there is the book of the prophet Malachi. It has been made the last book of the Old Testament in the Christian Bible and its final sentences contained these words:

> Behold I will send you Elijah the prophet before the great and terrible day of the Lord comes. He will turn the hearts of fathers to their children and the hearts of children to their fathers, unless I come and smite the land with a curse.
>
> (Malachi 4:5-6)

John the Baptist was the returned Elijah in Christian eyes. Indeed the New Testament even says that he dressed like Elijah and lived in the wilderness like him (Matthew 3:4; cf. 1 Kings 18). In popular folklore Elijah would return to herald the coming of the Messiah. Jesus, then, believed he was the Messiah. Perhaps early Christians claimed that the curse mentioned by Malachi was the terrible destruction of Jerusalem and the Temple by the Romans in 70 C.E.

190

Jesus seldom used the word Messiah and seems to have discouraged his followers from referring to him by that title. Therefore, it has sometimes been suggested that he did not believe himself to be the Messiah. However, at his trial he accepted the title, and Jews reading the gospels could scarcely doubt that the claim was being made. The feeding of the five thousand, whatever actually happened, was seen as the feast which the righteous would enjoy in the hereafter, a messianic banquet: and when Jesus said, 'You have learned that our forefathers were told, Do not commit murder..., do not commit adultery... do not break your oath..., but what I tell you is this...', he was setting himself above the teaching given to Moses at Mount Sinai. (The full account of this teaching is found in Matthew, chapter 5). The fact that in Matthew's gospel the teaching was given on a hillside, so that we now call it the Sermon on the Mount, was probably a way of linking it with the giving of the Torah. He also claimed to forgive sins (e.g. Mark 2:9). The messianic banquet and the forgiveness of sins were regarded as characteristic of the new age brought in by the Messiah. The gospels argue that Jesus has inaugurated that age, therefore he is the Messiah.

Jesus probably avoided using the word Messiah for two reasons. Firstly it was a term which already conveyed very firm ideas of a military deliverer and Jesus did not see his messiahship in this light. He took as his text from the Jewish Bible some words of the Isaiah scroll –

> The spirit of the Lord is upon me because he has anointed me;
> He has sent me to announce good news to the poor,
> To proclaim release for prisoners and recovery of sight for the blind;
> To let the broken victims go free,
> To proclaim the year of the Lord's favour.
>
> (Luke 4:18-19)

In the rest of Luke's gospel the meaning of this mission is explained as Jesus befriends the poor and lonely, criticizes the deeply religious who lack compassion, weeps for the people of Jerusalem and dies forgiving the repentant thief who is being crucified with him.

The idea of a spiritual messiah, perhaps even a messiah who would suffer, may not be unique to Jesus. Similar ideas may have been held by a group of Jews known now as the Qumran community who lived near the Dead Sea in the time of Jesus.

191

However, unlike Jesus they do not seem to have gone around the towns and villages of Palestine spreading their views. If a popular preacher like Jesus had begun by declaring himself to be the Messiah it is unlikely that he would have been given a chance to explain himself before either the people forced him to lead a military rising, or the authorities arrested him before the riots started.

Jesus the Son of God

The second reason why Jesus may have avoided the term Messiah may have been because he regarded it as inadequate. He was more than the Messiah. The Messiah was not expected to forgive sins, this was the right of God alone, in Jewish eyes. In this, and many other ways, Jesus seemed to be making himself God's equal. Also, his message appeared to be for the whole of humanity, not only the Jews, and the word 'Messiah' was meaningless to the rest of the human race. Perhaps this was one reason why Jesus often called himself 'son of Man' – another title found in the Jewish Bible, but less popular and obviously capable of being used anywhere to mean that Jesus was the representative of mankind sent by God.

Although 'son of Man' is the phrase most often found on the lips of Jesus, 'son of God' is the one favoured by Paul and most of the other New Testament writers. The use may have received some encouragement from Jesus, certainly an only son features prominently in some of his parables (Matthew 21:33-43 and 22:1-14), and the idea gains support from the Nativity stories in the gospels of Matthew and Luke where Jesus is in the womb of his mother, Mary, while she is still a virgin.

Unfortunately the term 'son of God' is now as embarrassing as the word 'Messiah' was in Jesus' day. The emphasis is all too often placed on biology rather than on a relationship. When Jesus used the word *abba*, daddy, when he addressed God, it was the father's love and the authority, responsibility and mission which the father had given his son which he had in mind. In the twentieth century some Christians accept the biblical narratives of Jesus' birth as historically true, others regard them as literary attempts to express this father-son relationship. Faith in Jesus ultimately depends on how one reacts to the claim that Jesus was God's special messenger.

The Experience of the Risen Jesus

In the years immediately after the end of Jesus' ministry the most compelling argument that was put forward by the Christians for their faith was their experience of the risen Jesus. Two thousand years later it is often this experience, and the loyalty to Jesus which stems from it, which unites Christians even if they disagree on other matters.

The New Testament contains many incidents which describe this experience. Often they indicate that the crucifixion brought most of the followers of Jesus to the point of despair. Then the unexpected happened:

> Two of Jesus' followers were on their way to a village called Emmaus, which lay about seven miles from Jerusalem, and they were talking about all these happenings. (The crucifixion and rumours that Jesus had risen from death.) As they talked and discussed it with one another, Jesus himself came up and walked along with them: but something held their eyes from seeing who it was. He asked them, 'What is this that you are debating as you walk?' They halted, their faces full of gloom, and one, called Cleophas answered, 'Are you the only person staying in Jerusalem not to know what has happened then in the last few days?' 'What do you mean?' he asked. 'All this about Jesus of Nazareth', they replied, 'a prophet powerful in speech and action before God and the whole people; how our chief priests and rulers handed him over to be sentenced to death and crucified him. But we had been hoping that he was the man to liberate Israel. What is more, this is the third day since it happened and now some women of our company have astounded us: they went early to the tomb, but failed to find his body, and returned with a story that they had seen a vision of angels who told them he was alive. Some of our people went to the tomb and found things just as the women had said; but him they did not see.'
>
> 'How dull you are!' he answered. 'How slow to believe all that the prophets said! Was the Messiah not bound to suffer thus before entering upon his glory?' Then he began with Moses (the Torah) and all the prophets, and explained to them the passages which referred to himself in every part of the scriptures.
>
> (*New English Bible*, Luke 24:13-27)

The story goes on the say that the two, husband and a wife, perhaps, still failed to recognize Jesus and that it was only when they reached an inn and began a meal that they realized who it was – as he took some bread, said a blessing over it and gave it to them. As they recognized him he vanished from their sight. Immediately they returned to Jerusalem to tell the rest of Jesus' followers of their experience.

These two were clearly Jews who were looking for the Messiah, nothing more or less, and hoped that Jesus was that Messiah. It seems that however carefully Jesus had explained himself to them, and to the twelve special disciples, they were unable to grasp what he had said. Only the resurrection made it all fall into place.

The gospels contain a number of similar incidents. Critics argue that all of them could have been hallucinations and suggest that the resurrection was invented by the despairing disciples to keep their spirits up. Christians would point out that the eleven surviving disciples (Judas, Jesus' betrayer had committed suicide) are often shown as disbelieving the claims made by the women, or Cleophas and his unnamed companion, to have seen Jesus, Of course, all these could be clever literary inventions. In reply, Christians would cite the case of Paul of Tarsus.

After Jesus himself and perhaps the disciple Simon Peter, Paul is the most important figure in the New Testament. He was the most famous early Christian missionary, but he began his career hunting down those who claimed that Jesus was the Messiah. He had no reason for wanting to believe in the resurrection, yet in the Acts of the Apostles, chapter nine, it is possible to read of his experience of the risen Jesus. Throughout the same book there are many other accounts of Jews and eventually Gentiles having a similar experience – just as one can find twentieth century Christians with similar claims.

The Church

The description of Jesus' ministry in the four New Testament gospels suggests that he acquired a following of men and women who did not belong to the pious religious groups of their day but to those who were almost regarded as outcasts, to the *am haraz*, the people of the land. In the Jewish Bible this phrase is applied to non-Jews and to Jews who inter-married with them. It is used in the New Testament (John 7:49) to refer to Jews who were regarded as casual in their observance of the Torah. Jesus' followers were criticized for not keeping the Sabbath properly, and so was Jesus, who defended them (Mark 2:23-26). He was also called the friend of tax collectors and sinners, men who worked for the hated Romans, and men and women who where careless in obeying the command of the Torah. 'Sinner' need not imply immorality, it could also be used of someone who worked on the Sabbath or broke the dietary rules. Some of the rabbis would not even speak to a woman who was not a member of his own family; Jesus had a large following of women as well as men. The earliest picture we are perhaps invited to have of Jesus is that of a rabbi whose followers were ordinary men and women seeking comfort, friendship and spiritual guidance. This was denied women, who could only observe synagogue worship and men who were not serious enough to begin by following the way of the Torah.

Disciples and Apostles

Eventually, Jesus chose twelve men as disciples. This word seems to have a special meaning, though it was also applied to his loyal followers generally (Luke 6:13, 19:37; John 4:1, 6:60, 66). It was used to describe an inner circle of twelve men who gave up their homes and jobs to be with Jesus permanently. These were his intimate companions whom he taught with the greatest care. During his ministry they were sent out two by two in order to prepare people for his teaching, as part of their training. Eventually, when Jesus' ministry was over they

195

became the first Christian missionaries, carrying the message entrusted to them to Jewish communities throughout Palestine and beyond. One of these men, Judas Iscariot, betrayed Jesus and then committed suicide. Before the other eleven began their missionary work they chose a successor. The story is told in the Acts of the Apostles, chapter one, an account which provides some very important information. Firstly, the eagerness of the eleven to restore their number to twelve which implies that twelve was considered important – probably because there were historically twelve tribes of Israel, one disciple for each tribe. Secondly, it lays down that candidates should possess the same qualities as the other eleven, namely that they should have been constant companions of Jesus since the beginning of his ministry, and they should have witnessed his resurrection. This was because their task was to tell others about these events as eye witnesses. The account names two candidates, unheard of before and never mentioned again – so, clearly, the New Testament does not tell us everything about Jesus and the early church. The new twelve, and later Paul of Tarsus, are given a new name 'apostles', a word which comes from a Greek word meaning 'to send'. The learners (disciples) were now sent out to be preachers.

The Message and Work of the Apostles

The Acts of the Apostles contains a number of sermons preached by Peter, Paul, the first Christian martyr, Stephen, and others. Their content is very similar and from them some idea can be obtained of what the message of the apostles was as they went, probably two by two, to Jewish towns preaching in synagogues and in the open air. In Acts, chapter two, there is an account of a sermon preached by Peter. It reads:

> Men of Israel, listen to me: I speak of Jesus of Nazareth, a man singled out by God and made known to you through miracles, portents, and signs, which God worked among you through him, as you well know. When he had been given up to you, by the deliberate will and plan of God, you used heathen men to crucify and kill him. But God raised him to life again, setting him free from the pangs of death, because it could not be that death should keep him in its grip.

196

For David says of him:
I foresaw that the presence of the Lord would be with me always, for he is at my right hand so that I may not be shaken; therefore my heart was glad and my tongue spoke my joy; moreover, my flesh shall dwell in hope, for thou wilt not abandon my soul to death, nor let thy loyal servant suffer corruption. Thou hast shown me the ways of life, thou wilt fill me with gladness by thy presence.

Let me tell you plainly, my friends, that the patriarch David died and was buried, and his tomb is here to this very day. It is clear therefore that he spoke as a prophet, who knew that God had sworn to him that one of his own direct descendants should sit on his throne; and when he said he was not abandoned to death, and his flesh never suffered corruption, he spoke with fore-knowledge of the resurrection of the Messiah. The Jesus we speak of has been raised by God, as we can all bear witness. Exalted thus at God's right hand, he received the Holy Spirit from the Father, as was promised, and all that you now see and hear flows from him. For it was not David who went up to heaven; his own words are: 'The Lord said to my Lord, "Sit at my right hand until I make your enemies your footstool."' Let all Israel then accept as certain that God has made this Jesus, whom you crucified, both Lord and Messiah.

(*New English Bible*, Acts 2:22-36)

The emphasis in this sermon is twofold, firstly that Jesus is alive, the crucifixion was not the end of the story, and secondly that Jesus is the Messiah. In the earliest days the followers of Jesus were sometimes called Nazarites (Acts 24:5) after the village where Jesus grew up, and some Jews may have preferred to use this name rather than the one which became most common – Christian. Because of the claim that Jesus was the Messiah, those who believed in him were given the nickname 'Christian', apparently at Antioch in Syria (Acts 11:26). The name is simply the Greek translation of the word 'messiah'. The apostles' task was to do what others could not do, give their personal testimony of Jesus' life, ministry and resurrection. Therefore, although Peter was the leader of the apostles, it was James, Jesus' brother, who took charge of the Christian community in Jerusalem. For Peter to have stayed in one place, no matter how important that city was, would have been to waste one indispensable witness. However, as time went on changes took place. Paul of Tarsus, an opponent of the new Jewish movement, became a Christian while on the way to Damascus to arrest any Christians he might find there. Eventually he became the most famous missionary of the early church, and an apostle, probably because of his vivid experience of the risen Jesus (Acts 9) and his understanding of the Christian message. Peter, on the other hand, seems to have settled in Rome. No one could tread the hard roads forever, travelling from city to city. Nothing could be wiser than that an ageing Peter, the leading apostle, should become Christian spokesman in the most important city in the world of his day, the capital of the Empire, Rome. There is good evidence that he died there, probably as one of the emperor Nero's victims.

Inspired Men and Women

In the sermon of Peter's which has already been quoted, the apostle referred to some words of the prophet Joel; 'This will happen in the last days: I will pour out upon everyone a portion of my spirit.' (Joel 2:2). The very men who when Jesus was with them, and especially after his arrest, and even after his resurrection, had been slow to believe, faint hearted and cowardly – none of them stood by him in his hour of need – now discovered that they were inspired. They could stand and face a hostile crowd. The threat of being killed like Jesus did not make them afraid. They even found that they had the gift of being able to preach, and to heal. God had kept the promise contained in the words of Joel.

Sometimes this inspiration worked against their own judgement and prejudices. Left to the apostles, Christianity might never have become more than a Jewish movement which hailed Jesus as a rabbi and the Messiah. Before long it would probably have been reabsorbed into Judaism and forgotten. However, Acts 10 and 11 tell of a strange incident involving Peter. He had a dream which, as he was hungry, was about food – which meats a Jew might eat and which he should avoid. He heard a voice inviting him to eat forbidden meat, which, when he refused, told him that it was for God to decide what was to be eaten or avoided, not him. The meaning of the dream was a puzzle to Peter until friends of a Gentile soldier came to the house to ask Peter to visit his home. Peter went, preached to him, his family and his friends. He was convinced that the spirit Joel had referred to, which had inspired him, was also in those Gentiles. Therefore, he baptized them, that is made them members of the Christian community.

In the Acts of the Apostles there are many descriptions of people receiving this inspiration and the power which Jesus possessed. Often the details almost defy belief and, not surprisingly, modern readers are sceptical. The Christian would ask such people to look at the changed lives of men like Peter and Paul and consider what they did. It may be that the experience of God's power and presence which they had, defies words, as religious experiences usually do, and that the accounts should not be taken literally. On the other hand, some Christians would point to similar experiences which man and women have had through the centuries. John Wesley, a famous English Christian of the eighteenth century, described what happened to him more simply than the New Testament described similar events, but one feels he is referring to the same experience.

> I think it was about five this morning that I opened my Testament to those words: (here he quotes them in Greek) 'He has given us his promises, great beyond all price, and through them you may... come to share in the very being of God'. (2 Peter 1:4). Just as I went out I opened it again on those words: 'You are not far from the Kingdom of God'. In the afternoon I asked to go St Paul's. The anthem was, 'Out of the deep have I called unto thee, O Lord –' (here he quotes the whole of Psalm 130, possibly because it expressed his mood of despair, but also because it reminds us that we cannot be perfect before God and so need his forgiveness).
>
> In the evening I went very unwillingly to a society in Aldersgate Street where one was reading Luther's preface to the Epistle to the Romans. About a quarter before nine, while he was describing the change which God works in the heart through faith in Christ, I felt my heart strangely warmed. I felt I did trust in Christ, in Christ alone for my salvation; and an assurance was given me, that he had taken away my sins, even mine, and saved me from the law of sin and death.

From Inspired Movement to Institution

The kind of ecstasy, excitement, enthusiasm and inspiration

199

that is found in the New Testament has never disappeared from Christianity, but any successful movement soon develops into an organization. The Jerusalem Christians met daily at first and may have shared all that they possessed with one another rather than having private property, but soon the number of widows and orphans who joined them meant that there was a possibility of the apostles spending so much time on food distribution that they were not available to meet their unique preaching responsibilities. So seven men were appointed to be deacons, or servers, to look after this charitable work. Where new Christian communities were set up, the apostles appointed leaders, called elders, to guide these churches and organize their worship.

There was no uniformity of organization in the church for some centuries. Until the fourth century the church at Alexandria elected its own elders and from them chose its own overseer now called a bishop (the Greek *episkopos*, overseer, was translated by the Germans as *bischof* which became bishop in English). Elsewhere the practice had developed of neighbouring bishops being invited to choose a successor when a vacancy arose. Only slowly did the bishop of Rome emerge as accepted leader of the church; this owed much to the qualities of men who became leaders of the Roman church, to the importance of Rome as the focus of the Roman Empire, and to the fact that in 313 Constantine, the Roman emperor, himself a Christian, recognized Christianity as a legal religion and gave it his support.

Sunday emerged as the Christian day of worship. It distinguished Christians from Sabbath-keeping Jews (though many Christians observed both for some time), but it also celebrated the beginning of creation, the day when Jesus rose from the tomb, and the day on which the apostles received the Holy Spirit according to Acts, chapter two.

In the Acts of the Apostles, baptism, the rite of acceptance into the church, confirmed the experience which men and women had already had of being possessed by the Holy Spirit. If often came to be an act by which the Holy Spirit was conferred upon those who wished to become Christians after they had completed a course of training lasting perhaps as long as three years.

The Lord's Supper, an intimate meal based on the last supper, which Jesus had shared with his disciples before his arrest, came to be the elaborate ceremony of the Mass, though the process took hundreds of years.

The spontaneity of the early movement gave way to something more formal, though not necessarily less sincere.

The Creeds

The apostles taught that Jesus was the Messiah, that he died in obedience to God's will, not just because men feared his influence or regarded his claims as blasphemous. To prove that God had willed Jesus' death they argued that Jesus had risen from the dead (something no human could do) through the power of God. This proved that God approved what Jesus had willingly done – and vindicated the claim that Jesus was God's son.

In the early, exciting, and often dangerous days there was little need to explain these things further. The enthusiasm of the apostles, their sincerity, and the experience of the power of inspiration was either convincing enough or not persuasive. However, as time passed keen Jewish and Greek minds began to work on the simple message and show how complex it was.

What did it mean to say that Jesus was God's son? Was Jesus divine or not? Was he always divine, or did he become divine as a reward for his act of obedient living and dying, like Orion or Hercules in some Greek myths?

What of the Spirit whose presence and power the apostles and many other Christians had experienced? Was this God too?

These and other issues Christians began to debate especially from the time of the emperor Constantine. When free from the threat of persecution they had leisure to do so and, patronized by the emperor, they found themselves attracting members for the wrong reasons. During the next 150 years a number of meetings, called councils, hammered out formulas of belief known as creeds. One of the briefest statements, known as the Apostles' Creed because it was argued that it summed up what they taught, reads:

> I believe in God the Father Almighty,
> Maker of heaven and earth:
> And in Jesus Christ his only Son our Lord,
> Who was conceived by the Holy Ghost,
> Born of the Virgin Mary,
> Suffered under Pontius Pilate,
> Was crucified, dead, and buried,

He descended into hell;
The third day he rose again from the dead,
He ascended into heaven,
And sitteth on the right hand of God the Father Almighty;
From thence he shall come to judge the quick and the dead.
I believe in the Holy Ghost;
The holy Catholic Church;
The Communion of Saints:
The Forgiveness of sins;
The Resurrection of the body;
And the Life everlasting. Amen.

Another formula of belief, the Nicene Creed, is a little longer. The Athanasian Creed is so complex that only highly trained theologians can understand it, and not all of them can explain it in terms that the average Christian can understand.

The creeds were attempts to settle disputes and provide statements about important matters of faith at a time when there was a fear that Christianity would stray from the path of truth. However, God cannot be defined, neither can the relationship of Jesus to God. The words 'Father' and 'Son' do not mean what they say when we see 'Dombey and Son' or 'Smith and Son' on a board over a shop. Some churches do not use creeds at all, believing that they create more problems than they solve, while other denominations include the creed in every major act of worship. Most Christians would agree that more important than any of these statements of belief is faith in the one God whose reality and nature is revealed in Jesus and experienced through the Spirit.

The Divided Church

Although the New Testament describes a church in which the directing influence of God's spirit maintained unity, it does not try to conceal the fact that there were rivalries, tensions and disagreements. Religions may be revealed by God but they are lived out by human beings. What is surprising, therefore, is not that Christianity became divided but that it remained united for so long.

It was in 1054 that the first split came. The eastern, mainly Greek speaking, Christians broke with the western church, based on Rome. The cause seemed to be a matter of doctrine, whether the Holy Spirit proceeded from the Father only or from the Father and the Son, but the real issues were far deeper. In language, temperament, history and tradition, and attitude towards Islam, East and West differed considerably. The final disagreement came in 1054 and since then Catholic and Orthodox branches of Christianity based on Rome and Byzantium (or Constantinople), until that city was captured by the Turks in 1453, have gone their separate ways.

The Reformation

Western Christianity remained united until the 16th century. From time to time critics had threatened its unity but they had been silenced and the church had gone on heedless of their demands for reform. When Martin Luther, a monk, spoke out in 1517, to his own surprise he succeeded in shaking the church where others had failed. The reasons for his success lay in the timing of his protest, which was accidental on his part. However, Martin Luther made his protest at a time when the corruption of the church had weakened it morally, politically and financially, and European kings were jealous of its influence upon their subjects and of the amount of money which left their countries each year for Rome. By now the bishops of Rome, better known as popes (from *papa* meaning father) were great landowners eager to rule Italy. They engaged in expensive wars and built up considerable debts. They had also decided to replace the ancient church of St Peter's in Rome, dating from Constantine's reign, with the splendid building which stands on the site today. This project increased their debts. A way of raising money was to sell indulgences. These were documents which stated that the persons for whom they had been purchased would be spared punishment of hell, the 'place' to which evil doers were sent after death. Normally, the church preached that if someone repented he would be forgiven and spared the torment of hell – but this time the church needed the money so much that little or no emphasis was placed on repentance. People were encouraged to think not only of themselves but of dead relatives, parents or perhaps children, their safety from eternal suffering could also be secured by purchasing these indulgences. Martin Luther, the theologian monk, attacked this latest abuse of power to forgive sins which Jesus had entrusted to the apostles and the church. The authorities thought they could silence this critic as they had others.

203

However, Martin Luther found himself supported by some German princes and a local dispute about one matter turned into a major revolt. Within a few years it became clear that the whole claim of the popes of Rome to be successors of St Peter and therefore Jesus' earthly representative was being called in question. Taking their cue from Martin Luther, rulers in many parts of Germany – in Scandinavia, Scotland and England – broke with Rome and established national churches. England under Henry VIII broke away, although FID DEF still appears on coins because the Pope had previously called him 'Defender of the faith'. Henry, an opponent of Martin Luther, used the opportunity to banish papal authority from his kingdom and declare himself head of the church. He established what eventually came to be called the Church of England.

This great upheaval in western Christianity is called the Reformation because its initial purpose was to reform the church by persuading it to respond to the criticisms which many of its members were making. Those who continued to accept the authority of the Pope came to be called Roman Catholics and the rest, Protestants, although the term originally applied only to some German princes who protested that the Holy Roman Emperor, their overlord, had gone back on his word to permit them to establish their own churches in their territories.

The Split Widens

Many Christians who rejected the authority of the Pope doubted whether kings would be any better as leaders of the church. Martin Luther had turned to his Bible in his argument with the Pope and they turned to theirs. Everyone can find in the Bible what he wishes if he looks hard enough and ignores one verse in favour of another, so it is not surprising that very soon dozens of new churches were to be found in western Europe. Some were very short lived, quite literally. Their members were persecuted by Roman Catholics who regarded them as heretics, that is deviants from the faith, and by Protestant kings who considered them to be traitors. Either by fire, as heretics, or by hanging, for treason, they were put to death. Despite persecution some groups survived and the Baptists, Lutherans, Presbyterians, Society of Friends and other denominations (the name given to the separate churches which made up Christianity) survived. In

England, of course, because a national church was established, Roman Catholics were often persecuted, not for heresy but for treason. At other times, for example in the reign of Mary Tudor, Henry VIII's daughter, Protestants were burnt as heretics. While this turmoil was going on the Roman Catholic Church belatedly underwent its own reformation but it acted too slowly and was unable to win back many of the reformers who had rejected the Pope's authority.

For a hundred years or more Christians engaged in a power struggle which only ended when European powers turned their attention to building overseas empires. Meanwhile, Catholic Spain had conquered and converted, often by the sword, the people of South and Central America. Between the Spanish in the south, and the French of Canada in the north, British refugees from religious persecution (both Catholic and Protestant) were learning to live peacefully together in the country which was to become the United States of America.

Mission

Christianity and Islam are the world's two great missionary religions. Jesus sent out his disciples as apostles. The word missionary simply means one who is sent, and refers to the thousands of people who have continued the apostles' work. The spread of the Christian gospel falls into a number of phases.

1. The initial explosion. Within 50 years of the resurrection of Jesus, Europe, as far as Rome, parts of north Africa and probably India had been reached by missionaries. The main expansion was in Europe. Some Christians took the gospel into areas beyond the Roman Empire, such as Russia, but most of the effort went into converting Britain, Gaul and eventually Germany.
2. Once the new world of America was known, missionaries began the work of converting their native populations.
3. In the 18th and 19th centuries the European powers began the conquest of India and the colonization of Africa; missionaries went with the conquerors and often ahead of the colonists.

Now that the world is dominated by the major religions there is little prospect of mass conversions taking place as they

205

did in the past. England and Thailand will not become Muslim; Egypt and Pakistan will not become Christian. Missionary work will still continue but at the level of individual conversions, as in the early days of Christian expansion, and the work will increasingly be done by indigenous Christian, Muslim or Buddhist groups. The white European, or American, is too much associated with the days of empire and colonization for him to establish Christianity in the Sudan, Burma or Pakistan; the citizens of those countries must do it, if anyone can.

In recent years, Christians have also recognized that what they often took from Europe to Africa or elsewhere was not so much Christianity as western culture. They built cathedrals in Lahore, or Delhi, like those in Britain. They even encouraged the use of English or Latin as the language of worship and taught European hymns and hymn tunes. The younger churches of Asia and Africa are gradually developing patterns of worship and organization suited to their own cultural circumstances, which seem much healthier than the European transplants of yesteryear. Mission has given way to the rise of what are called indigenous churches. Christian leadership may eventually pass from Europe to these other Christian areas – the Pope may be a South American, or an African, and the archbishop of Canterbury a West Indian.

The Ecumenical Movement

Long before the French and British colonies began their struggle for independence, missionaries began to reflect upon the divisions of Christianity. It was possible for inhabitants of a village in the Punjab to be visited by Baptists one week, Anglicans another, and the Roman Catholics, and probably other Christians besides, each claiming to be the true church, preaching the pure message of Jesus. There was little need for the missionaries to ask why the bewildered villagers did not give up their Hindu, Sikh or Muslim faith. What was the point of changing when the Christians could not agree among themselves and often denounced one another. Those Indians and Africans who became Christian often protested that the European arguments of four centuries ago meant nothing to them. They wanted to be Christians, not Anglicans or Roman Catholics.

The upshot of this was the Ecumenical Movement which might be said to have begun at the Edinburgh Missionary Conference of 1910. Its intention was to find ways of ensuring

Christian co-operation, rather than competition in the mission field. All churches, with the exception of the Roman Catholic, were represented. The word ecumenical comes from a similar Greek word meaning one world. Alexander the Great had the vision of one world ruled, of course, by himself, a world happy to enjoy the benefits of Greek culture. Now Christians had a similar hope, one world united by faith in Jesus. The prospect was spoilt by one thing, the scandal of disunity and the same people who dreamed of a Christian world began to work for a united Christianity.

Within a few years Europe plunged the world into war. With it perished any chance that there might ever have been of a Christian world. Eighty years later it is possible to see that there never was a chance of converting the whole world to one faith, be it Christian, Marxist or Muslim, but in 1910 Ethiopia, China and Japan were almost the only countries in the world which were not Christian or under European Christian influence, and of these Ethiopia was the oldest surviving Christian country in the world.

If mission suffered as a result of the 1914–18 war, the ecumenical movement did not. Its supporters continued their work for church unity and were eventually rewarded with some success, though it was only after another war (1939–45) that the Protestant churches formed the inter-denominational World Council of Churches in 1948. However, by that time acts of reunion had taken place in Scotland and Canada, for example, and in South India in 1947.

Reunion is often most difficult where the original division started and prejudices and vested interests are strongest. So, in England, the only attempt at reunion to succeed has been between Congregationalists and Presbyterians who, in 1972, came together in the United Reformed Church. Discussions took place between Methodists and the Church of England but agreement could not be reached.

Between 1962 and 1965 the Roman Catholic church held an assembly called the Second Vatican Council at which it reconsidered its doctrines and policies. Since then it too has taken part in ecumenical activities and discussions and now works closely with protestant denominations and the Orthodox churches.

Inter-faith Dialogue

Contact with the religions discussed in this book, and others,

207

has not only prompted missionary work but also discussions with members of these faiths. In the course of lecturing about Judaism, and other religions, some Christians have met members of these traditions and come to the conclusion that the God Christians experience through Jesus is present in the life, worship and beliefs of these men and women. They have found their own faith enriched, not undermined or threatened, as they share a common concern about prayer, peace, or preserving the environment with other people of faith. So, while some Christians are working to bring together Christians of different denominations, others are engaged in developing co-operation and understanding between people of different religions. Many Christians, of course, are trying to do both. Two notable organizations committed to increasing mutual respect and friendship are the World Congress of Faiths, which was founded in 1936, and the Council of Christians and Jews, set up in Britain in 1942, at a time when Nazi persecution threatened Judaism with extinction. More recently the Standing Conference of Jews, Christians and Muslims in Europe, founded in 1971, has

Many Christian children attend lessons at church on Sundays. Often these take place at the time of morning sermon. Sometimes children gather with their parents for part of the service before withdrawing to their own classes.

added its weight to this work. This exchange of views, and sharing of interest in the spiritual future of mankind which often results in practical acts of co-operation, in comparing racial and religious prejudices, as well as combined Jewish-Christian visits to Israel, is known as inter-faith dialogue.

The Church of Tomorrow

Beyond saying that Christianity will survive into the twenty-first century, there is little that one can say with certainty and the rest of this chapter must be personal opinion.

If the church is to do more than survive, if it is to be a positive spiritual force in the world, the inspiration must probably come through the new churches of Africa and Asia and the revitalized churches of South America. European Christianity is too much caught up in its colonial history, a nostalgia for yesterday and a struggle for economic survival to produce the revolution which Christianity needs. It talks about helping the underdeveloped, or colonially exploited areas of the world, but spends its money preserving its architectural heritage. It talks about church unity but allows vested interests to suppress it. It refuses, for the most part, to ordain women to the ministry and denies them the fulfilment which they probably found during Jesus' lifetime. It continues to tolerate racism. The institutions and outlook of the church are out of date. A new reformation is overdue. When it will happen, how and where it will take place, no one can guess. It might even be in Europe, for no one would have expected a rather conservative scholarly monk – Martin Luther – to have ignited the fuse of the explosion which shook western Christianity in 1517. Christians must always remember that God has a habit of upsetting their predictions.

The Bible

Interpreting the Jewish Bible

Jesus was a Jew. As such, the sacred writings which he knew very well and used were the books of the Hebrew Bible, which Christians now refer to as the Old Testament. It has already been suggested that Jesus can best be understood as a man who began to teach Jews as a rabbi, a person who knew his scriptures well and was skilled in interpreting them.

Those who regarded Jesus as the Messiah would recognize his teaching as the Oral Torah, the unwritten interpretation also given to Moses at Sinai, which had been passed on safely to succeeding generations of Jews. There is a hidden period in the life of St Paul during which he lived in Arabia (Galatians 1:13-20), presumably during those years he was carefully instructed in the teaching which Jesus had given his disciples. When he began preaching he would pass on to the converts what he had received.

Judaism, in the time of Jesus, had not yet decided finally which books were to be counted as scripture. All Jews were agreed that the Torah, the first five books, attributed to Moses, were inspired. They had been revealed to Moses at Sinai. The Pharisees, a radical group of devout Jews, also regarded the prophetic books and the writings, psalms, proverbs and other texts as scripture but the priests, especially a group known as the Sadducees, refused to give this status to any books other than the Torah. Jesus and, therefore, the early Christians clearly accepted the whole of what became the Hebrew Bible, the *Tenakh*, as divinely inspired. When Paul wrote some years later, 'All scripture is inspired by God' (2 Timothy 3:16), he may well have been meaning that the prophets and writings as well as the Torah were to be regarded by Christians as authoritative.

The first task of the Christian church, following the example of Jesus, was to interpret the Hebrew Bible in accordance with their belief that Jesus was the Messiah. We can see something of this process at work in St Matthew's gospel. Repeatedly the writer mentions something that Jesus did and follows it with the words, 'this was so that the scripture might be fulfilled': then he quotes a passage from the Jewish Bible. The letter to the Hebrews and many other New Testament books make similar attempts to show that the Hebrew scriptures prepared the way for Jesus.

The First Christian Writings

The oral tradition of Judaism probably explains why Jesus never wrote a book. Rabbis did not write, they taught their disciples who, in turn, taught others. This perhaps also explains why very few New Testament books were written by apostles – many scholars doubt whether the gospels of Matthew and John, or the letters of Peter, were actually written by the apostles who bore these names. The first Christian writings that we are aware of are letters written by Paul to the young churches. They do not contain the teachings of Jesus directly, though the Acts of the Apostles does contain some words of Jesus not found in any of the gospels, 'Happiness lies more in giving than in receiving' (Acts 20:35). These letters were written to explain the Christian message to men and women who had already heard it from the lips of the apostles but needed to ask questions about it and found difficulty in working out how to be a Christian. Should slaves obey their masters? Should Christians, like Jews, avoid eating pork, or could they eat any meat? These were the kind of questions they asked – and more theological ones such as, what will happen when the final judgement takes place?

The Growth of the New Testament

It is hardly likely that Paul thought he was writing letters that would ever form part of the Christian scriptures and be read almost 2,000 years after he sent them to Corinth, Thessalonica or Rome, or to his younger Christian friend Timothy. Perhaps some readers began to regard them as a gloss upon the message Paul preached, as a kind of written form of Christian oral Torah. Anyway, for whatever reason, copies of the letters began to circulate and be collected.

Next came the Acts of the Apostles, a very badly named book. It scarcely mentions any other Christian messengers besides Peter and Paul and any explanation of its purpose

211

must provide some answer to why they are so prominent. The solution may be that they were highly suspect in Rome, and may even have died under Nero's persecution. Acts defends them, showing them to be godly men, not criminals.

Most well known are the gospels which many people think were written first because they hold pride of place in the New Testament. In fact, probably not one of them was written until Paul had penned his last letter. It is quite likely that they were produced to replace the apostolic witness. The decision to write the first, Mark's, may have been triggered off by the shock of Peter's execution in Rome around 64 C.E. Finally, mention must be made of an unusual book, the last in the Bible, called Revelation. This is a book full of fantastic imagery, so popular among cranks that it has been called the fertile mother of foolish theories. The only other piece of literature like it is Daniel, in the Old Testament. Both are to be regarded as examples of the apocalyptic. The word *apocalypse* means something which reveals what is hidden, something which explains secrets, but in a way which only special people understand. With Daniel, the special people were Jews suffering persecution, with Revelation the people were Christians suffering persecution, probably in the reign of the emperor Domitian. To the persecuted, these strange books brought hope; to their enemies, who might read them, they were meaningless. They were riddles. Like riddles they are bewildering but once they have been unravelled the meaning is simple. In both cases it is, 'Hold on, times may be grim, but God will deliver those who trust in him'.

It might be rash to provide a list of New Testament books in their probable chronological order, but here is an attempt to put them into a fairly general order,

Paul's letters

pre-60 C.E.   Thessalonians 1 and 2
Galatians
Corinthians
Ephesians, Philippians, Colossians, Philemon
(perhaps all written during the same imprison-
ment)
Romans
Timothy 1 and 2, Titus 1 and 2

60-70 C.E.   Acts of the Apostles (though perhaps Luke later
revised it when he had written his gospel).
Gospel of Mark

212

	Gospels of Luke and Matthew
	Gospel of John
Later	The three letters of John
	The Letter to the Hebrews
	Revelation (perhaps about 96 C.E.)
	Letters of James, Jude:
	The two letters of Peter.

Incidentally, although the word 'book' has been used throughout this chapter, it may be that Paul wrote his letters on scrolls. The book form might not yet have been invented. It has been suggested that Christians were the first to use it, to make possible quick reference from one passage to another.

No original manuscript of any of these books survives. The earlier copies date from the second or third centuries, though earlier fragments have been discovered. The Jews who became Christian generally came from those who were more concerned with understanding the teaching of the Torah than with handling the scrolls reverently. So far as the writings of Paul and others were concerned, the church was more interested in preserving the teachings, the message of Jesus, than keeping old manuscripts.

The New Testament Canon

Until the 4th century there was no final agreement on the books that should be regarded as scripture, other than the Jewish Bible. By approximately 200 C.E. twenty books seem to have been agreed, but seven remained in doubt – Hebrews, James, Jude, 2 Peter, 2 and 3 John and Revelation. In 367 C.E. an Egyptian Christian scholar, Athanasius, listed the 27 books which he recognized as scripture. He was a highly respected scholar and the list, which included the seven disputed books mentioned above, received general approval. A number of other books, for example the letter of Barnabas (not to be confused with the 15th century forgery known as the Gospel of Barnabas), which some churches favoured, were omitted from the list. These 27 books came to be known as the New Testament canon, the group of documents which contained the true teachings of the Christian church.

Two factors determined whether a book found its way into the canons or not. Both are linked with respect. One was usage. For 300 years a book like Paul's letter to the Roman Church or Mark's gospel had been used continuously, read and re-read, worn out and recopied, because the churches found them useful, in fact indispensable. Secondly, it was claimed that all were written by apostles or had close apostolic connections – so Mark was linked with Peter, Luke with Paul, James and Jude with Jesus. The Letter to the Hebrews was thought to have been written by St Paul, though few scholars now hold this view and some early Christians had their doubts. Though the traditional association with Paul ensured its inclusion, it was clearly the convincing message of the book that won support for it. The Gospel of Peter, the Gospel of Thomas and the Acts of Paul, claimed to be apostolic but were rejected.

The Authority of the Bible

Authority, as we have already suggested, depends on more than authorship. Shakespeare wrote some inferior plays which survived because they were written by him but they are rarely performed because few would go to see them. When Christians read the letter to the Hebrews, by its unknown author, they soon become so immersed in its ideas and message that the question of authorship becomes unimportant, they find themselves being spoken to by God. Herein lies the authority of scripture. If it convinces readers by bringing them face to face with God, as revealed in Jesus, it has authority, they will heed and obey its teachings, if not, it will be no more religiously significant than a play by Shakespeare and perhaps far less effective as a work of literature.

When Christians make decisions the Bible always influences them directly, or indirectly. Some will turn to its pages and read them carefully and prayerfully for very precise guidance. Others will listen to the advice of a church leader, the Pope or the archbishop of Canterbury, who make their decisions after considering the traditional view of the church over the centuries, which has itself taken into account the message of the New Testament. Even groups like the Society of Friends, who seek to be guided by the inner light of God's spirit within them, give full place to the principles of the Bible in making their decisions, for they do not believe that God is perverse and unpredictable, changing his mind from one day to another. As he is consistent, through reading the Bible one can discover guidance for the present and the future from the way he has worked and spoken in the past. These different attitudes to the Bible are clearly demonstrated in Christian worship.

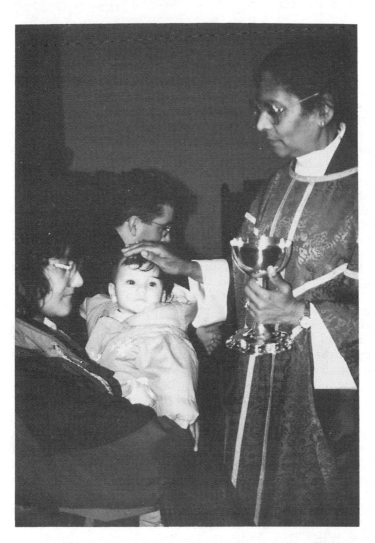

One of over 1600 Anglican women priests at work in Britain

Christian Worship and Festivals

The evidence of the New Testament is that Jesus was an observant Jew. In Luke's gospel the first account of his ministry states that Jesus 'went to the synagogue on the Sabbath day as he regularly did' (Luke 4:16). There are also references to him going to the Temple in Jerusalem and to his eagerness to celebrate the Jewish Passover festival with his disciples before his arrest. The apostle Paul hunted down Christian Jews in every synagogue where their presence was reported (Acts 22:19). His own final arrest took place while he was worshipping in the Temple (Acts 21:30). It would therefore appear true to say that Christian worship began in the Jewish place of worship, in the Temple, and the synagogues of Palestine and the rest of the Roman Empire. In addition, Christians met to pray and 'break bread' in private houses, perhaps a reference to the early importance which they attached to continuing to commemorate the meal the disciples had eaten with Jesus. A paragraph in the book of Acts provided an outline of the life of the Jerusalem Christians, demonstrating clearly the importance of worship and close fellowship in their lives. It also indicated that from the outset the purpose of Christian worship has been to praise God.

> They met constantly to hear the apostles teach, and to share the common life, to break bread, and to pray. A sense of awe was everywhere, and many marvels and signs were brought about through the apostles. All whose faith had drawn them together held everything in common: they would sell their property and possessions and make a general distribution as the need of each required. With one mind they kept up their daily attendance at the temple, and, breaking bread in private houses, shared their meals with unaffected joy, as they praised God and enjoyed the favour of the whole people. And day by day

the Lord added to their number those whom he was saving.

(Acts 2:42-47)

Early Developments

Daily gatherings would not be possible for everyone, especially when Christianity spread into the Gentile world of the Roman Empire and attracted slaves. They would have no free time of their own, in theory. They did not even possess their own bodies. If they could slip away from supervision it would probably be in the early morning before the household woke up.

Although groups of Christians might meet daily, the first day of the week gradually became special. It even came to have a distinctive name. Among the Jews only one day was named – the Sabbath. The rest were merely numbered. However, the writer of Revelation calls the first day 'the Lord's day' (Revelation 1:10). Perhaps he was suggesting that the day of the Lord had come, spoken of by the Hebrew prophets, but the name was applied to the first day for a number of reasons. It was the day when God said, 'Let there be light', and creation began. Jesus, the light of the world, began the act of spiritual recreation. On the first day of the week Jesus rose from death, so the choice of that day by a group which proclaimed his resurrection as a central part of their message, was natural. The Acts of the Apostles asserts that the apostles received the Holy Spirit on the first day of the week. Finally, as Christianity grew away from its Jewish parent it probably felt the need to have its own special weekly holy day. The observance of the first day became a mark of Christian identity, distinguishing them from other Jews, though some Christians observed the Sabbath as well for some centuries.

Baptism, which seems to have been a spontaneous response to the will to become a Christian in New Testament times, developed into a highly symbolic ritual, preceded by as much as three years preparation and probation in some cases. The ceremony included anointing to exorcise evil spirits. This was followed by immersion in purified water, free from demonical powers, to wash away sins, and represent the burial of the past life. Finally, the cleansed person entered the church to receive the Holy Spirit by the laying on of hands. When the bishop had put his hands on the candidate's head, made the

217

sign of the cross, and blessed him or her, the new Christian joined a celebration of the Lord's Supper where, in addition to bread and wine, they were given milk and honey as a sign that they had entered the Promised Land. This would be their first communion they had attended for in those days (in the second and third centuries) only the baptized were allowed to attend the commemoration of the Last Supper. Services were divided into two parts. The first, which included hymns, scripture readings and an address or sermon, was open to anyone who seemed seriously interested in the young religion. Of course, as Christianity was illegal, attempts would be made to exclude police informers. The second part of the service took the form of a ritual based on the Last Supper and included the Lord's Prayer.

Christian Worship in the 20th Century

The information in the preceding paragraph comes from a book called the *Didache* whose date and place of origin are uncertain, though it was popular and influential in the third and fourth centuries. Between the *Didache* and the twentieth centuries Christian worship has changed considerably but certain essentials have remained unaltered.

For many Christians the Lord's Supper remains the most important act of worship, whether it is called the Mass, Eucharist, or Holy Communion. Baptism is still the rite through which people become Christians, though usually total immersion has been replaced by sprinkling, and most people are baptized as babies at the request of their parents. To retain the element of personal decision and preparation, an act of confirmation has been introduced. Its intention is to ensure that someone who was baptized as a child does not slip accidentally into becoming a full member of the church. Some training and education has to be undergone; personal promises are made in front of a bishop. Only then may a person share in the Holy Communion, by receiving the bread and wine.

The Sunday-by-Sunday worship of Christians takes two forms, that of a service centred upon the Holy Communion, or one which concentrates on prayer, praise and the Bible, without a celebration of Holy Communion. The difference of emphasis is often shown on church notice boards where the reader's attention will be drawn either to the Holy Communion, perhaps celebrated daily and at the Sunday service, or to

A Roman Catholic priest consecrates the bread and wine at the Mass

a statement saying 'the preacher next Sunday will be...' on a noticeboard which perhaps relegates the Communion service to one Sunday in the month.

Bible-centred services are often called services of the Word. Besides readings from the Bible, both Old and New Testaments, there will be a sermon based on a biblical text, often explaining one of the Bible readings. The hymns may have been inspired by the Bible and may include one of the Psalms from the Old Testament. Such services are similar to the public worship of the early church to which anyone might be admitted.

Communion services usually include a service of the Word in an abbreviated form but, after the sermon, attention switches dramatically from the pulpit to the communion table or altar and to the words spoken by Jesus at the Last Supper, first written down by Paul in his letter to Christians at Corinth.

> For the tradition which I handed on to you came to me from the Lord himself: that the Lord Jesus, on the night of his arrest, took bread and, after giving thanks to God, broke it and said: 'This is my body, which is for you; do this as a memorial of me.' In the same way, he took the cup after supper, and said: 'This cup is the new covenant sealed by my blood. Whenever you drink it, do this as a memorial of me.' For every time you eat this bread and drink the cup, you proclaim the death of the Lord, until he comes.
>
> (1 Corinthians 11:23-26)

The climax of the service is the blessing, or consecration, of the bread and wine which is then shared among the congregation. In some churches they come forward and kneel to receive these from the priest, in others they remain seated and the bread and wine are brought to them.

Private Devotion

Public worship has always been important to Christians. They are taught to regard themselves as 'the body of Christ', that is as his representatives in the world. However, each Christian should also grow in fellowship with Jesus by prayer. When Jesus' disciples asked him to pray – he taught them how to do so, as other rabbis taught their followers. He did not prescribe special times or command them to kneel or stand. Go into a private place, somewhere where you can be alone, he told them. This was to discourage ostentation. A Christian should not pray in order to impress others but consciously to experience, enrich and develop the relationship which he always has with God, whether he is mindful of it or not.

The Lord's Prayer

The prayer which Jesus taught his disciples is to be regarded as a nucleus for all prayers. In modern English it reads:

Our Father in heaven,
May your name be kept holy,
May your kingdom come,
May your will be done on earth as it is in heaven.
Give us the food we need for today:
Forgive us the wrongs that we have done,
As we forgive the wrongs that others have done to us:
Do not bring us to the time of testing, but
Save us from the evil one.

(Matthew 6:9-13)

It affirms belief in God's love and power; he is a providing father, but it places severe limits upon the natural human inclination to ask for non-essentials, and lays a definite requirement upon the Christian who would experience God's forgiveness to be forgiving. It also recognizes that the world is a place of testing and bids the disciple to ask God to help him overcome all threats to maintaining his loyalty to God.

Besides this prayer, which Christians use everyday in public worship and private devotion, they may also speak to God intimately, from the heart, using whatever words come to mind. Some will turn to prayer books and to Bible reading notes to help them pray and study the Bible. Others will adopt methods of meditation borrowed from the East. Many Roman Catholics use a rosary to help them meditate upon the joys, sufferings and glories of Jesus and his mother.

The times chosen for private devotion vary. Some choose to rise early to pray for the day which lies ahead of them. Others will look forward to a time of quiet when the day's activities are ended.

Festivals

The Christian year begins with *Advent*, the season of preparation for Christmas (the *advent* means the arrival and refers to the coming of the Word of God into the world as a man). Advent Sunday is always the one nearest to St Andrew's Day (30 November).

Christmas itself is a combination of Christian theology and non-Christian practices. It commemorates the event whereby, so Christians believe, the creative Word of God became flesh and lived a fully human life. The precise date of Jesus' actual birth is not known. There is no evidence of the church celebrating this occasion before the fourth century. A calendar compiled in 354 C.E. states the observance of the Nativity in Rome in 336 C.E. The date of December 25 was chosen by the western church to Christianize the Roman pagan festival of the birthday of the unconquered sun, which the populace of the city was unwilling to give up. The merrymaking and presents are relics of this Roman tradition, as are the greenery and lights, though these have also a German and Celtic association. The eastern church observes Christmas on January 6th, the Feast of Epiphany, when they celebrate the baptism of Jesus. Western Christians remember the visit of the Wise Men on this day.

It probably comes as a surprise to many people to discover that Christmas was not an early Christian festival, yet only two of the four gospel writers were interested in describing the Nativity, and they produce very different accounts. It was not until the 6th century that a scholar named Dionysius Exiguus, in 527, calculated the year of Jesus' birth and the custom of using A.D. (*anno domini* – in the year of our Lord) began. Later scholarship has shown that Dionysius was incorrect and that Jesus was born four or five years earlier, if Herod the Great was still alive as Matthew's gospel claims.

Easter was the greatest occasion for early Christians, though here again pagan customs, as well as a pagan name in the English-speaking world, have been absorbed by it. The message of the apostles was that Jesus, who had been crucified on the day before the Sabbath, had been raised to life by God on the day after the Sabbath. Easter is the festival which commemorates this event.

The death of Jesus coincided with the Jewish festival of Passover but eventually, at the Council of Nicaea in 325, the church decided that Easter should be celebrated on the first Sunday after the spring full moon. The eastern church now uses a different calendar so west and east may vary in the timing of their celebrations by as much as five weeks. In the West, Easter is preceded by a period of fasting, known as Lent, during which Christians remember Jesus' forty days of fasting before he began his ministry, and prepare to share with him in spirit the agony of the cross on Good Friday, and the ecstasy of the resurrection on Easter Day.

Whitsuntide (or Pentecost) falls seven weeks after Easter and is the festival at which Christians celebrate the gift of the Holy Spirit to the apostles, as described in the Acts of the Apostles, chapter two. Like Passover it is the Christianizing of an earlier Jewish festival, the one on which Jews remember the giving of the Torah at Sinai. The custom grew up for new converts, dressed in white, to be baptized on this day, hence the name Whitsunday.

Less universally celebrated are Ascension Day, on the fifth Thursday after Easter, when the Ascension of the Risen Jesus is remembered, and Trinity Sunday, the Sunday after Whitsunday, which bears witness to the Christian claim to worship one God in three persons, Father, Son and Holy Spirit. Corpus Christi, on the Thursday after Trinity Sunday, and the Feast of the Annunciation (March 25), when the angel Gabriel told Mary that she was to be the mother of Jesus, are other festivals celebrated by Roman Catholics (and some other Christians) with special services, though not always with a public holiday.

Christian Ethics

The Law of Love

Jesus was once asked which were the most important commandments of the Torah that should be kept. The story is almost reminiscent of the challenge put to the rabbi Hillel who is supposed to have been asked to put the Torah into a nutshell – to cover as much as he could of its essence in the time he could remain standing on one leg. Almost before the man had lifted a foot Hillel replied 'Do not do to your neighbour what would be hateful if it were done to you. This is the Torah. All else is commentary. Now go and study it.' Jesus' reply to his questioner was:

> Love the Lord your God with all your heart, with all your soul, with all your mind. That is the greatest commandment. It comes first. The second is like it. Love your neighbour as yourself. Everything in the Torah and the prophets hangs on these words.
>
> (Matthew 22:37-40)

A similar account in Luke's gospel describes Jesus being asked to explain the meaning of the word neighbour. 'Who is my neighbour?' asked his questioner (Luke 10:30). Jesus told the story of a Jew who was attacked by robbers and left for dead. Various people passed by but ignored him. At last, a Samaritan stopped. He was someone despised and disliked by Jews for claiming to be Jewish but worshipping at another Temple, not at Jerusalem, and having a different version of the Torah. As a 'pseudo-Jew' he was worse than a Gentile. In the story this was the man who stopped and behaved in a neighbourly manner.

Jesus also commanded his disciples to 'Follow me', not 'Follow the Torah', and once said 'I am the way, the truth and the life'. Christians, therefore, are immediately invited to follow a person rather than a code of discipline or certain instructions. In the New Testament there is very little evidence of Jesus satisfying his disciples' wish for precise

224

regulations. Once when he was asked to decide between two brothers over an inheritance dispute he said that his mission was not to settle such arguments; on another occasion a disciple, perhaps feeling rather smug, asked how often he should forgive his enemy, suggesting seven times, which was one more than the usual requirement. Jesus replied, 'Until seventy times seven!'

The Need for Discipline

There is also evidence in the New Testament that the apostles felt the need to provide the young Christian community with discipline. Paul sometimes felt it necessary to tell the people to whom he sent his letters to separate themselves from immoral men and women who called themselves Christians but lived like pagans. It had become necessary to impose some rules upon the community which had been founded on the principle of love.

Christianity has always existed uneasily between the requirements of law and love. Christians have consequently always been ahead of public opinion in seeking prison reform, pressing for the abolition of capital punishment, and pleading the case of pacifism. On the other hand, some Christians feel called to be chaplains in the armed forces, or to demand severe punishment for criminals in order to secure a just and safe society. Whichever side Christians stand on in the debate about society and justice, however, they would all agree that punishment and all forms of social action and organization should be redemptive in purpose. Christianity has no place for revenge, for retributive punishment, or for using actions purely in order to deter others. There should always be a concern for the individual.

Here Christianity faces another tension, that between society and the individual. It would seem that one of the criticisms levelled against Jesus was that he was a threat to the social and religious order. This was also a charge levelled against the early Christians – they threatened to turn the world upside down, to invert its standards and values. Sometimes Christianity has been used to support the existing social order, and sometimes to bring it down. It has championed liberty of conscience, though often the church itself has had imprisoned and executed those who dare to disobey it in the name of Jesus.

To someone standing outside the Christian faith it must

often seem that Christians are in complete disarray on ethical matters. There seems to be no agreement at all. This is true and inevitable, though one must remember that there is no disagreement that such things as theft or murder are wrong. Differences arise when men and women try to put love into practice. The consequences can be the apparent illogicality of rejecting pacifism but at the same time denouncing euthanasia, or abortion, on the grounds that taking human life is wrong, or accepting pacifism while permitting euthanasia and abortion.

To be a Christian is to face the world in the company of Jesus. The Bible and the tradition of the church are there to guide and these provide many Christians with all they need to make personal decisions. However, there remain more than a few who would say that they feel compelled by the Holy Spirit to depart from tradition whenever the teachings of Jesus are repudiated.

Major Beliefs

The focus of Christianity is Jesus. It is through his example that the Christian claims to know and understand God, to make sense of life and the world, and to discover how to live. The starting point of a study of Christian belief must be the life and ministry of Jesus himself.

In the first chapter we saw that the New Testament presents Jesus as claiming to be the Messiah, but more than the Messiah, the son of man, the representative of mankind. The apostles called him 'Lord', and 'Son of God', preached to Gentiles as well as Jews and declared that he was the saviour of all humanity, past, present and yet to be born.

The Meaning of the Crucifixion and Resurrection

The crucial event which the apostles had to wrestle with and explain to the world they wished to convert was the crucifixion of Jesus. Rome prided itself on justice and, although some Romans might be cynical of the government, they would scarcely be inclined to believe the story put about by two frequently imprisoned and probably finally executed men named Peter and Paul, about a man, Jesus, who was put to death after a personal appearance before the Roman governor of Judaea, Pontius Pilate. Consequently, the Acts of the Apostles goes to great pains to vindicate the apostles. The gospels give considerable attention to the arrest, trial and death of Jesus, drawing attention to Pilate's weakness in sentencing a man he knew to be innocent, and calling soldiers as other witnesses to Jesus' innocence, as well as the thieves who died alongside him.

However, the trump card in the apostolic argument with their opponents was the claim that Jesus had risen from death, been seen by them, and could be experienced by anyone who put his faith in him. The resurrection also proved that the death of Jesus was more than the deed of weak or wicked men, it was an act of loyalty to God, vindicated by God in the resurrection. 'He would not suffer his holy one to see corruption' (Psalm 16:10, quoted in Acts 2:27, 13:35). The death of Jesus was in some ways an act of God.

To explain how something as terrible as the death of an innocent man would be part of God's plan, the apostles turned to clues provided by Jesus and to the ideas and language which Jews and Gentiles of the day might understand. Once Jesus said, 'The son of man did not come to be served but to serve, and to give his life as ransom for many' (Mark 10:45). These few words have probably provoked as much Christian thought as any others.

The idea of ransom is well understood in all cultures, a person is taken prisoner and his loved ones have to buy his freedom. Applied to Jesus this suggested that mankind had fallen into enemy hands and somehow Jesus' death was effective in ransoming them. St Paul explored this notion as far as he could, linking it with the story in Genesis of the disobedience of Adam and Eve which resulted in their rejection from the ideal life of Paradise to a rough existence of pain and toil, culminating in death. Disobedience had made man the captive of sin, by which Christians mean rebellion against God, and each person therefore suffered the penalty of death. The obedience of Jesus had ransomed everyone; men and women might now rise from death to eternal life as Jesus had done, through faith in Jesus.

Sacrifice was common in the Roman and Jewish world, so sometimes Christians speak of Jesus' death as a sacrifice, an expiation for sins. If this analogy is to be helpful in understanding the meaning of the crucifixion it must not be pressed too far. The words of St Paul must always be remembered, 'God was in Christ, reconciling the world to himself' (2 Corinthians 5:19) and some words in the first letter of John 'God is love: and his love was disclosed to us in this, that he sent his only son into the world to bring us life. The love I speak of is not only love for God, but the love he showed to us in sending his son as the remedy for the defilement of our sins' (1 John 4:10). If Jesus is a sacrifice, he is the sacrificial victim offered by God to assure us of his love. He is not the price demanded by a vindictive God eager to punish and reluctant to forgive. This is one of the reasons why Christians insist that Jesus is God, to prevent people falling into the error of seeing God and Jesus as the contrary principles of justice and love struggling against one another.

Sometimes the New Testament writers emphasized the exemplary nature of Jesus' life. He was the model of obedience, so much so that even though he was the son of God, and as such might rightly demand the respect usually shown to a prince, to use a popular analogy, nevertheless he lived in the world as a humble man, the servant of all, and even accepted the ignominious death of a common criminal. His life and death was a reminder of some words in Isaiah 53, an Old Testament passage describing the servant of God. The conclusion was that Jesus was recalling Judaism to its role of being a suffering witness to God, and inviting his followers to be servants, an appropriate message to a church whose members were often slaves and frequently confronted with suffering. The cross gave them the example of love and discipleship.

The Greek world, in particular, looked to men of wisdom and learning to enlighten them. It is not surprising, therefore, to find St Paul writing to the Greek city of Corinth to say that Jesus is the revelation of God's glory (2 Corinthians 4:6). This idea is not particularly associated with explaining the meaning of Jesus' death, but when one reads John's gospel carefully it soon becomes apparent that the whole of Jesus' life and ministry was an enlightening activity. The pessimist might consider life and, especially, death to be meaningless, the example of Jesus was used by Christians to argue that they were wrong.

One of the most popular New Testament ways of explaining the significance of Jesus' death was as a victory over evil. People in the ancient world believed it to be inhabited by evil spirits and demons, and to be in the power of evil forces. Christians often saw themselves involved in a struggle against such spiritual enemies who inspired an emperor like Nero to hunt them down and persecute them. Jesus had cast out evil spirits: Mark's gospel, above all, showed Jesus fighting and defeating evil and wickedness of all kinds, natural phenomena, hunger, disease, demons, human hatred and, finally, death.

Christianity has never stated that any one of these explanations of the significance of Jesus' death and resurrection is the correct or approved one. So much depends on the individual believer's personal experience of Jesus. Someone who is very conscious of having lived a corrupt and selfish life might emphasize the belief that Jesus bore his sins on the cross and ransomed him from the power of evil. Another person whose life has been aimless might find in the life and death of Jesus an example to imitate, and in the resurrection the power and inspiration to achieve this goal. Whatever the particular view might be, however, there will be agreement that Jesus died for others and that his death and resurrection is the assurance of God's underlying love.

To sum up this section: Jesus is God and Lord (the one to whom Christians give their love and loyalty), he is also man, the brother of all humanity, and the servant of man and God.

God

Christians believe in one God but they say he can be experienced in three ways. He is the creator and sustainer of the universe. He is experienced as Lord and brother, through Jesus. His grace, that is his understanding love, and his power, are inwardly experienced: this inner presence of God is called the Holy Spirit.

Christians also call God 'Father' and believe that his dominant characteristic is love. Creation and the world of everyday experience might be regarded as neutral, some people see it as lovely and beautiful, others see ugliness and cruelty. The Christian believes that God is love because of what Jesus taught, because he believes that Jesus is God, and because of his own experience of God's love, through Jesus.

Heaven and Hell

It might seem odd that a religion which emphasizes love has a belief that those who reject God's love live eternally separate from God.

Before examining this idea it is necessary to say that Christianity believes very strongly in life after death. The evidence upon which this belief is based is the resurrection of Jesus and the experiences which it is possible to have during this life of qualities like love which are eternal. The belief is not in everlasting life, that beyond death life is resumed and goes on forever; it is in eternal life, an existence of a different kind but one which can be known and appreciated now, before death, especially through love.

Understanding Christian views about heaven and hell has been made difficult because of the simple pictures the people often have in their minds. They imagine heaven to be a place of delights and hell a place where the souls of the dead are endlessly tortured. They also imagine that selection for heaven and hell is based on good or bad conduct. Sometimes

Christianity has encouraged this latter belief, using the promise of heaven, or the threat of hell, to encourage people to be obedient to the Church and State and to live morally.

However, heaven and hell are really about attitudes, In the Bible the emphasis is upon the choice of obedience or disobedience, and not even upon how obedient or disobedient one is. Is one for or against God? Heaven, or eternal life, are convenient terms to explain the unbroken relationship with God that can be enjoyed by those who want it. Hell is the corresponding word, referring to the state of those who consciously and willingly reject God.

A few further important points need to be made. First, the notion of hell as a place of physical torment must be removed. Love and cruelty cannot exist together. No one who believes in God as loving can also believe that he vindictively punishes those who reject him. Perhaps the final state of souls which refuse eternal life is death, ceasing to exist all. No one knows, but Christians would say that if we return to the simple idea of heaven as a place, the lock is on the outside. Anyone who wishes can enter by turning the key. God locks no one out.

Eternal life with God is not a condition and a relationship which is offered only to Christians. One must say this for three reasons. Firstly, it is possible to call oneself a Christian and to be a baptised member of a church but still be a rebel against God. Secondly, it may be that Christians have presented God so badly that decent people have preferred not to want anything to do with him. An American Indian chief in the Caribbean was offered the choice of death by burning if he refused to become a Christian, and eternal life if he became a Christian. He chose death, saying that if his conquerors were going to heaven he would rather not spend eternity with them and the God they believed in! Thirdly, many may know the being to whom Christians give the name God without awareness of this. In their commitment to truth, love, justice, and the needs of humanity they may already possess eternal life. Exploring these points further, it would be difficult for Christians to claim that 'only Christians can be saved', to use a popular expression meaning that only baptized Christians can enjoy eternal life with God.

The Church

The fellowship of Christian believers is called the church. It began with the apostles and other followers of Jesus but eventually split into many different sections, known as denominations, each emphasizing different aspects of belief, organization or practice. Although one church might not recognize the claim of another to represent fully the true form of Christianity, nevertheless each denomination believes a number of things about itself.

First, that God as Holy Spirit is present in the work,

Some Christian churches baptize babies but this baby is, in fact, being dedicated. Baptism will follow on confession of faith as an adult.

worship and life of the denomination. Sometimes the church is called, 'the body of Christ' to express this belief.

Secondly, it is through the church that its members, as a body, develop their relationship with God as he is known in Jesus. God's forgiveness, love and power pass into the community of Christians and are received by them through prayer, worship and obedience. Traditionally each Christian receives these gifts of forgiveness, love and power at baptism. They are strengthened through regular prayer and worship and obedient living. Many Christians emphasize the importance of the rite known as the Lord's Supper, Eucharist, Mass or Holy Communion, based on the last meal which Jesus had with the disciples, as the principal means of spiritual nurture. Baptism and the Eucharist are therefore called sacraments, symbols of God's undeserved love, known as grace, or channels through which it is received. Sometimes they are known as the means of grace. Roman Catholics recognize

The minister shakes hands with members of his congregation after a service.

seven sacraments. To the two already mentioned are added, Confirmation, Penance, Extreme Unction, Marriage & Orders, (the ritual by which a man is consecrated deacon or priest).

Thirdly, the church should be the means by which God's grace reaches the world at large. In other words, the church has been given the responsibility of presenting God to the world as Jesus did, by serving mankind, as well as by teaching.

Besides the visible church of Roman Catholics, Anglicans, Pentecostalists, Quakers, Baptists, the Eastern Orthodox and many other denominations, there is the invisible church. This does not only mean 'the communion of saints', those Christians who now live in God's eternal presence, it also includes everyone who is serving God in the world, whatever name he may use to describe himself.

No one who looks carefully and seriously at the Christian churches and the world in which they exist can believe that the victory of love, truth and justice is complete. Christians believe that Jesus' Life might be compared to a shaft of sunlight breaking through the clouds. (Some of them would see the work of other witnesses to truth, men and women of faith, mentioned elsewhere in this book Jewish, Hindu, Muslim, Sikh, and many others, as other people who affirmed the existence of a benevolent reality to whom they give the name God.) To return to the metaphor of the sun, it exists but it is often obscured. Similarly, God's power and love does not always seem real. Christians, therefore, believe in an age when love, truth and justice will rule, though they have different ideas of how this will come about. Some believe that Jesus will return, not incognito, as a man, but as Lord, and will establish the kingdom of God on earth. Others believe that he is already present as Lord, that his power and love exist in the hearts and lives of all who are loyal to God. They do not look for an age to come, they seek greater faith to recognize the present reality of the Holy Spirit in their lives.

Christianity Today

To some extent the whole of this section has been a personal expression of what Christianity is and what it means to the writer, who is a Christian. Against critics, I would defend myself by saying that I hope I have not misrepresented the faith, and I hope too that I have perhaps enabled Muslims, Jews and others who read these words to gain some impression of what it means to be a Christian – in terms of actions, beliefs and values, as well as the basis upon which Christian life is built.

Christianity is, above all, the exploration of a relationship between the individual and Jesus. It is not, however, only a purely personal affair. There is the experience of other Christians to guide and help, living members of the church, those who wrote the New Testament, and those who have lived during the intervening nineteen centuries.

The story of Christianity is therefore an ongoing story of a community, or group of communities called churches, and individual Christians trying to be faithful to the truths which they believe they have experienced in Jesus. A Polish pope, after five centuries of Italians, and the growing importance of black Christians who do not regard Jesus as a white man, or Christianity as a European religion, will have growing impact. In Britain churchgoing is often a leisure-time minority activity, attracting more followers than soccer but fewer than angling, while Christianity is seen to be one of many other faiths, five of which have been placed alongside it in this book.

In these circumstances, Christianity is reconsidering itself but the task is not easy for churches exist in time, even though they may preach about eternity, and their members are human beings, even though they may be concerned about spiritual development. Consequently, the upkeep of increasingly expensive buildings and the preservation of old loyalties often absorb the churches' wealth and prevent denominations from uniting.

A number of issues face Christianity as it looks towards the future. The following are just a few of them:

Attitudes towards and relationships with other faiths, particularly those covered in this book.

Attitudes towards secularism, whether it be simple materialism or the ideals of humanism and Marxism.

Attitudes towards racism and gender.

Attitudes towards the imbalance of wealth in the world.

As it considers these, it may rediscover its own unity and its role as the servant of God and mankind. Growing more like Jesus, it may learn again what it means to be the body of Christ.

In the same way, individual Christians need to pass from using terms which are no longer very meaningful or helpful, such as son of Man, son of God, or Christ, to discovering in their experience who he is. For Christianity is not a collection of beliefs, or a series of ritual activities, it is a living relationship with God as revealed in Jesus its Lord.

ISLAM

RIADH EL-DROUBIE

Introduction

The Land of Islam

In the year 570 C.E. a child was born in Makkah and was named Muhammad. Forty years later he received a message from God and was ordered by Him, to invite the people to this message. The people of Makkah were hostile to Muhammad and he was forced to flee in 622 C.E. to Medina about 270 miles from Makkah. After organizing his community in Medina, and in the tenth year after leaving Makkah, he returned and destroyed idolatry in all Arabia. After his death his successors (the caliphs) carried the message to the neighbouring countries known today as the Middle East. In less than one hundred years they conquered Spain and part of France; their fleet controlled the Mediterranean. Turkey, part of the Balkans, Persia, the Caucasus and part of Russia accepted Islam. The subcontinent of India (known today as India, Pakistan and Bangladesh) and many parts of South East Asia adopted the new faith. Also, many parts of Africa became Muslim – Morocco, Algeria, Tunisia, Libya and Egypt in the north, Sudan and Somaliland in the east, as well as Nigeria in central Africa.

The People of Islam

You will see that the people of Islam are of different nationalities and they have different customs, dress and ways of life, but all submit to one God and follow the message of Prophet Muhammad (Peace be upon him). Today, in Britain, we have many Muslims who come from different countries, their colour of skin differs, they wear different clothes and eat different food.

The Meaning of Islam

Muslims believe that the message of Islam did not start with the revelation to Prophet Muhammad. It has its origin with the creation of Man. The message sent to Muhammad is the final one and therefore Muhammad is the last of the prophets.

If you are living in an area where Muslims dwell, you might have heard the words 'Assalam Alaikum', with these words Muslims greet each other. It means 'peace be upon you'. The word *Assalam* is an Arabic word. Arabic is the language of Prophet Muhammad and is spoken by over 120 million Arab Muslims in the Middle East and the area around it.

The Arabic language is very beautiful and rich; from one word many meanings can be derived. It is from the root word *salam*, which means submission, that the word *assalama* comes. *Islam* means submission to the command of God as it is given to Prophet Muhammad. The word *assalama* means to enter into peace; Islam is the religion of peace.

If a person does enter into peace with God by following His commandment, he will be at peace with the whole world and will find peace within himself. That is why the religion of Islam is so called because it requires from every believer peace and submission to the message of God, as given to Prophet Muhammad by the angel Gabriel. The believer in this message is called a Muslim.

The Birth of Muhammad

In 570 C.E. Prophet Muhammad was born on 12th Rabi-ul-Awwal of the Arabic Calendar, in the town of Makkah. His father, Abdullah, died before he was born. His grandfather Abdul Muttalib, as the head of the family, named him Muhammad (the praised one) and took him into his care. Although the family was not very rich, according to the Arab custom of those days, Muhammad was given to Halima, a Bedouin woman, for nursing at her camp in the desert. He spent five years in her camp and then was brought to his family in Makkah. His mother, Amina, took him to visit her family and his father's grave in Medina; on the way back to Makkah she was taken ill and within a few days she died. The child and maid returned to Makkah alone.

At the age of eight his grandfather died and the young Muhammad was taken into the care of his uncle, Abu Talib.

Muhammad's Youth

Muhammad spent his youth helping Abu Talib in his trade, and they were always on the move with the caravans. He went to Syria with his uncle at the age of twelve and on this journey met a Christian priest who told Abu Talib to take care of the boy as there was a great future for him, for he had the signs of a prophet.

From childhood, Muhammad was dissatisfied with the society he lived in. It is best described as a world of ignorance. The city of Makkah, as well as the rest of Arabia, and the world at large, was in deep moral decay. The people worshipped idols and images. Arab society was divided because the tribes were at war with each other. They were a nation without any government or educational institution. Muhammad's dissatisfaction with his community led him to think about the people and the universe, about the poor and the rich and about idols and God. He grew up in a different way from others in his society; he did not like gambling or drinking wine, he never took part in any idol worship. He was always known among the people to be trustworthy and of high moral conduct and was called Al Amin (The Trustworthy).

Muhammad's Marriage

The people of Makkah knew of Muhammad's high morals and many asked him to work for them. When he was nearly 25 years of age, a very rich merchant's widow named Khadijah heard about Muhammad, his honesty and other fine qualities. She sent for him and asked if he would lead her caravan of merchandise to Syria. He agreed and returned to her with a good profit. She was very pleased with his honesty, kindness and responsibility, and offered herself to him in marriage. Khadijah was older than Muhammad; he was 25 and she was 40. They had three sons who died in infancy and four daughters who survived. She was his only wife for 25 years and she gave him all the support he needed.

The Black Stone

When Muhammad was 35 years of age, the Quraish, the noble tribe of Makkah, decided to rebuild the Ka'aba at Makkah as the walls were cracking after the great flood. The building work went very smoothly until they reached the place of the black stone when they differed as to who should have the honour of putting it back in its original place. A fight nearly broke out until they agreed to get someone else to arbitrate. They decided that the first man to pass by should be the judge. While they were talking they saw Muhammad approaching. They were happy to see him, as all the people of Makkah used to respect him. He asked them to hand him a *thoub*, large sheet of cloth, which he placed under the stone and asked one man from each tribe to take a corner to lift up the *thoub* and carry it to the required place. The black stone was lifted back into the wall by them. By this decision a possible war was prevented.

Muhammad the Prophet

From time to time Muhammad sought peace from the busy city of Makkah and went away to Cave Hira in the Mount of Noor (Light) to meditate and seek guidance from the creator. One day during the month of Ramadan, at the age of 40, he heard a voice asking him to read. He was very frightened. The voice repeated itself three times, then Muhammad said, 'I cannot read'. He was then asked to repeat the following verses:

> Proclaim! (or read!)
> In the name
> Of thy Lord and cherisher,
> Who created –
> Created man, out of
> A (mere) clot
> Of congealed blood:
> Proclaim! and thy Lord
> Is most bountiful –
> He who taught
> (The use of) the pen, –
> Taught man that
> Which he knew not.
>   (Qur'an 96:1-5)

These were the first few words from God given by the angel Gabriel to Prophet Muhammad. When Gabriel left him he was trembling and full of fear and rushed home to tell his wife. Khadijah took Muhammad to her cousin, Waraqah, a Christian monk, who was old and blind, but he was learned as he had studied the books of the Christians and the Jews. Waraqah told them of the story of the Prophet to come, and that Muhammad would be that prophet. He also told them that people would fight him and his followers would suffer. A few days later Muhammad received this command:

> O thou wrapped up
> (in a mantle)!
> Arise and deliver thy warning!
> And thy Lord
> Do thou magnify!
> (Qur'an 74:1-3)

Opposition to the New Message

When Prophet Muhammad received the command to deliver the message of Islam to the people, he defied his elders and declared the message in Makkah. The first to believe in him as a prophet of God was his wife, Khadijah, then Abu Bakr, one of Mecca's notables, Ali, the young son of his uncle Abu Talib, and Zayed, his servant.

Due to the success of the new message, the fear of the Quraish was increased as they found that its acceptance would abolish all their idols, preach equality between slaves and masters, and the right of the poor in the wealth of the rich. The Quraish took an original stand and served punishment on everyone who welcomed the message.

As the sufferings and hardship of the new believers intensified, Prophet Muhammad advised his follows to migrate to Abyssinia (Ethiopia), where there was a Christian king who was just and wise, and he told them to stay there until God put an end to their sufferings. When the Quraish heard that the Muslims had reached safety in Abyssinia, they sent a delegation to the king demanding the return of the Muslims as rebels in opposition to their fathers' faith. The king, after hearing both sides, refused and the delegation returned.

The Quraish tried many methods of stopping the spread of the new message. The leaders appealed to Abu Talib, who was

241

not himself a Muslim, either to stop Muhammad from preaching the new religion or to withdraw his protection to him as head of the family of Hashim. Abu Talib spoke to his nephew the Prophet and told him about the Quraish delegation's demand. The Prophet's answer was, 'O uncle, by God, if they place the sun in my right hand and the moon in my left in order to stop me preaching God's message, I will not do so until God gives me success, or until I die'. Abu Talib refused the Quraish's demand.

The condition in Makkah became worse for the Muslims, although their number was increasing. At that time a few people from Medina adopted the faith of Islam and invited the Prophet and his followers to emigrate to their city. This migration is known as *Hijrah*.

The Prophet at Medina

Before the arrival of the Prophet in Medina, the inhabitants of the city were divided into many tribes and were at war with each other. The first task the Prophet had after arriving was to establish law and order in the city. He established a state on the basis of his religion of equality and freedom. The Arabs, Jews and other communities were placed on an equal footing. He defined the rights and obligations of each community.

The Battle of Badr

During the second year in Medina, while the Prophet and his followers were engaged in establishing the new community, the hostility of the Makkans was growing and a war between them and the Muslims became almost inevitable. At this time the trading caravan of the Makkans from Syria was passing. The leader of the caravan asked the Makkans to send a protective force to meet him near Medina. This made the Makkans believe that the Muslims wanted to attack their caravan; therefore they thought they would take the opportunity of crushing the Muslims. A battle took place at the Badr valley, near Medina. The Muslim force was 313 in number, poorly armed, against 1,000 Makkan men, strongly equipped. The chief of the Makkans was killed early in the battle, and while the army was in confusion, the Muslims pursued them and took seventy prisoners. The Muslim casualties were only 15 dead.

The Battle of Uhud

The defeat of the Makkans at Badr made them seek revenge. In the third year after emigration, the Prophet received a message from Makkah that the Quraish and their allies were sending an army of 3,000 strong men, fully equipped, to avenge the death of those killed at Badr. The Prophet accepted the advice of the Muslims who wanted an open ground for the battle and went out to encounter the Quraish army with 700 Muslim warriors, near the mount of Uhud, The Prophet organized his men and put 50 of them on the top of the mountain, telling them not to leave their place whatever might happen.

The two armies met and the Muslims defeated the Makkans again. The men on top of the mountain, seeing the Makkans running away, left their place and went down. When the Makkans saw that, they went around the mountain and attacked the Muslims from the back. There was a great battle and the Prophet was wounded and many of the Muslims were killed, but the Makkans returned to Makkah without having destroyed the new faith.

The Battle of the Trench

Prophet Muhammad had a pact with the Jews of Medina, that they would not fight each other and they would not help each other's enemies. The Jews did not keep their promise and tried to kill the Prophet. The Prophet ordered the Jews to leave Medina but they refused. Only then, did Muhammad drive them out of the town. When they left they wanted revenge, so they sent a delegation to Makkah with a promise to fight on their side. The Makkans went out with an army to destroy the Muslims hoping this would be the final battle.

The Muslim community was not very strong and not very well equipped. The Prophet asked the Muslims what they should do and one of them suggested they dig a trench around the city. The Makkans arrived, but could not cross the trench. They set up camp around the city and waited. After a few days there were heavy winds and storms which destroyed the camp and forced the Makkans to return home unsuccessful.

The Conquest of Makkah

In the eighth year after Hijrah the Makkans declared the truce between themselves and the Muslims as null and void: the Prophet took this opportunity and marched on Makkah with an army of 10,000 men. Muhammad took all the necessary precautions to make this march a secret. The Makkans did not realize the situation until the Prophet and his army were very near Makkah. They were not able to defend the city. The Prophet ordered his followers not to fight at all unless they were attacked. Muhammad and his detachment entered from the upper part of the city while others entered from different sides. The caller cried, 'He who enters his house and closes his door is safe, he who enters the Grand Mosque is safe, and he who enters the house of Abu Sufyou is safe.' On entering the Great Mosque, the Prophet destroyed all the idols, repeating the Qur'anic revelation (17-81):

> And say: truth has (now)
> Arrived, and falsehood perished:
> For falsehood is (by its nature)
> Bound to perish

The people of Makkah gathered around the Prophet. He addressed them: 'How do you think I should act towards you?' 'As a generous brother, and a son of a generous brother,' was the reply. He said, 'I shall speak to you as Yusuf (Joseph) spoke unto his brothers, I shall not reproach you today, God will forgive you. He is the most merciful and compassionate.' He then ordered Bilal to call for prayer from the top of the Great Mosque.

The Farewell Pilgrimage

The Prophet returned to Medina after the conquest of Makkah. From Medina he sent many delegations and letters to other countries informing them about Islam.

In the tenth year after Hijrah he left Medina for pilgrimage to Makkah. When he stood at the mount of Arafat he gave a sermon known today as the 'Farewell Sermon'. He outlined the important aspects of Islam, and on that day God revealed to him the last ayat (verse) of the Qur'an:

> ... This day I have
> Perfected your religion

244

For you, completed
My favour upon you,
And have chosen for you
Islam as your religion

The Death of the Prophet

After his farewell pilgrimage the Prophet returned to Medina.
Soon afterwards he fell ill. During his illness he stayed at his
wife Aisha's house, close to the mosque. She nursed him and
looked after him. On Monday, 12th Rabi-ul-Awwal, 11 years
after Hijrah, at mid-day, he died there and was buried the
next day in the same house, which was later added to the
mosque during its expansion.

The Status of the Prophet in Islam

If we read the Qur'an, or speak to Muslims, we find that
Muhammad is considered to be a man chosen by God from
his birth to be a prophet. God made him and moulded him a
suitable bearer of God's final message to the people.
God said in the Qur'an (3:164):

God did confer
A great favour
On the believers
When He sent among them
An apostle from among
Themselves, rehearsing
Unto them the signs
Of God, sanctifying them,
And instructing them
In scripture and wisdom,
While, before that,
They had been
In manifest error.

The choice of an apostle from among the people is an
indication that he is a human being like any other, and is such
an example to the people that the message can be implemen-
ted by everyone. The Qur'an also states (3:144)

Muhammad is no more
Than an apostle: many
Were the apostles that passed away
Before him...

245

This verse indicates that all apostles are human beings, given messages for the people. None of them is entitled to be worshipped or act as God for there is only one God (Qur'an 112):

> In the name of God, most Gracious, most Merciful
> Say: he is God,
> The one and only:
> God, the eternal, absolute;
> He begetteth not
> Nor is He begotton;
> And there is none
> Like unto Him.

From this we can clearly see that Muhammad is the messenger of God and, undoubtedly, he is no god or son of God, but he is a man, like any other man, deputed by God to carry his message to the people.

God told the Prophet (Qur'an 28:56):

> It is true thou wilt not
> Be able to guide everyone,
> Whom thou lovest; but God
> Guides those whom He will.
> And He knows best those
> Who receive guidance.

God also told him (Qur'an 7:188) to

> Say: I have no power
> Over any good or harm
> To myself except as God
> Willeth. If I had knowledge
> Of the unseen, I should have
> Multiplied all good, and no evil
> Should have touched me:
> I am but a warner,
> And a bringer of glad tidings
> To those who have faith.

The Sources of Islamic Law

The main source of Islamic law is the Qur'an, which is the word of God revealed to Prophet Muhammad, from the time it was first sent down to him in the Cave of Hira, in the Mount of Noor, near Makkah, until just before his death. The Qur'an which the Muslims have today is exactly the same as that which Prophet Muhammad dictated, recited and arranged, chapter by chapter and verse by verse. It is divided into 30 sections with 114 chapters (*surats*), 86 of them revealed to Muhammad in Makkah, and 28 in Medina. Each chapter starts with the verse: 'In the name of God, most gracious, most merciful'. The total number of verses (*ayats*) are 6,239. The Qur'an is the focal point of Islam and its main source for the behaviour of the individual and society. In it, Muslims find solutions for their daily life. The beauty of the Qur'an lies in its language and its unique code of law; it is also a book of historical facts about the past. Its basic objective is to awaken the soul to the sovereignty of God. It outlines the principles covering the entire life of men, not only personal matters, but the relations between man and his inner self, between man and man, and between man and God. From the time of early Islam, Muslims, from their childhood, learn the Qur'an by heart at the mosque. They read from it at least five times a day at their prayers. As the Qur'an is the word of God, Muslims have a special respect for those who carry the Qur'an in their hearts, these people are called *Hafiz*. Also, Muslims have a special respect for the book itself. This respect is illustrated in the manner in which the Qur'an is written and beautifully decorated. They hold it with respect and it takes a special place in the home, nothing is placed over it. Muslims believe that a home without a copy of the Qur'an is not a blessed house. A Muslim must be clean to hold or read the Qur'an and, if the book it too old to handle, it must be burned.

The second source of Muslim law is the *Sunnah* which is the practice of Prophet Muhammad, part of his mission as a Prophet. The word *Hadith* is used for the sayings of Prophet Muhammad, or the reports by word of mouth of what he said or did. From the beginning, people were interested to know what the Prophet did and said, so that they might learn something about their religion. After his death, and at the time of the expansion of the Muslim land, these sayings were transmitted by reliable people and were written down by different learned men. Of all the *Hadiths*, the following six books are the most authoritative: The Sahih of Bukhari, The Sahih of Muslim, Sunan Abu Daud, Sunan Al Tirmidhi, Sunan An Nisai, Sunan Ibn Majah.

A further source of law is *Qiyas*, meaning measurement. When trying a case a judge may find a definite precedent in the Qur'an or in the Tradition of Prophet Muhammad. If not, the judge has to look for cases with a similarity and make comparisons to arrive at a decision. This process is called *Qiyas*.

The term *Ijma* means 'the agreement of the religious scholars' on new matters. The duty of the ruler, or the judge, is to consult the learned Muslims and follow the rule of the majority.

If one cannot find a relevant passage in the Qur'an, the *Sunnah*, or in the *Tradition of the Companions (qiyas)*, or cannot get an agreement of the Muslim scholars (*ijma*), the duty of a Muslim is to make his own decision (*ijtihad*) on the basis of his faith and knowledge of Islam. This is only permitted in certain circumstances, and for certain people.

The Teaching of Islam

As the Qur'an continued to be revealed to the Prophet, the teachings of Islam were made clear to the people through his practice and speech. The teaching of one God and the equality of all people was revolutionary in the pagan society of Arabia. The requirements of the Muslims to look at the creation of God and learn, was one of its first principles. Islam also stresses the moral value of each action, and makes morality the basis of salvation. To lift up the soul and recognize the needs of other members of the community, Islam lays down a few principles which every Muslim has to adhere to. These principles are divided into five basic beliefs and five observances, as follows:

The Pillars of Faith

a) *The Belief in One God.* The main principle of Islam is faith, and faith is based on the pillar of the belief in One God. Besides this belief in the oneness of God and submission to him, whenever a Muslim starts doing something he always begins by saying '*Bismil-Lahil-Rahaminr-Raheem*' (In the name of God, Most Gracious, Most Merciful). These are the key words of Muslim life, repeated many times every day not only during daily prayers but on waking and on going to sleep, when starting work and on sitting down. It is especially said before eating. Also, a Muslim calls upon God by repeating one of the beautiful 99 names or attributes mentioned in the Qur'an (7:180) 'The most beautiful names belong to God: so call on him by them'. These names are repeated at all times – all day long. Among those names are: The Merciful, The Compassionate, The Wise, The Venerable, The Giver of Life, The One, The Guide.

To help Muslims repeat the 99 names of God without losing concentration the beads (*misbaha*) are used. The 99 beads are divided into three sections of 33, each marked by a bead of a different design. Sometimes a smaller string of beads of only 33 is used.

b) The Belief in the Angels. Muslims believe that angels are spiritual creatures who have no material desires or needs. They have been given various duties by God, like the angel Gabriel, who was given the duty of conveying the message of God to various prophets.

c) The Belief in many Prophets but One Message. Adam was the first man on earth, as well as being the first prophet. He received guidance from his Lord. The descendants of Adam multiplied greatly and were scattered all over the land. Muslims believed that God has chosen many prophets throughout history and revealed his message to them to guide their people. The Qur'an (2:136):

> Say ye: We believe
> In God, and the revelation
> Given to us, and to Abraham,
> Isma'il, Isaac, Jacob,
> And the tribes, and that given
> To Moses and Jesus, and that given
> To (all) prophets from their Lord:
> We make no difference
> Between one and another of them:
> And we bow to God (in Islam).

Through the ages, and especially after the deaths of the prophets, these messages were either destroyed or falsified. God therefore needed to send a new messenger with a more comprehensive message to suit the development of mankind. Among these prophets and messengers were Abraham, Moses, Jesus; and Muhammad was the final messenger.

d) The Belief in the Day of Judgement. Muslims believe that life on earth will come to an end and all our deeds will be counted for reward or punishment. The Qur'an (53:29-42):

> That Man can have nothing
> But what he strives for;
> That (the fruit of) his striving
> Will soon come in sight;
> Then will he be rewarded
> With a reward complete;
> That to thy Lord
> Is the final goal;

e) The Belief in the Qadar. The word *Qadar* means the timeless knowledge of God. Every movement in this universe is with

God's knowledge and his determination. Man has been given the means to choose for himself each action he makes and God has the pre-knowledge of what man's action will be. God, in his love for man, sent different prophets and messengers to guide him through his short life to the eternal world in the hereafter.

These are the articles of faith and belief in the Qur'an. Islam requires action and submission as much as belief, for belief alone is unacceptable.

The Five Pillars of Observance

a)   *Ash-Shahadah (The Creed)*. Islam is built on many pillars as Prophet Muhammad said. The main pillar is the Creed, the *Ash-Shahadah*, the words of which mean 'There is no god but Allah and Muhammad is the Messenger of Allah'. These words are pronounced when a person adopts Islam.

A story we are told in our childhood explains the meaning of the Creed. The story is of a father and his young son. One day the man asked his son to go with him to help him. The work that day was to steal fruit from a neighbouring orchard. The man asked his son to stand near the gate and to shout if anyone approached. When the man entered the orchard and stretched his arms out to pick the fruits, his son shouted, 'Father, father, someone is watching you!' The man ran up, asking, 'Where Where?' The son pointed his finger to heaven and said, 'He is watching you father'. This story is told when learning one of Prophet Muhammad's sayings – 'Worship God as if you see Him. Remember, if you do not see Him, He sees you'. Muslims feel the presence of God around them all the time, and their behaviour is bound by His presence.

b)   *Salat (The Five Daily Prayers)*. A Muslim in prayer can turn his face in any direction, facing the heavens at any time and raising his hands up asking God to ease his difficulties, or to grant his wishes. This form of prayer is called *Du'a*, or supplication. A Muslim has to perform another type of compulsory prayer five times every day. This is called *Salat*. The times of these prayers are at dawn, mid-day, in the afternoon, just after sunset and at night. There are *three* conditions:

i)   *To have a clear conscience* in the presence of God. It means to have a clear mind and a clean soul with an intention to pray.

ii)   To be clean bodily. The ablution is an essential part of prayer. Every Muslim must start in the name of God and wash his hands three times and rinse his mouth three times, then his nostrils three times, followed by washing the arms to the elbow three times, starting with the right hand first, then with moist hands to go over the head, ears and neck, then wash the feet to the ankles three times. During this action of washing a prayer of supplication is said.

iii)   A clean place for prayer. Muslims can pray in any place provided it is clean. They can pray on the grass in the park, in an office or factory, on any clean floor, on a sheet of paper, or in a splendid mosque. When a Muslim travels or goes to a place where he is not sure of finding a clean area, he carries a small prayer rug with him. This rug, according to tradition over the centuries, must conform to special conditions. First, it must be simple in colour, usually only four – black, red, blue and white, and with a design of an arch, indicating the *mihrab* (niche) with a hanging lamp in the middle. This design is called the 'Prophet's Window'.

When hearing the *Adhan*, the call to prayer, from the top of the minaret of the mosque, every Muslim goes quickly to the mosque in answer to the call. At the mosque (or alone at home), when everybody is assembled for prayer, a second call is made – the minor Adhan, or *Iqamat*, as a sign for the worshippers who are ready, to begin prayers.

Turning towards Makkah, south-east in the UK, Muslims stand in rows behind the *Imam*, leader of the prayers. When a Muslim raises his hands above the shoulders with palms facing Makkah and says: '*Allahu Akbar*' (God is Greatest) it indicates the throwing of all worldly thoughts behind him and he stands in the presence of God. The right hand is put over the left one and both are placed on the heart. Then, the worshipper reads the opening chapter of the Qur'an, *Al Fatiha*, as follows:

> In the name of God, most gracious, most merciful,
> Praise be to God,
> The cherisher and sustainer of the world;
> Most gracious, most merciful;
> Master of the Day of Judgement.
> Thee do we worship,
> And Thine aid we seek.
> Show us the straight way,

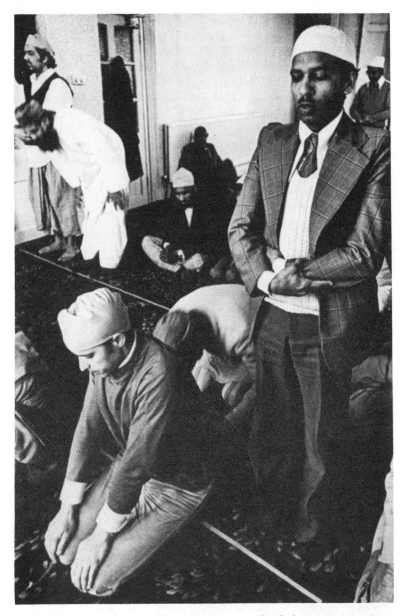

Muslim men at prayer. This shows several of the prayer positions which represent respect and complete submission to God.

The way of those on whom
Thou has bestowed Thy grace,
Those whose (portion)
Is not wrath,
And who go not astray.

The prayer consists of movements representing respect and complete submission to God. The last of the movements, where the worshipper says '*Assalamu A-Laykum wa rahmatullah*' (Peace and Mercy of God be upon you) is a greeting and prayer to those on one's left and right, wishing them peace as experienced oneself during prayer.

A special prayer, known as the Juma prayer, is said on Fridays (Qur'an 62:9)

O ye who believe!
When the call is proclaimed
To prayer on Friday
(The day of assembly),
Hasten earnestly to the remembrance
Of God, and leave off
Business (and traffic):
That is best for you
If ye but knew!

Another prayer position. Notice that all heads are covered.

254

Friday in Arabic is *Yawm al Juma*, the day of assembly, when Muslims gather at the mosque at noon to pray and listen to a sermon. The Imam gives a sermon on the affairs of the Muslim community, with some Islamic teachings according to the occasion, then he leads the prayer. Muslims believe in the story of creation. God created the heavens and earth in six days but he did not rest on the seventh day, or on any other day, for God does not feel fatigue. Friday is a holiday because it is a blessed day when Muslims come together and worship.

Friday is a holiday in the Muslim world and most Muslims in the UK go to the nearest mosque during the lunch hour. In Islam all the prayers are said in Arabic and the sermon usually is also in Arabic. A summary of the sermon may be given in a language understood by the congregation. For instance, in the UK an English summary is given.

c) *Payment of Zakat*. There is a great difference between *Zakat* and *Sadaqa* (charity). *Sadaqa* can be given by any Muslim person from what is surplus to his needs, and it can be given to any person he likes, Muslim or non-Muslim.

Zakat literally means 'purification of wealth.' It is not a tax or charity and it has no equivalent in other religions. It is an obligation on Muslim men and women who possess enough wealth to give a portion of it away. There is Zakat on every kind of wealth, on money, land, goods, houses and cattle. The amount on money, gold and silver is $2\frac{1}{2}\%$ each year which is to be given to any of the eight Muslim categories mentioned by God in the Qur'an: the poor, the needy, Zakat collectors, converts, prisoners, debtors, wayfarers, and 'in the way of God'.

Under the last category it could be used in any way which benefits the community if members of the other seven are not in need. It could be used for education, hospitals, mosques and the propagation of Islam. It is the duty of the Muslim government to collect and distribute Zakat, but in a non-Islamic country it is the duty of every individual Muslim to make sure it is paid to the right person. In the UK where it can be hard to find such deserving persons, Muslims send Zakat to the mosque in their area.

d) *Siyam (Fasting during Ramadan)*. *Siyam* in Arabic means the abstention from food, drink and sexual intercourse from dawn to sunset during the month of Ramadan. The purpose

255

of fasting is manifold. In the Qur'an (2:183) is the exhortation: 'that you may learn self-restraint'. To this effect Prophet Muhammad said: 'Fasting is a shelter. When one of you is fasting, let him not behave in an obscene or foolish manner. If someone intends to fight against him or scold him, let him just say: I am fasting! I am fasting!' Also: 'He who does not keep away from falsehood and false conduct, God has no need for him to abstain from food or drink.'

Fasting has other effects on Muslims such as establishing equality among the rich and poor as well as the promotion of sympathy towards the needy. It gives the strength to break bad habits and increase the will-power in general. Every night during the month of Ramadan there are *Salatul-Taraweeh* prayers at the mosque, usually followed by a lesson on Islam.

During this month the first revelation of the Qur'an was sent down to Prophet Muhammad. Muslims commemorate this by celebrating *Lailat-ul-Qadr* (The Night of Power). In most Muslim countries the night of the 27th day of Ramadan is observed. The celebration and prayers take place throughout the night. The Qur'an (chapter 97) refers to it as follows:

> We have indeed revealed
> This (message)
> In the night of power
> And what will explain
> To Thee what the night
> Of power is?
> The night of power
> Is better than
> A thousand months.
> Therein come down
> The angels and the spirit
> By God's permission,
> On every errand:
> Peace!. . .this
> Until the rise of morn!

Eid-ul-Fitr is the Festival of Breaking the Fast of Ramadan. When Prophet Muhammad arrived in Medina after his immigration from Makkah he found the inhabitants of Medina celebrating many pagan festivals which were against the principles of Islam. He declared to the Muslims that God had given them two important festivals that they could celebrate and enjoy, namely *Eid-ul-Fitr* and *Eid-ul-Adha* (Festival of Sacrifice), Eid-ul-Fitr comes at the end of

Ramadan to celebrate the fulfilment of the fasting. Every Muslim, young and old, male and female, takes part and prepares for this festival. The children wear new clothes and enjoy the gifts and a good sum of money to spend, while all the family goes to the mosque in their new clothes at dawn. After dawn prayer they wait for the festival prayer to start at about an hour after sunrise. Before the festival prayer they have to pay *Zakat-ul-Fitr* (the charity of breaking the fast). When the prayer is finished they go to visit the cemetery to pray for their dead relatives and to remind themselves of the hereafter during the celebration. Following this they go home for a substantial breakfast. Later in the morning visits are exchanged between the neighbours. The head of the family, with some other members, will knock on the doors of their neighbours and greet them by saying *Eid Mubarak* (blessed Eid). They will spend a few minutes with each neighbour before moving on to the next. The rest of the family stays at home to receive other neighbours coming to greet them.

Eid cards are sent during Ramadan to the relatives and friends living away. On the second and third day the family visits nearby relatives.

e)   Hajj (Pilgrimage to Makkah). Hajj is the journey taken by Muslims to the Sacred House (Al-Masjid Al-Haram) in Makkah to perform the religious duties of Hajj. (The Qur'an refers to this in chapter 3:96-97.) Makkah has become the centre of the world for over one billion Muslims. Every Muslim hopes to go to Makkah for Hajj once in his life, in response to the command of God. Every year over two million people from all over the world come to Jeddah by air, sea and land. In 1995 over five thousand people went from Britain; most of them were Muslim settlers and a few were converts.

Before arriving at Jeddah, at a certain point beyond which the pilgrims will not enter unless in the state of *Ihram*, the male pilgrims remove their ordinary clothes and put on two seamless white sheets of cloth, one covering the lower part of the body and the other thrown over one shoulder covering the upper half of the body. Women put on clean, plain, white dresses reaching to the ankles and with long sleeves. *Ihram* is a state in which a person is spiritually and physically near God. All the way to Makkah the pilgrims chant '*Labbaika Al Lahumma Labbaik*', meaning 'Here we come in answer to your call O Lord'. On reaching Makkah they go seven times around the Ka'ba. This act is called *Tawaf*. From there pilgrims proceed towards the two hills of Safa and Marwa, where they walk briskly seven times between the two hills. On the ninth day of *Dhul-Hijjah* the pilgrims go to Mount Arafat, situated about 15 miles from Makkah. The Arafat plain is large enough to accommodate all the pilgrims. Pilgrims spend the day in prayer and meditation until sunset when they move to a place called Muzdalifah where they spend the night in the open air, praying and reading from the Qur'an. They also collect pebbles for the following day's ritual. Early on the 10th, *Dhul-Hijjah*, they return to Mina where they stone the three pillars representing the devil who tried to tempt Isma'ail to rebel against his father Ibrahim.

After stoning the first pillar, the pilgrims sacrifice a lamb in the tradition of Prophet Ibrahim. Muslims all over the world make such sacrifices, even in the UK where Muslim butchers prepare the sacrifices for them. This day is called *Eid-ul-Adha*, the festival of sacrifice.

Hajj is a demonstration of the brotherhood and equality of Islam. It is the largest annual meeting in the world where Muslims meet fellow Muslims to get to know each other and to show their commitment to God by the acts of sacrifice and the hardship of the journey – forsaking the material life for a few days. They also hope to gain a personal knowledge of the birthplace and the historical sites of Islam.

Eid-ul-Adha (Festival of Sacrifice). This festival follows the completion of Hajj (pilgrimage), to be celebrated by those Muslims who went to Makkah and undertook Hajj.

Following the practice of Prophet Ibrahim, who sacrificed a lamb in fulfilment of the command of God when He spared him the sacrifice of his son Isma'ail (*see* Qur'an, chapter 37:99-109), it is also celebrated by all Muslims the world over. The celebration follows the pattern of Eid-ul-Fitr, but there is no Zakat-ul-Fitr (charity of breaking the fast). After returning home from the festival prayer, families sacrifice a lamb or a cow, according to their means. Usually the meat is given to the poor and neighbours; some is kept for the family.

Visits and greetings cards are also exchanged. The days of Eid-ul-Adha and Eid-ul-Fitr are the only feast days in Islam.

On completion of Hajj (pilgrimage) Muslims travel from Makkah to Medina to pay their respect to Prophet Muhammad.

The Islamic Calendar

The Islamic calendar is based on the lunar system, i.e. the

orbiting of the moon around the earth. The month starts from the new moon and ends with the next new moon, making it either 29 or 30 days. The day starts from sunset, continuing to sunset the next day. This makes the Islamic year shorter than the solar year by ten to eleven days. The Islamic calendar moves forward against the solar year so the same festival will be ten or eleven days earlier each year. If say, *Eid-ul-Fitr* falls on the 11 October this year, next year the same festival will be on the 1 October. If you have a chance to look at the Islamic calendar you will see the year 1417 A.H. begins on the 19th May 1996. The movements of the festivals and Ramadan can be seen in the following table:

Hijrah Year	Muslim New Year begins	Month of Ramadan	1st of Shawwal (Eid-ul-Fitr)	10 Dhul-Hijja (Eid-ul-Adha)
1416 A.H.	31 May 1995	22 Jan 1996	21 Feb 1996	30 Apr 1996
1417 A.H.	19 May 1996	10 Jan 1997	9 Feb 1997	19 Apr 1997
1418 A.H.	9 May 1997	31 Dec 1997	30 Jan 1998	9 Apr 1998
1419 A.H.	28 Apr 1998	20 Dec 1998	19 Jan 1999	30 Mar 1999
1420 A.H.	17 Apr 1999	9 Dec 1999	8 Jan 2000	19 Mar 2000
1421 A.H.	6 Apr 2000	28 Nov 2000	28 Dec 2000	7 Mar 2001
1422 A.H.	26 Mar 2001	17 Nov 2001	17 Dec 2001	25 Feb 2002

There could be a one day difference either way to the above dates, depending on the sighting of the new moon with the naked eye.

The Muslims always put A.H. after the year to indicate that it is After Hijrah, i.e. the migration of Prophet Muhammad from Makkah to Medina. The Islamic calendar was adopted by the second caliph, Umar, ten years after the Prophet's death.

Although the New Year's day is not a public holiday, it is celebrated in all Muslim counties by gatherings at the mosques and people listening to the stories about the Prophet's life and the suffering of the Muslims in Makkah before their migration to Medina.

Jerusalem and the Night Journey to the Seven Heavens

There are many miracles in the life of every prophet, and one of the miracles of Prophet Muhammad was the Night Journey to the Seven Heavens, through Jerusalem. It happened at a very difficult time during Muhammad's life when the Makkans rejected and humiliated those who followed him. To make it worse, news was brought to him of the death of two people dear to him, his uncle and

259

protector, Abu Talib, followed a few days later by his wife, Khadijah. The Quraish intensified their fight against the Prophet and to escape them he went to Taif, a town about 200 miles south of Makkah. Here he was rejected and forced to return.

It was at this time that the Journey to the Seven Heavens took place as an assurance of God's support, to give Muhammad some sign from God so as to provide him with the strength to carry out his mission. One important point to remember is that this journey from Makkah to the Seven Heavens went through Jerusalem, underlining the importance of this great city to the Muslims. The Qur'an (17:1) refers to it as follows:

Glory to (God),
Who did take His servant
For a journey by night
From the Sacred Mosque
To the farthest mosque,
Whose precincts we did
Bless, – in order that we
Might show him some of
Our signs; for He
Is the one who heareth
And seeth (all things).

In early Islam, Muslims used to face Jerusalem in their prayers until the command of God changed the direction of the prayer from Jerusalem to Makkah after Muhammad's Journey to the Seven Heavens. The journey through Jerusalem emphasizes the importance of the city (Qur'an 2:144).

One night when the Prophet was asleep, the angel Gabriel came and awakened him and took him to al-Buraq, an animal of the size of a horse with two wings. This creature was so fast that the distance from Makkah to Jerusalem, and then on to the Seven Heavens, took only part of the night. In Jerusalem, the Prophet met other prophets – Abraham, Moses and Jesus. In the Seven Heavens he also met the prophets and saw many of God's signs. During his visit in the Heavens, Muhammad received the command of the 'daily prayer'.

When the Prophet was questioned in public about his journey by the Makkans, he described to them many things he saw on the way to Jerusalem and told of the caravans on the way back to Makkah. The Makkans could not believe

260

what they heard and hurried to Abu Bakr, the close companion of the Prophet. They told the story to Abu Bakr in the hope that he would also disbelieve it, but he answered them, 'If he told of the revelation which came to him within the hours of the day and night and I believed him, then this is not strange to me.' When they asked the Prophet, his answer was in the affirmative – he *had* told Abu Bakr immediately afterwards.

Although Muslims differ as to whether the journey was by soul and body, or by soul alone, it seems that a miracle took place. The Qur'an refers to it in chapter 17 indicating two important aspects: the five daily prayers were commanded by God for every Muslim; the meeting of Prophet Muhammad with the prophets before him indicated that Islam was *not* a new religion but a continuation of the same message given to the earlier prophets.

The Family

Islam is the religion which covers all aspects of life, regardless of time or place. All the systems in Islam are based on a godly moral code, with great consideration for the spiritual and material needs of men, in this world and in the hereafter.

Islam pays much attention to the family, the foundation of the society. This is made clear in the Qur'an which does not deal with any other subject as much. It is concerned with marriage and makes recommendations; it deals with the marriage contract (*Nikah*); the rights and duties of husband and wife; divorce; and the tradition (*Sunnah*) of Prophet Muhammad enforces that. From all this we see the family in Islam is built on three principles: Love, Mercy and Justice.

Marriage and Divorce

From the Qur'an (30:21):

> And among His signs
> Is this, that He created
> For you mates from among
> Yourselves, that ye may
> Dwell in tranquillity with them,
> And He has put love
> And mercy between your (hearts):
> Verily in that are signs
> For those who reflect.

Marriage, in Islam, is a bond of love and mercy. It not only unites man and wife but extends unity to all relations; brothers and sisters, uncles and aunts, grandparents, etc. Relatives hold different positions according to seniority within the family. The marriage is based on love first and then mercy. Muslims do not believe in, and are forbidden pre-marital sexual relations.

When a man likes a girl, he negotiates through his family and presents himself to the girl and her family. After introducing himself to them, he enquires about their interests

262

and conditions for the marriage of their daughter. When both parties agree, the engagement is announced and the wedding date is fixed. In marriage, Islam makes it necessary for the man and woman to accept each other. The man must give a dowry to his wife-to-be, this is to be fixed before marriage, but if the woman likes she can free her husband of any part, or all of it, if she desires. The amount of this dowry is not specified, it depends on the standards of the two families, and the smaller it is, the better. The marriage can be performed at any place and by any upright Muslim man, who may officiate in the presence of at least two adult male Muslim witnesses. In this country, most Muslims go to the mosque and ask the Imam to perform the ceremony.

The Imam opens the ceremony by recitations from the Qur'an. The first few verses from 'The Women', chapter 4 in the Qur'an are the most suitable for this occasion:

> In the name of God, most Gracious, most Merciful,
> O Mankind! reverence
> Your Guardian-Lord,
> Who created you
> From a single person,
> Created, of like nature,
> His mate, and from them twain
> Scattered (like seeds)
> Countless men and women;
> Reverence God, through whom
> Ye demand your mutual (rights),
> And (reverence) the wombs
> (That bore you): for God
> Ever watches over you.

This is followed by a short talk about marriage and the duty of husband and wife towards each other, and towards their future children. The rings are then exchanged. The man may have any kind of ring except gold. The guests congratulate the bride and the bridegroom saying, '*Baarakal-Lahu Lakum wa Baaraka Alaykum*' (May God bless you and invoke His benediction upon you). A big feast follows. There will be some music and songs within the limits of Islam.

Married couples are thus described in the Qur'an (4:34):

> Men are the protectors
> And maintainers of women.
> Because God has given

The one more (strength)
Than the other, and because
They support them
From their means.
Therefore the righteous women
Are devoutly obedient, and guard
In (the husband's) absence
What God would have them guard.

and (2:187)...

They are your garments
And ye are their garments.

Islam permits polygamy but never imposes it; it is only permitted under special circumstances. Two of the conditions are: justice and ability; justice by the husband to treat his wives equally, and ability to maintain them and their children on equal footing. Due to development in the Muslim world, this custom has diminished; it exists only in rural areas.

The man has no right to get married unless he is able to do justice to his wife. Justice here is not only in a materialistic sense which a judge could decide, but it is a moral obligation which the person concerned can feel. The remembrance of God is an essential part in the preserving of this justice. The poor members of the family are the responsibility of the more fortunate ones; and the weak are the responsibility of the strong.

Regarding divorce the Qur'an (4:35) states:

If ye fear a breach
Between them twain,
Appoint (two) arbiters,
One from his family,
And the other from hers:
If they wish for peace,
God will cause
Their reconciliation:
For God hath full knowledge:
And is acquainted
With all things.

If, for one reason or another, a marriage does not work out, Islam permits the couple to divorce, Prophet Muhammad said 'Among legal acts, divorce is the most odious to God!' However, a marriage bond should not be broken right away. Reconciliation must be attempted to save the marriage. An arbitration by the families between husband and wife must attempt to bring the man and his wife together again. If this fails, then divorce procedures take place. This could be done in court and the man has the authority to pronounce the divorce, but the woman has the right to obtain the divorce.

There are three kinds of divorce in Islam: the first is the revocable divorce which permits the husband to retake his wife without a new marriage contract; the second is the minor, irrevocable divorce when the two parties can come back together with a new marriage contract; thirdly, there is the major, irrevocable divorce where they may not marry again, unless the woman marries another man and lives with him, then, if divorced or widowed, she could remarry her first husband.

Children

Children are the gifts of God and joys of life. Every infant is born according to the *Fitrah* (true nature of submission). Islam makes it the responsibility of the parents to look after their children and give them a good chance in life. This means providing them with a sound education and good manners, enabling them to be valuable members of the Muslim community. The duty of the children towards their parents is best described in the Qur'an (31:14–15):

> And we have enjoined on man
> (To be good) to his parents:
> In travail upon travail
> Did his mother bear him,
> And in years twain
> Was his weaning: (hear
> The command), 'Show gratitude
> To Me and to thy parents:
> To Me is (thy final) Goal.'
>
> But if they strive
> To make thee join
> In worship with Me
> Things of which thou hast
> No knowledge, obey them not;
> Yet bear them company
> In this life with justice
> (And consideration), and follow

The way of those who
Turn to Me (in love):
In the end the return
Of you all is to Me,
And I will tell you
The truth (and meaning)
Of all that ye did.

When Muslim parents are blessed with a child, it is bathed and the call to prayer (*Adhan*) is said softly into the right ear of the baby. The *Iqamat* (Minor Adhan) is then said into the left ear. When the child is taken home from hospital the act of *Tahneek* is performed by an older member of the family. This is done by placing a small part of a very soft date or honey into the mouth of the infant and a *Du'a* prayer is said.

On the seventh day, the *Aqeeqah* celebration takes place, the child is given a name. The selection of the right, correct name of a child is very important in Islam. The best names are those which are derived from the name of God (Allah), like Abdullah (servant to God), or Abdul-Rahman (servant of the Merciful), or such names as that of Prophet Muhammad, or derivatives like Mahmood and Ahmad. One or two sheep or goats should be slaughtered and a feast held. Friends and neighbours are invited and some meat is given to the poor. Also, on this day, the baby's hair is shaved and gold or silver equal to the weight of the hair, or the value of such, is given to the poor. The *Khitan* (circumcision) of a male baby is performed on this day. If it is not possible, then it should be done before the boy reaches the age of seven, or at the latest, twelve.

Parents

A man came to Prophet Muhammad asking: 'O Messenger of God! Who among the people is the most worthy of my good company?' The Prophet said, 'Your mother'. The man said, 'Then who else?' The Prophet said again, 'Your mother'. The man asked again, 'Who else?' The Prophet said once more, 'Your mother'. The man continued to ask, 'Then who else?' Only then did the Prophet say, 'Your father'. The Prophet also said: 'Paradise lies at the feet of mothers.'

A group of Muslim children outside a house in Wolverhampton which has been converted into a mosque.

Death

All that is on earth
Will perish:
But will abide (for ever)
The face of thy Lord,
Full of majesty,
Bounty and honour.
                    (Qur'an chapter 3:185)

Every soul shall have
A taste of death:
And only on the Day
Of Judgement shall you
Be paid your full recompense.
Only he who is saved
Far from the fire
And admitted to the garden
Will have attained
The object (of life):
For life of this world
Is but goods and chattels
Of deception.
                    (Qur'an chapter 55:26-281)

It is reported that Prophet Muhammad during his last illness said: 'Allah, forgive me and have mercy on me and join me to the companion on high' (God). He also said: 'Allah, help me over the hardship and agony of death.'

Death is the end of the present life but it is not final as it is only a temporary separation from the loved ones who will all be brought back to life on the Day of Judgement and, if God wills, reunited once more.

When death approaches, the dying should be urged to affirm the unity of God by asking them to repeat the *Ash-shahada* – that there is none worthy of worship except God. The dying person should also utter a prayer for forgiveness and mercy from God, helped by a reading from the Qur'an by others present. Chapter 36 – 'Ya-Sin' is always read on such occasions.

On hearing the news of a death, the following is said: 'To God we belong, and to him is our return.' Relatives and friends gather at the home of the deceased. They extend their comfort and solace to the immediate family members, recite the Qur'an and pray for God's forgiveness and mercy for the person who has died.

There is a positive rule for washing the body and covering it with *Kafan* (a shroud). Great respect should be shown. The body is to be washed at least three times with soap, starting with the parts of the body as for the ablution for prayer. It is then wrapped in a special way with three pieces of white cotton cloth. Scent or perfume is also used.

Prophet Muhammad strongly urged Muslims to bury the dead without delay. The body is usually put on a bier (a coffin may be used), and carried on men's shoulders either to a mosque, or direct to the burial ground for the funeral prayer (*salat-ul-janazah*) which is necessary for every dead Muslim, male or female. This prayer is a common obligation (*fard kifayah*) for Muslims, meaning that it should be observed by at least a few, but not necessarily by all, who are associated with the event.

The coffin should be positioned in front of the Imam who stands facing *Qiblah* – towards Makkah. The funeral prayer is offered in congregation and there is no bowing or prostration. The body is then carried to the burial place. Whenever the procession passes other people on the way, they stand still to show respect. None shall speak evil of the dead and all must engage themselves in exalting the virtues of the deceased and praying for him.

In Muslim countries the mourning period varies, from seven days in some to 40 days in others, and even up to three months. During this period no joyful events may take place such as weddings, etc. This applies not only to the immediate family of the deceased but to all distant relatives as well.

On the death of a Muslim a post-mortem is forbidden except in very special circumstances. The dead of Muslim faith should always be buried among Muslims in a Muslim cemetery, and cremation is absolutely forbidden. Further, a Muslim should be buried preferably at the place of death (it is unnecessary to send a body back to the place of birth).

Way of Life

We have mentioned earlier that Islam spread to different countries, to different people, and that their faith united them and made them one nation. What is this factor which unites Muslims, and how does it affect their way of living in spite of all the differences in food, clothes, and customs, all around the Muslim world?

Halal and Haram

Halal means lawful and permissible, and *Haram*, unlawful or forbidden. Prophet Muhammad said: 'What is lawful is clear, and what is unlawful is also clear. Between them there are doubtful matters which many people do not know, so whoever guards himself against those doubtful matters he purifies his religion and his honour and whoever falls into the doubtful, falls into the unlawful.'

Muslims look at things in life according to the teaching in the Qur'an or in the tradition of the Prophet Muhammad. They have one important rule, that everything is lawful unless explicitly forbidden. Also, anything leading to the unlawful is forbidden, and Muslims know that only God has the right to lay down what is lawful and what is unlawful. All bad things are forbidden and good intentions do not justify committing the unlawful. Many things which people might think are not bad, Islam forbids, like lending money for interest, gambling, or sex outside marriage.

Food

One of the most important considerations is that everything man eats must be obtained by lawful means. Beyond this principle there are certain foods and drinks mentioned in the Qur'an (2:173) as forbidden:

> He hath only forbidden you
> Dead meat, and blood,

270

And the flesh of swine,
And that on which
Any other name hath been invoked
Besides that of God.
But if one is forced by necessity,
Without wilful disobedience,
Nor transgressing due limits,
Then is he guiltless.
For God is oft-forgiving
Most Merciful.

Also, from the Qur'an (5:93-94):

O ye who believe!
Intoxicants and gambling,
(Dedication of) stones,
And (divination by) arrows,
Are an abomination, –
Of Satan's handiwork:
Eschew such (abomination),
That ye may prosper.

Satan's plan is (but)
To excite enmity and hatred
Between you, with intoxicants
And gambling, and hinder you
From the remembrance
Of God, and from prayer:
Will ye not then abstain?

According to the above command of God, Muslims consider all pig meat and fat, and all kinds of alcohol, however small in quantity, as forbidden. Muslims are required to slaughter animals for food in the manner described, in the tradition of the Prophet Muhammad. The method of slaughtering the animal stipulates that the actual slaughtering must be carried out by a Muslim and the windpipe, jugular veins and the oesophagus (gullet) must be cut. During the action of slaughtering the name of God must be invoked to signify that one does not take the life of any of God's creatures wantonly, but only for food, with God's permission. 'Eat not of (meats) on which God's name hath not been pronounced: that would be impiety...' (Qur'an 6:121).

Islam considers everything forbidden as harmful to the body or mind of the individual. Qur'an 7:157:

271

... For He commands them
What is just and forbids them
What is evil; He allows
Them as lawful what is good
(And pure) and prohibits them
From what is bad (and impure)...

After the declaration of what is lawful and what is unlawful, God invites the Muslims to 'Eat and drink: but waste not by excess, for God loveth not the waster' (Qur'an 7:31).

Dress

There is no Muslim dress as such, although Islam considers decency, modesty and morality important; anything which gives a false impression or reflects pride, is forbidden. Men are forbidden to wear pure silk and gold, while women are permitted to do so. This is because Islam considers the wearing of silk and gold by men, and the luxury and pride in the wearing of them, is not in keeping with the hard and responsible life which men have to lead. Women should also not be extravagant in their usage. Islam stresses the point that women should keep their femininity and men their manhood. Women should not dress like men, and men should not imitate women. The Qur'an lays down women must dress to cover their bodies and the clothing should not be light or transparent. The same applies for men.

Social Life

We have noticed that all Islamic activities, including prayer, have in some way or another a social characteristic. This is because Islam is concerned for the development of human nature. Islam permits gatherings of people, male and female, in most circumstances according to the needs of Muslim society and individual responsibility. The equality between men and women does not mean they do not play different roles to fulfil their different responsibilities. Islam puts the prime responsibility for the family, and society, on men, but this does not mean that women cannot leave the house or take up work outside their own homes. In the early days of Islam, during the time of the Prophet, and for some time afterwards, women took a full part in the affairs of everyday life. Mature men and women are allowed to mix, with certain limitations, as this cannot be avoided in life.

The Mosque

The Parts of the Mosque

The mosque in Islam is called *massjid* or *jami'a*. The *masjid* is a place of prostration. The Prophet said: 'The whole earth has been made a place of prostration for me'. This is the reason why Muslims can pray at any clean place on earth, *Jami'a* is a bigger place of worship to accommodate large numbers of the community for *Salat-ul-Juma*, (Friday prayer), or Eid prayer.

The mosque usually has two main sections – the inner part, or the sanctuary, and the outer part, or courtyard. The inner part is the main part of the structure. It is built to face Makkah. The first wall facing Makkah has to be distinguished from other walls by an arch built inside the wall, facing towards Makkah. This is called the *mihrab* which is the place where the Imam stands to lead the prayer.

In the early days of Islam, the Jews were called to their prayer by a horn, the Christians by bells. Muslims found a

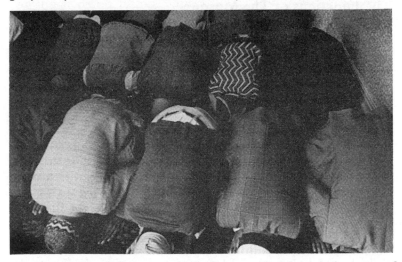

Muslims express their unity and obedience to God through the action of bowing before him during prayers.

273

different way when one of the companions of the Prophet made a suggestion, following a dream in which he heard the call to prayer. The Prophet ordered Bilal, the Abyssinian, to go up on the roof and call the faithful to prayer. He was the first *muezzin*.

In the early days the muezzin went up on to the roof of the mosque and called the *adhan*. Later on, when Muslims conquered many lands, the muezzins found higher platforms such as towers, to call for the prayer. These developed later, in the seventh century, into minarets. The outline of minarets became one of the important features of the mosque.

An important part of the Friday prayer is the sermon. The Prophet used to stand on a three-stepped platform called *minbar*. Later on, they were developed into glorious wooden pulpits, inlaid with ivory, with more than 33 steps in some cases. The place of the minbar is immediately on the right hand side of the mihrab.

Kursi al-Qur'an (lecterns) were introduced at a time when the Qur'an was written in the form of a book, which, in those days proved too heavy to be held in both hands. Again, it developed into the shape in use today. The earliest one known of is in Quniya (Turkey) and dates back to 678 A.H. (1297 C.E.).

The Functions of The Mosque

The mosque is unlike any other place of worship. It is a unique institution which moulds the conduct of worship to the foundations of everyday life. The unity of God reflected in His creation is represented in the structure of the mosque. The distinctive architectural character helps the worshipper to submit to God without any mediator. The use of the mosque for other purposes helps the organization of the Muslim community.

Before the development of society the functions of the mosque were more diverse than they are today. Compared with town mosques, we find mosques in rural areas serving different purposes. The mosque is, however, the heart of the Muslim community, where people meet and discuss their problems. It is also used as an educational institution and as a place for Muslims seeking refuge. In the early days of Islam, the mosque was the administrative centre where the Prophet, and the Caliphs after him, used to sit and direct the administration of the state. It was a place where foreign

274

delegates were received and housed, and the command headquarters of the army.

The School (*Al-Madrasah*)

One of the most important functions of the mosque is that of acting as a school for the Muslim community. The Prophet himself used to teach and train Muslims and today the function is continuing. Everywhere in the Muslim world you come across the Qur'anic school for teaching the Qur'an and the Tradition of Prophet Muhammad. One of the important mosque schools is the Al Azhar Mosque in Cairo where most of the world's Muslim teachers of theology graduate. Others are in Kairouan in Tunisia, at Lucknow in India and Najaf in Iraq.

In Britain today we find these Qur'anic schools in every mosque. Although they are old fashioned in their methods of teaching and differ a great deal from those in the Muslim world, they are the only source of religious instructions in this country for Muslim children.

The Imam

The word Imam means 'a leader'. The Imam's function is as a teacher and prayer leader at the mosque. He has no divine authority, but as a man of knowledge the Muslims seek his advice on everyday matters, and they are perfectly at liberty to accept or reject it.

Young boys receive instruction in the Qur'anic school.

275

The Muslim Community

One morning in 1965 I received a long letter from an inmate of the county of Kent Prison, telling me his life story and requesting some information about Islam. He mentioned that due to bad health and his interests he had been given the responsibility of making an index of all articles published in the newspapers of the county of Kent from the year 1800 to the year 1965. He had found many interesting cuttings about Muslims, especially those which were dated around 1820. Among the many cuttings, he came across one of a geological excavation during which a coin, minted at the time of King Offa of Mercia (707-796 C.E.), was found. On one side was written in Arabic: 'There is no god but Allah and Muhammad is the Messenger of Allah'. This an indication that the history of Islam in Britain goes back far beyond the time of the Empire.

It is reported that the first official delegation from the Muslim world arrived in London in the year 1394 C.E., at the request of King Richard II who had ordered the building of Westminster Hall, which is part of the Parliament building. The architect and builders of the famous hall were unable to join the arches of the central dome above the hall. After their failure, the king was advised to seek the assistance of some Muslim architects from the Muslim world, who were the inventors of this type of arch. After some time the Muslim architects arrived and they were able to make the arches meet at the central point of the dome. Since then, Muslims have been welcome in this island, although their numbers were few and did not increase until recent times. In 1889 the building of the Woking Mosque, in Surrey, highlighted the significant number of Muslims in Britain.

It is estimated that the number of Muslims in Western Europe is over 13 million, with more than one million in Britain, many of them from Commonwealth countries. There is no doubt that commerce, trade and cultural scholarships have contributed to the introduction of Islam in Britain, as was the case with many countries overseas, where Islam spread through the Muslim merchants trading with non-Muslim countries.

The population of the Muslim community in the UK has been increasing due to immigration from Pakistan and India and other countries with Commonwealth links. Many of the first generation now have grandchildren in schools sharing their lives with British youngsters. Since their arrival in the UK, Muslims have tried to adapt themselves to their new environment which differs greatly in regard to faith and the social and moral life. They have many different organizations of their own, but also make an effort to participate in activities with the host community in order to further a better understanding, and to establish a better society for all.

The dialogue between Muslims and non-Muslims has increased tremendously over the past few years. This interest came as a result of changes in the Muslim world, which occurred not only because of oil, as some observers may relate, but also because of the new awakening of faith. This happened at the same time as changes in Europe which resulted in a parallel decline of faith in God and the decline in moral standards.

It was said that the first large number of Muslims reaching the shores of UK in contemporary history were those from Yemen and Aden. They were very good seamen, employed by the British Navy. They, and some of their descendants today, are concentrated near the ports of Liverpool and Cardiff.

At the end of the Second World War most of the Muslim countries were under British rule. The education system was geared to the British system and western civilization. The Muslims who came to the UK in the hope of a better living standard were able to establish mosques and Qur'anic schools as soon as they stepped on this soil.

The need for a central mosque in London was felt as early as 1926, when the late Sheikh Hafez Wahaba, the then Saudi Arabian Ambassador in London, started to establish such a scheme. He was able to secure £50,000 from the Nizam of Hyderabad of India and £20,000 from the late Agha Khan. As the Muslim countries were under British rule and a large number of Muslims participated in the Second World War, the British Government purchased the site of the present London Central Mosque on the edge of Regent's Park from Lady Ribbersdale. The site was handed over to a trust formed by the Muslim Ambassadors in London, with a committee of

277

three Ambassadors, under the chairmanship of Sheikh Hafez Wahaba of Saudi Arabia, and the Iraqi and Egyptian Ambassadors as members. In November 1942 King George VI inaugurated the opening of the Islamic Cultural Centre. Thus, we find no truth in the claim that the site was in exchange for a site for an Anglican Church in Cairo, arranged by the British and Egyptian Governments.

Efforts to start building the mosque were hindered due to lack of funds and sometimes due to events, like the Suez crisis. In 1954, the foundation of the mosque was laid by Sheikh Wahaba, but the magnificent design by the Egyptian Architect, General Ramzy Omar, was rejected by the Fine Arts Commission on the grounds that the design conflicted with the surrounding buildings by Nash, the famous Georgian architect. After many upheavals, in 1969 the trustees of the mosque set up an international competition and appointed a jury of three well-known architects, Sir Robert Mathew of the UK; M.A. Ahad of Pakistan and Blanco Solo of Spain. Fifty-two designs from 17 countries were received and after careful study of the designs, the needs of the Muslim community and the conditions of the Fine Arts Commission were met; there were four winning designs. The first was an English design by Sir Frederick Gibbard, an eminent architect who designed Liverpool Cathedral; the second, a modern Turkish design; joint third, a traditional Moroccan and a traditional Egyptian design. The first winning design was built in 1972 and it took four years to complete at a cost of over £4 million.

The problems which Muslims face in Britain are fundamentally that of adaptation to a completely different environment. A Muslim must mould himself gradually to fit into a new society. This may lead to conflicts between his own values and the values of the surrounding community.

To understand these problems one must take a look at the Muslims in the western countries, with the Muslim community in the UK as an example. The immigration of Muslims to this country is not a new factor in Muslim society. Muslims have travelled in the past far away from their homelands for many reasons. The belief in God had abolished all frontiers between the countries, and it became their duty to look into the wonders of the universe which God created. Muslims were at one time a great maritime power. They went from Morocco to Spain and southern Europe in 710 C.E. and from Turkey to Eastern Europe in the early eleventh century. It is claimed they landed in America long before Columbus.

Muslims, like all minorities, tend to cling together and do not attempt to mix easily with the people of this country, with the exception of a few. The reason is that the English people keep themselves to themselves and do not accept foreigners for a long time, during which period they keep up a superficial relationship with them. It is true that Muslims, or any other immigrant group or minority, should accept some of the customs and way of life of the majority but, if the customs and daily way of life conflict with the principles of their faith one cannot hope for a full integration but only for toleration and acceptance of differences.

To explain this, one of the most common social events which bring people together are parties or pub visits. In most parties alcohol is consumed and flirtation with the opposite sex takes place, both unacceptable to Muslims. Even clubs run by the various churches favour the above-mentioned social life. Muslims have to boycott gatherings of this kind.

Language difficulties are not serious, as is testified by the overwhelming majority of the first generation of Muslims who had little knowledge of English on arrival in Britain and became fluent after only a short while, with the exception of some women from the sub-continent of India, who do not leave their houses and so have little contact with the host community.

All these problems, however, can be overcome if a Muslim has the right contacts with his community and with the British people. Moreover, there are many ways of becoming integrated in a foreign environment, for example through joining professional societies with a high standard of morality. Unfortunately, most of these organizations and societies intend changing Muslims' behaviour. Some religious organizations even try to convert Muslims to Christianity.

It may not be out of place here to emphasize the psychological aspects of this problem. Whether Muslims are practising Islam or not, the discipline in eating habits is the first and most important line of resistance of their faith. This resistance is not something superficial. It is sincere, something deeply ingrained in their vary nature, instilled from childhood. If circumstances make them yield on this point, it is a most painful moral decision and the effect on their morale is often disastrous – the feeling of having lost everything. Many people even cease to offer prayers as they feel themselves unfit for this holy function. In short, the shock has an eroding effect on faith.

The majority of Muslim immigrants are from Pakistan and India and Bangladesh. The fact is that to every immigrant the local authority, especially the health departments, education departments and the employment offices, look upon them, the immigrants, as second class citizens. Instead of seeking their help during times of need, immigrants keep away from these departments as much as they can.

During recent times some English people have shown sympathy towards immigrants and offered their help and friendship, something Muslims welcome and appreciate – these efforts have resulted in trust and understanding.

SIKHISM

PIARA SINGH SAMBHI

Introduction

The youngest of the religions examined in this book, Sikhism, has more in common with Hinduism than the semitic traditions of Judaism, Christianity and Islam.

Sikhism began in the Punjab region of north-west India and this is where its numerical strength still lies. Twelve million of its 14 million adherents still live in the provinces of the Punjab and Hiriyana, though before 1947 the word Punjab referred to much of the land between Peshawar and Delhi, watered by the tributaries of the river Indus.

The first noticeable Sikh migrations were to other parts of the world which were under British rule, or were English speaking. After 1849, when the Sikh kingdom of the Punjab was annexed by the armies of Queen Victoria, Sikhs enlisted in the British army. Towards the end of the century they were to be found serving in Singapore, Hongkong and other parts of south-east Asia and the Pacific. When their period of service was over, some Sikhs remained as policemen, watchmen or security guards in the lands where they had been discharged and brought their families to join them. Soon after the turn of the 20th century they had reached Vancouver in Canada and from there moved southwards into California. At about the same time other Sikhs were to be found among the Asians who followed the flag into East Africa.

The year 1947 saw the partition of India into the countries of Pakistan and India, with the frontier running through the middle of the Sikh homeland. The Sikh response to an upheaval which affected some 3 to 5 million people in north-west India was often to move from the crowded Punjab countryside, with its limited opportunities, to Dehli, Bombay and other cities. A people already widespread throughout the world now began to disperse from the Punjab into other Indian provinces.

Some Sikhs, but only a small number, had found their way to Britain before the First World War. Others came in the interwar period. Most, however, came from India or East Africa at the same time as Hindus and Muslims, and for the same reasons. During the 1950s they filled job vacancies, especially in textile mills, which Britons from the declining industries of coalmining and the docks, were unwilling to do. The need of Britain, and many other European countries, for workers coincided with the closing of traditional host countries to migrants, either as a result of new policies following independence, or saturation. More recently Sikhs, no longer able to come to Britain to find work, have turned to the Arab states of the Middle East.

The Sikh man, wearing his often brightly coloured turban, is easily identified in a crowd. For this reason he is perhaps the most noticed of Britain's citizens, even though he is outnumbered two-to-one by Muslims and three-to-one by people of Caribbean origin. The number of Sikhs in Britain is about 250,000.

The Sikh Gurus

Sikhism began with the preachings of Guru Nanak, the first Sikh Guru. Guru Nanak was born in 1469 at Talwandi (now called Nankana Sahib in his honour) which is a small town about fifty miles to the south-west of Lahore in Pakistan. He belonged to a well-to-do middle class Hindu family and received a fairly good education. Nanak was a precocious child with an immensely inquisitive nature. At an early age he showed great interest in spiritual matters, and the frequent discussions which he had with the itinerant holy men furnished him with the basic knowledge and practices of Hinduism, Islam and various yogic cults. He was married and had two sons. For about 14 years he worked as a storekeeper for the provincial governor, Nawab Daulat Khan, at Sultanpur; but his early thoughts of spiritualism replaced his interest in worldly pursuits. Guru Nanak spent most of his leisure in meditation and in solitude. However, the decisive moment in his life came when he was about 30 years of age. Most of his biographers describe his mystical experience as follows: one morning when Nanak was meditating, after taking a bath in the river Bein near Sultanpur, he was summoned to the presence of God who charged him with the mission of preaching his name.

After the receipt of this divine call Guru Nanak resigned his job and took to preaching. During the course of his intermittent but extensive tours of India, and the adjoining Islamic countries, he visited important religious centres of the various communities and had discussions with their leaders. In his later life he settled down as a farmer at Kartarpur, on the River Ravi in the Punjab. His family joined him and soon a community of followers grew up around him. A few days before his death, in 1539, Guru Nanak nominated his most devoted disciple, Angad, as his successor.

Guru Nanak laid strong emphasis on the fatherhood of God and the brotherhood of man. Worship and piety had no meaning if they failed to promote truthful conduct and compassion for the less fortunate, he said. Religious hypothesis and social institutions which hampered the growth of equality and fellowship needed to be discarded. The life of a recluse and the monastic ideal were rejected because they failed to provide for the love and service of fellow human beings. Priesthood is not honoured in Sikhism, because it encourages formality. Family life is central to the religious approach advocated by Guru Nanak. The love of God and the fulfilment of the obligations of a family life could be attained by a threefold discipline of *Nam Japna, Dharam di Kirat Karni* and *Wand Chhakna*.

Nam Japna means the remembrance of God. This is the conscious repetition which keeps God in our mind and in our thoughts and which leads to a feeling of his presence. For remembrance of God, or meditation, God's word is essential, because the word dwells upon the attributes of God and fills us with emotions of love for him. It bolsters up the mind to shun evil and inculcates thoughts of prayer and thankfulness.

Dharam di Kirat Karni means honest work, or work done honestly according to one's ability and capacity. It means no fraud, no adulteration or corruption in any business, trade or profession. Work is bad when it leads to unfair and untruthful means being employed.

Wand Chhakna means the sharing of the product, or profit, of one's honest work with others. It should be done, however, in a spirit of service, believing wealth to be the gift of God, and in thankfulness to him for providing such an opportunity of serving his fellow beings.

Guru Nanak provided the basic ideas and institutions of *sangat* (congregational worship) and *pangat* (common dining) and his nine successors amplified and translated his precepts into practice, according to time and circumstances. Guru Angad (1539-52) improved and perfected the existing *Mahajni* script for the writing of the Punjabi language in which the hymns of Guru Nanak were expressed. He named it *Gurmukhi* and made concerted efforts to popularize it for the education of the younger generation. Guru Amar Das (1552-74) succeeded Guru Angad in 1552 at the ripe age of 70 years. He strengthened the Sikh movement with the appointment of missionaries, and invited his followers to his headquarters at Goindwal twice a year, on the days of Baisakhi and Diwali. For the obliteration of caste distinctions among his followers he made it obligatory for all visitors to take food in the common kitchen (the *langar*) before seeing him. It is a religion of the masses and not of the classes, he said. He championed

284

the cause of women by appointing them as missionaries and by denouncing the practices of widow burning (*suttee*) and veiling (*purdah*). Guru Ram Das (1574-81) founded the city of Amritsar in 1577 which became a rallying point for the Sikhs, and made arrangements for collection of contributions from his followers for welfare works. Guru Arjan (1581-1606) compiled the Sikh scripture and built a central place of worship for the Sikhs, known as *Harimandir* (the House of God) in the midst of the town built by his father Guru Ram Das.

By this time the Sikh religion had established itself as a distinct system of thought and a way of life. Its popularity with the masses alarmed the Hindu and Muslim orthodoxy alike. Hindus regarded it as an erosion of their cherished ideals and the Muslims thought that it had checked the growth of their proselytising activities. The succession of Jehangir to the Mogul throne helped the opponents of the Gurus. He ordered the arrest and execution of Guru Arjan on a charge of helping his rebellious son, Khusrau. Thus Gur Arjan became the first martyr of the Sikh faith.

Guru Hargobind (1606-44) succeeded Guru Arjan and a reconciliation between the Guru and the king was soon effected by mutual friends like Mian Mir, who was a Muslim Sufi saint. The Guru prepared the community to resist any interference by the government in their religion in future. He therefore embarked upon a programme of militarizing the Sikhs for which the Guru was detained for some time by the Emperor Jehangir. In the later years of his Guruship of forty years he had to fight a number of battles against the government troops. On the whole, things remained quiet for a long time; and Guru Har Rai (1644-61) and Guru Har Krishen (1661-64) concentrated on matters spiritual.

In 1669, Aurangzeb, the Emperor of India, issued orders to suppress the religious freedom of the non-Muslims including the Sikhs. Guru Tegh Bahadur (1664-75) led the people to resist. The Guru was arrested on sedition charges and beheaded in Delhi in 1675. His son, Guru Gobind Singh (1675-1708), the tenth and last Guru of the Sikhs, succeeded him. He founded the order of the *Khalsa* in 1699 (the brotherhood of saint-soldiers). This was, however, not a departure from the path of spirituality. The aim was not territorial conquest but the defence of religious freedom. Guru Gobind Singh gave a distinctive external appearance to the Sikhs, with its five sacred symbols, including the unshorn

285

hair and the turban. He died on October 7, 1708 at Nanded (south India) and a day before his death he declared that after him the Sikhs were to look upon the scriptures, the Adi Granth, or Guru Granth Sahib, as their guide and the symbolic representative of all ten Gurus.

(*N.B.* In the following pages reference to the Adi Granth is abbreviated to AG.)

Sikh Beliefs and Teachings

God

For a Sikh, belief in the existence of God is essential.

> You are clearly present in the world, O Lord,
> Because all crave for your name.
>
> AG 71

The opening statement of the morning prayer of the Sikh begins:

> The True One was in the beginning
> The True One was before all ages began
> The True One is, also
> Nanak says, the True One shall ever be.
>
> AG 1

A complete knowledge of God and his creation is impossible. 'Men, according to different understandings, have given different descriptions of thee, O Lord,' said Guru Gobind Singh. 'No one knows the state and extent of God' (AG 879); 'God alone knows how great he is,' (AG 5) said Guru Nanak. God is the creator, 'God is invisible, but he is ever visible through his nature' (AG 1042); 'God is behind creation and does not sit apart from it and is immanent in every form of life. God is hidden in every heart and every heart is illumined by the Divine Being' (AG 597). It is the function of the godly, the saints and seers, to make people aware of this latent presence of God in everything and lead them to God-consciousness. Guru Nanak and his successors were such inspired teachers of mankind. Their revelations are preserved in the Guru Granth Sahib, the Sikh scriptures which form the basis of the Sikh teaching.

The Sikh concept of God is monotheistic. This means that God is the one only supreme reality worthy of worship. 'My God is one, brethren, my God is One,' (AG 350) said Guru Nanak. This recognition of God's oneness and uniqueness has been further emphasized by such assertions that 'This alone is his merit that there is none other like him, there never was, nor will there ever be another' (AG 349) and 'no one equals him'. Such affirmations about the nature of God rule out both a belief in incarnation and the practice of idolatry.

> Burnt be the lips that utter the belief,
> God takes birth, He does not become incarnate
> And dies not.
>
> AG 1136

and

> He who thinks that a stone is God
> Worships in vain
> He who prostrates before stones
> Labours to no purpose.
>
> AG 1160

God is the creator. He is also the sustainer and the destroyer as well.

> When the Creator projected himself
> All creatures of the earth assumed various shapes
> But when you draw creation within yourself, O Lord,
> All embodied beings are absorbed by you.
>
> Guru Gobind Singh

How and when this universe came to exist is known to him alone. 'When he so willed he brought the universe into being' (AG 1036). God alone is autonomous, while all else depend on him for their continued existence and sustenance.

Prayers and petitions must be addressed to God alone:

> Whosoever cries out and begs at the Lord's door is duly heard and blessed.
>
> AG 349

and

> There is no other place to go except God
> And he is but one.
>
> AG 60

We must concur with Guru Nanak who said:

> I am convinced of one thing, that there is but one Lord of all creation, and I should not forget him.
>
> AG 2

The saints and seers have used a large number of names to describe God, according to their experience and understanding.

> Your names are countless, O Lord, I do not know their end,
> but of one thing I am sure, that there is not another like you.

AG 87

The Sikh Gurus made the practice of using most of the names of God which were then current among the Muslims, Hindus and yogic cults in their hymns. The one most favourite with Guru Nanak was *Sat Nam* – The Eternal Reality. *Waheguru* (the Wonderful Lord) is another name for God which is very popular with the Sikhs.

Man

Man, like everything else, owes his existence to the will of God:

> He sends us and we take birth
> He calls us back and we die.

AG 1239

The spirit that illumines the human soul, however, equally sustains all other beings:

> None has been created without it
> They follow the path according to their understanding
> And judged in the same way 'come and go'.

AG 24

The reason why man has been regarded as the crown of creation is perhaps that he alone among the created has the freedom to decide how to act.

> Other forms of life are subject to you (Man)
> Your rule is on this earth.

AG 374

Man consists of a body and a soul. Both are complementary to each other. The body is subject to death and decay but the soul survives till it merges with the supreme soul that is God. The soul lives on because 'God resides in the soul and the soul in turn is contained in him' (AG 1153). God and the soul of the individual are in essence one and the same. 'The drop of

289

water (soul) is in the Ocean (God) and the quality of the Ocean is in the water' (AG 878). The body is important because the soul itself lives through the body. It is therefore regarded as the 'Temple of God'.

The beautiful mansion, the body, is the Temple of God
In it He has installed His Light infinite.

AG 1256

The body as such has to be kept pure and sound by thoughts and deeds and must not be harmed by ascetic exercises and penances. It has to be cared for and properly fed for singing God's praises and serving his people.

Life is a mystery. Some people are good, some are wicked, some are rich, some are poor, some are healthy and some are crippled. If God is the father of all, and we are God's children, then why is there so much suffering and iniquity in the world of man? Sikhism attributes suffering to the law of *karma*, i.e. a man reaps what he sows. An individual is placed in a given situation, good or bad, at the time of his birth according to his past actions. This may be called his fate, or his limitation, but man is an intelligent and a moral being by nature. He has the freedom to choose between right and wrong. Predestination is responsible only for his present. He has the opportunity to mould his future if he listens to the word of God and makes a conscious effort to improve his life.

O Man, you are blessed with human birth
It is opportunity given to you to meet your Lord.

AG 378

or

O, my soul, you have emanated from the light of God
Know your true essence.

AG 1022

Good deeds and good company can help man in his spiritual improvement, otherwise he will not progress far. The law of karma operates both progressively and regressively, i.e. man, according to his actions, changes his being and surroundings. If his record is good he may be born into a good family, but if the record is bad, he may fall to the lower plane of animals or birds. This cycle of repeated birth and death can be brought to an end only by God himself. On becoming conscious of his limitations and short-comings, an awakened soul turns to

God for grace. Man can strengthen this link with God by singing his praises and with the offering of good deeds. Man can go no further:

I have come to your feet O God.
Help me to meet in the way you like.

AG 104

Death is not the end of man. It is a stage in the development of his spirituality and ultimate unity with God. At the end of a span of life conduct is adjudged in the light of man's accumulated actions and the future course is determined accordingly.

Having created mortals, God has installed in their hearts, to record their accounts, the seat of Dharma.

AG 463

With the grace of God he can be ushered into the eternal presence, or granted another round of birth to enable him to improve his conduct, if found wanting. Sikhs have no concept of spatial regions of heaven and hell. They are the conditions of life in this world. The very birth with the lower forms of life, or a life full of sufferings and miseries is regarded no less than hell. The man who is happy and prosperous is nothing short of being in heaven. The belief that this world is for action only and the next world is for retribution and requital does not stand the test of everyday experience of life.

To become God-like is the Sikh ideal of man. A life in tune with the will of God is salvation. Complete realization of man in this world is not an unfulfilled dream but a possibility worth striving for. Constant remembrance of God paves the way for his grace and salvation. To become God-orientated man has only to rid himself of self-centredness.

Engrossed in Ego we attain not the True one.
But when Ego vanishes we attain the highest state.

AG 226

A conscious effort is therefore called for diverting the mind from pursuing selfish ends towards altruistic ends. *Sewa* and *Simran* provide the necessary equilibrium to a life otherwise dominated by self-aggrandizement. According to Guru Nanak, 'Without practising virtue there can be no worship of God' (AG 64). Meditation is a means of involving God and unveiling his presence within us. 'The true one is not away

291

from us. He resides within us' (AG 421). God–consciousness leads to the realization of God.

> When God consciousness fills the heart
> One gets salvation whilst living.
>
> AG 412

But

> Rare are such men in the world whom after testing
> God has gathered unto his treasury.
>
> AG 1345

Such a man is called 'Jivan Mukht', i.e. liberated one while alive. He is a Brahm Gyani, i.e. endowed with the knowledge of God. He is no longer subject to the laws of karma. His 'coming and going' has ceased. He leads others on the path of spirituality.

> They are not subject to the law of transmigration,
> The servants of the Lord come for doing good to others.
> They infuse spiritual life, inspire devotion and
> Unite men with the Lord.
>
> AG 749

A life of contemplation is not considered incompatible with the everyday life of a householder. Physical renunciation of the world is not recommended for the attainment of spiritual enlightenment. Renunciation of evil desires is praiseworthy, but not cessation of work and abandonment of family responsibilities. True renunciation is a mental attitude of detachment from worldly possessions and association.

> By contemplating truth, light dawns.
> Then amidst sensual pleasures one remains
> detached. Such is the greatness of the True
> Guru that living with his wife and children
> one obtains salvation.
>
> AG 661

Other Important Sikh Teachings

Sikhism recognizes the potential divinity of all human beings and therefore ensures them an equal right of worship irrespective of sex and social status. 'The One Lord is the Father of all and all of us are his children' (AG 611); 'therefore,' said Guru Nanak, 'who can be called bad, who can be called good? For we see the same God within all' (AG 353). Sikhism discourages intolerance. People of all classes and creeds are welcomed to its places of worship, to the hospitality of their free kitchen, and the use of the educational and charitable institutions run by the Gurdwara committee.

Meditation of the name of God and singing his praises constitute the Sikh mode of worship. In place of elaborate rituals, pilgrimages and other practices, purity of life and service of humanity are insisted upon. Guru Nanak taught 'Truth is above everything but higher still is truthful living' (AG 62). Stress is laid on the practice of religious life and not on formalism or ritualism.

In Sikhism there is a strong denunciation of idlers, parasites and beggars. Work is no less important than worship. 'He alone has found the right way who eats what he earns through toil, and shares his earnings with the needy' – Guru Nanak (AG 1245). A Sikh is to acquire wealth and not to abjure it, but hoarding and the show of wealth is condemned. Any surplus wealth is to be used for alleviating the sufferings of the poor, and not for indulgence in luxury and intoxicants.

Sikhism advocates the middle path, between the ascetic and the epicurean – the life of a householder. All the Sikh Gurus, except the eighth, who died as a child, had normal family lives discharging their obligations as householders as well as being the spiritual mentors of their people. For the attainment of salvation or union with the Lord, retirement from domestic and social responsibilities is not recommended. A life of service and devotion in the world of human ties is preferred to the life of a recluse and a mendicant. 'One does not reach God by despising the world', Guru Arjan (AG 962).

Sikhism does not consider the use of force immoral in all circumstances, 'When all other means have failed, it is righteous to draw the sword', said Guru Gobind Singh. Peace at any price is not the slogan of the Sikhs. They will not sit back and see rape and murder of defenceless people. They believe that war can be justified, to defend freedom and oppose injustice.

The Sikh religion discourages the belief in good or bad omens, in impurity at birth and death, in the effect of the conjunction of stars or constellations and in the worship of tombs or graves.

Sikhism does not frown upon leisure. It is not an extra in life. It is a necessity, like working and praying and sleeping.

Physical recreations and hobbies, film and television watching, intellectual pursuits, can all in one way or the other enrich the human personality. However, a Sikh should be careful to see that his leisure is not anti-social. There should be no room in his leisure for such things as gambling and drinking, cheap and immoral entertainments and undesirable company.

The Role of the Guru

The term Guru in the Indian tradition is mostly used to mean a spiritual guide and instructor, but in Sikh parlance it is only applied by Sikhs to the ten Gurus – to Guru Nanak and his nine successors. In the Sikh scripture, however, the term Guru was often used by the Sikh Gurus and others in its traditional sense of a religious preceptor, as well as for God himself. The role of the Sikh Gurus, however, was a little different and distinct from the traditional Gurus, in the sense that instead of imparting knowledge of God to the people on the basis of the existing scriptures available to them, they acted as revealers of truth, that is knowledge of God. This ultimately formed the basis of Sikhism, as distinct from Hinduism, and the Sikh Gurus became its founders.

All human beings are potentially capable of the realization of God because 'God resides in the soul, and the soul in turn is contained in him' (AG 1153). A godly person , or a saint, is one who has realized this truth. The human Gurus were perfect examples of saintliness.

The enlightenment comes from God. God is therefore the Guru of all, including the ten Sikh teachers.

> Creating all, O God. Thou art the supreme Guru.
> I am devoted to Thee and bow before thy feet.
> Guru Nanak AG 1187

Such is the human predicament that, engrossed in the day to day affairs of life, a person rarely has time to think of matters spiritual.

> Man is awake, and yet he is being robbed.
> The worst of it is, that he is enjoying it.
> He is wearing the noose of worldly attachment round
> His neck and he is involving himself more and more.
> AG 1330

The souls who have realized God are called 'Gurmukhs' (God-orientated). These saints and seers show the way and guide the seekers of truth on the path of spirituality.

In the Sikh credo there is no provision for intercession, and priestly mediation. Man turns to the Guru for instruction because of his wisdom and his moral purity. The Guru provides a link between man and God. 'The Guru is the ladder, the boat, the raft, by means of which one attains to God' (AG 17). However, the disciple has to make the necessary effort to accept the love of God by following the Guru's instructions.

> The whole world enjoys the sight of the Guru.
> But none will be saved by the mere sight of him.
> One must mould one's thoughts according to the Guru's word
> Otherwise the dirt of egoism will not be removed, nor
> Will his love be fixed on God.
>
> Guru Amar Das AG 594

The human Guru and the disciple can go no further by their efforts. Salvation is achieved only by the grace of God (AG 2). When the disciple has reached the stage of bliss then no difference is left between the human Guru and the disciple. Both are equal:

> Nanak! behold this pleasure, from the Guru
> Came into being another Guru.
> The Creator caused it to be so
> The light has blended with light.
>
> Guru Amar Das AG 490

The disciple may become as enlightened as his master.

The Guru brings about the transformation of the personality of the disciple with the help of the word of God, called *bani* or *shabad*. The change is wrought by the message and the human Guru is only the vehicle. This is believed to be God's method of self-disclosure and communication with human beings. For this reason a Guru is sometimes called the voice of God. The supremacy of the word of God, therefore, has been emphasized time and again by the Sikh Gurus in their utterances.

> True Guru is the Word
> The word is the True Guru that shows the path
> Of liberation.
>
> Guru Ram Das AG 131

The word is my Guru. By fixing my attention
On it, I become its disciple.

Guru Nanak AG 943

The message is regarded not less than God himself:

The Gurbani is God himself and it is through it
That man becomes united with God.

Guru Amar Das AG 39

This emphasis on the importance of God's word led Guru
Gobind Singh to declare the Adi Granth, which is the
repository of the word of God, to be the Guru of the Sikhs
when he decided to put an end to the human institution of
guruship of which he himself was the last representative.

Sikh Worship

The Gurdwara

A Sikh place of worship is called a *gurdwara*, that is the House of the Guru and the dwelling place of God, although, of course, Sikhs believe that God is omnipresent. The Guru Granth Sahib, the Holy Scriptures of the Sikhs, is their Guru. A gurdwara is a place where the Guru Granth Sahib is installed.

The building could be a temporary hut, a room in a house, or a large palatial building dominating its surroundings, like a medieval church. The place acquires its sanctity from the presence of the Guru Granth Sahib installed therein. The siting of the building and its design are not dictated by any consideration of orientation whatsoever. In India there are several beautiful and imposing gurdwara buildings commemorating the places where the Gurus were born, stayed, preached or died. These are known as historical gurdwaras and are great centres of pilgrimage.

In Britain, however, most of the gurdwaras are ordinary dwellings adapted for the purpose, or redundant Christian places of worship. There are new purpose-built gurdwaras in Bradford, London, Coventry, Huddersfield and Nottingham. The size of the gurdwara depends on the resources of the local Sikh community.

At present there are over eighty gurdwaras in the United Kingdom. In large cities like Glasgow, London, Birmingham and Manchester there is more than one gurdwara with an impressive attendance on Sundays. Most of the gurdwaras are named after Guru Nanak and Guru Gobind Singh; some other names such as Gurdwara Singh Sabha, Ramgarhia Sikh Temple or simply the Sikh Temple are also common. The different names, however, do not mean that there are sects in Sikhism. All the gurdwaras provide the same type of facilities and religious service to the community as a whole. People attend one or the other according to their convenience and to the relative attractiveness of the service on a particular occasion.

Small or large, ordinary or distinct, a gurdwara building can be recognized from a distance by a yellow triangular flag with a Sikh symbol called a *khanda* emblazoned on it. The khanda, known by its central symbol, is made up of three parts: a *khanda* (two edged sword), a *chakar* (quoit), two *kirpans* (swords). Sikhs are saint soldiers. The symbolic representation of the weapons of war on their religious flag testifies to this dual role of the Sikh brotherhood. The flag hangs from a pole fully draped in yellow cloth and surmounted with a metal khanda at the head of the pole. The flag stands in the compound on the gurdwara or attached to one of the walls. The Sikh emblem on the flag is usually of blue. The flag post is called *Nishan Sahib*.

The doors of the gurdwaras are open to all communities and creeds. A visitor to a gurdwara, however, is required to observe a few customary rules of etiquette. He should take off his shoes and cover his head before entering the hall or the room where the Guru Granth Sahib is installed upon a specially made resting place on a raised platform, called *Manji Sahib*, under a canopy. He should not carry any cigarettes or tobacco on his person and must not be under the influence of

Shoes outside a gurdwara in India. The whole world is God's creation but as worshippers stand in God's presence, before the Guru Granth Sahib, they take off their shoes as a mark of respect.

299

drink. On approaching the Guru Granth Sahib a Sikh will kneel or prostrate himself in front of it before making an offering of money or food to be used in the Guru's service. He will not turn his back upon the book and after saluting the assembly with the words '*Wahe guruji ka khalsa, waheguruji ki fateh*' (Hail to the Khalsa of the Wonderful Lord, victory to the Wonderful Lord) in a low voice, will find a seat in the congregation. All sit crosslegged on the carpeted floor and nobody should sit with feet pointing directly towards the scriptures. Men and women worship together, although they sit separately.

The most sacred thing and the centre of attention in the gurdwara is the Guru Granth Sahib, the Sikh scriptures. It is opened and closed with great reverence. In a procession it is carried upon the head or in a *palki* (palanquin) on a decorated vehicle. A home which possesses a copy will accord it the same respect, giving it a room of its own, often an upstairs room in Britain, again emphasizing the idea of dignity. Not only is this influenced by the thought of one's devotions being disturbed by people walking and making a noise in the room above, there is also a wish to avoid the possibility of someone walking over the place where the sacred book is

The granthi *waves a* chauri *over the Guru Granth Sahib as a gesture of respect.*

300

installed. At the time of worship, a trained reader called the *granthi* sits behind the Guru Granth Sahib with a *chauri* in his hand. (This is made of nylon or yak hairs embedded in a wooden or silver holder, though sometimes a bunch of peacock feathers is used.) This is a symbol of royalty. Every now and then the granthi waves the chauri over the Guru Granth Sahib. The Sikhs accord the scriptures precisely the position once enjoyed by the living Gurus. Upon leaving the room they will press the palms of their hands together and bow towards the scriptures. There are no altars or statues inside the holy precinct and the use of the term 'temple' which is often used to describe a Sikh place of worship, therefore seems to be highly inappropriate. It is really a place of congregational worship.

Attached to the gurdwara is a free kitchen (*Guru ka langar*). The institution of the langar is as old as the faith itself. People partake of a meal sitting together in rows, irrespective of their creed or status. It helps in the promotion of equality, brotherhood and social integration. It is no less a practical example of the Sikh ideal of *wand chakna*, sharing one's earnings with others. People contribute in cash and in kind for its efficient functioning as liberally as they do for other religious works.

In most of the gurdwaras facilities are also made available for the lodging of pilgrims, travellers, or the needy for a short stay.

The gurdwara buildings in many cases now house literacy classes for the instruction of the young in the faith and language of the Guru Granth Sahib. There is no adequate provisions in British schools for the teaching of Gurmukhi, in which the Sikh scriptures are written and worship is offered. The necessity and importance of this work therefore can never be over-emphasized if the Sikhs are to preserve their identity and culture.

For the Sikh community a gurdwara is a socio-political institution as well as a place of worship. Arrangements for the solemnization of social ceremonies such as birth, death and marriage are made by the managing committee for the benefit and convenience of the community as a matter of course. Catering facilities for private cooking are made available to them and the necessary household utensils and crockery are also provided for serving meals to the guests.

It provides a forum for the discussion of social and political problems affecting the community, and a clearing house for the dissemination of information which could be taken advantage of by the community as a whole.

In the absence of suitable entertainments at home, or outside, elderly Sikhs, both men and women may feel lonely and bored. Gurdwaras provide a social environment for them where communication is no problem.

A gurdwara is the only convenient place of meeting for the Sikhs and provides an important link between them and other communities. The initial contacts with the Sikhs by the host community invariably take place through the members of their managing committees. Sikhs never hesitate to play their role in activities arranged by the organizations set up to deal with a particular problem, racial, religious or political. Sometimes a day is fixed for the public to visit the local gurdwara. Talks are arranged and literature on Sikhism and the Sikh way of life is distributed among the visitors.

Gurdwaras are thus multi-purpose institutions. They not only impart spiritual instructions but also feed the hungry, lodge travellers, educate the young, shelter the destitute and even provide a meeting place for social contacts.

Gurdwaras are managed by committees appointed by their congregations. Sometimes there are formal elections but often men and women are informally invited to serve the congregation. In the Punjab the historical gurdwaras (those associated with the human Gurus) are managed by a central organization, the Shromani Gurdwara Parbandhak Committee.

Private Meditation and Public Worship

A Sikh is expected to rise early in the morning and after taking a bath, if possible, or the necessary ablution, to meditate on the name of God:

> After taking a bath, meditate on your Lord and your body and mind become pure.
>
> AG 611

> In the ambrosial hours of the dawn repeat the true name and meditate on His greatness.
>
> AG 2

Most Sikhs know *Japji* (the morning prayer) by heart. They will recite it while getting ready for work before breakfast. Some will read it from a *gutka* (a booklet of daily prayers), sitting on a sofa, or crosslegged on the carpet. Women will hum it while preparing the meal or doing the household chores. Many families will listen to it recorded on cassettes. Children are taught to say *Waheguru, waheguru* (Wonderful Lord) – a few times to start with. The rosary or mala is popular with the older generation. It is usually made of wool with 108 knots tied in it. They will go on repeating the popular chant *Sat nam waheguru* (The True Name and Wonderful Lord) for quite sometime. Women will recite the *Sukhmani* (a popular composition of Guru Arjan) during the day, or read the scriptures. There are set prayers also for the evening and bed time.

In the highly industrialized western society, with its shift systems and untimely working hours, keeping to the Indian ideals of early rising and meditation seems to be difficult. A Sikh is, however, free to say his prayers at any time of the day when the opportunity presents itself.

Sikhism is not merely a faith, it is also a community of followers, a brotherhood. Prayers to God can be offered at any time and at any place but they must also be offered in public, in association with other members of the community.

> The highest and the most beneficial deed is the Lord's praise in the holy congregation.
>
> AG 642

> Holy congregation is the school of the True Guru.
> There we learn to love God and appreciate His greatness.
>
> AG 1316

Congregational worship is therefore, an obligation for a Sikh and a gurdwara is a symbol of collective unity. Arrangements for the daily morning and evening services exist in most gurdwaras. The services open with a random reading from the scripture and are followed by set prayers designed to be recited at the morning and evening services respectively. The weekday services, on the whole, are short and thinly attended except when a touring party of *Ragis* (singers of sacred hymns), or a speaker, is available to address the congregation.

Sunday is the day when most Sikhs will take their families to the gurdwara. At daybreak the service will start with readings from the scriptures. As soon as a party of Ragis arrives, the singing of *kirtan* (devotional songs) will start. It may continue for an hour or much longer.

A large part of the Sikh scriptures is in poetry which has

been set to music, and the singing of these verses (called *shabads*) to the accompaniment of musical instruments is the main feature of the Sikh congregational worship. Shabads are sung in slow and sustained tones to create a feeling of serenity. The words are pronounced clearly and correctly without musical embroidery so that the display of virtuosity is restrained. What is important is the message; poetry and music are brought in only to enhance its emotional appeal, and not to the extent that people should start dancing or swinging their heads. Outbursts of such emotional fervour are decried in strong terms. Appreciation at the end of the performance is shown not by clapping hands but by a full-throated shout of *Sat Sri Akal* (Timeless God is True) by the congregation, if invited by the Sikh presiding over the function, with his solitary shout of *Bale so Nihal* (whoever shouts shall be happy).

Kirtan is followed by lectures and speeches. If a speaker is available he will be requested to give a discourse on *Gurmat* (Sikh theology) or to talk about some other matter of concern to the community. Time has to be allocated for the performance of a marriage ceremony, which takes about an hour. Appeals for collection of funds for charitable purposes could be addressed to the worshippers by the management. The service will close with the recitation of *Ardas* (the formal prayer of the Sikhs which is said standing) and distribution of *karah prashad*. This is a cooked mixture of flour or semolina, sugar, water and *ghee* (clarified butter). The purpose of this sharing of food is symbolic. No one must leave the Guru's presence hungry, and by eating together the worshippers show that they are one united family of equals.

The Scriptures

The Guru Granth Sahib

The *Guru Granth Sahib* is the scripture of the Sikh faith. Collections of the teachings of the Sikh Gurus had been in circulation for over a century, for the guidance of the Sikh communities scattered over the Punjab and beyond. Guru Arjan, the fourth in succession to Guru Nanak the founder of the faith, felt the need of a central collection which he compiled in 1604. The collection also included and sanctified selections from the writings of some prominent non-Sikh saints of medieval India; Hindus like Namdev and Ravidas, and Muslims like Kabir, Sheikh Farid and Bhikhan. The purpose of the inclusion of their token contribution to an enormous volume of 1,430 pages was to show that truth is not the monopoly of any one religion, that it is approachable by diverse paths and the grace of God is available to all who love God. This historical document exists and can be seen in the Gurdwara Shish Mahal at Kartarpur, India. It is known as the *Adi Granth*. A revision was commissioned by Guru Gobind Singh, the tenth and last Sikh Guru, who added hymns of his father, Guru Tegh Bahadur to the existing sacred material. The compositions of Guru Gobind Singh were collected by Bhai Mani Singh, his disciple, in a separate volume called the *Dasam Granth* – the book of the tenth Master, some years after the Guru's death. Guru Gobind Singh did not nominate any human being to succeed him as Guru. Instead a few days before his death in 1708 he bestowed the status of Guru on the scripture and since then the Sikh scripture, the Adi Granth, has been called the *Guru Granth Sahib*. *Granth* comes from the Sanskrit meaning a collection; *sahib* means lord or master and represents the Sikh mode of expressing respect and veneration.

The Granth opens with Sikh creed, known as the *Mool Mantra* – the basis of the Sikh belief. Freely translated it reads:

> There is but one God. Truth by name, the creator, all pervading spirit, without fear, without enmity. Whose

existence is unaffected by time, who does not take birth, self existent, who is to be realised through his grace.

Most of the hymns of the Granth are concerned with the recitation and enlargement of these divine attributes. These hymns of devotion are arranged according to the Indian musical pattern, and as such it is not possible to pinpoint the doctrinal statements in logical sequence. Certain ideas emerge as dominant by virtue of repetition and can be tabulated under various headings to form the principles of the Sikh faith.

1. It advocates the worship of one God, family life, and equality of human beings.
2. It rejects image worship, physical renunciation of the world, and beliefs in omens and miracles.
3. It discourages formalism, bigotry and monasticism in religion, and condemns the use of beer, spirits, wine and drugs.
4. It accepts the theory of karma and transmigration of the soul along with a belief in the grace of God.
5. It also provides insights into the religious, political and social conditions prevailing in India during the Middle Ages. Any reference to the events relating to the private or public lives of the Gurus, however, is conspicuous by its absence. The Granth is a collection of devotional hymns with almost no narrative material.

The Guru Granth Sahib is of central and paramount importance in the life of a Sikh. No ceremony, religious or secular, is complete without it. It is the focal point of worship in the gurdwara or elsewhere. Its complete reading is undertaken on the eve of the Sikh festivals, before the marriage and after the death of a Sikh. In its presence they are named, initiated and married. On moving to a new house, or on the opening of a new business premises, it is taken there and a few passages are read from it before invoking the blessings of God for the success of the business, or the happiness of the family. Though great reverence is shown to the Guru Granth Sahib by Sikhs, it should not be concluded or asserted that Sikhs worship the book. They worship God alone and nothing else. The book is the basis and not the object of worship; its true worth lies in its teachings, not in its physical form or presence.

Dasam Granth

The second sacred book of the Sikhs is the *Dasam Granth* – the book of the tenth master. It was issued in 1734 in the name of Guru Gobind Singh by Bhai Mani Singh, one of his close disciples. Sikh scholars are not unanimous in attributing the whole of it to Guru Gobind Singh, but no attempt has ever been made to sift the compositions and to produce an authorized version of the Dasam Granth. In volume and size it is as big as the Guru Granth Sahib itself, but it differs from it both in content and approach. The collection consists of a number of books as various in subject matter as in length. It includes *Jap Sahib* (meditation), *Akal Ustat* (the praise of the Lord) and *Shabad Hazare* (priceless hymns). Weapons are glorified, with the object of inculcating the spirit of bravery and heroism among the Sikhs, in *Shastar Nama* (inventory of arms). Other sections are mainly autobiographical and historical, in which the Guru states his mission of reformation and tells of battles with the hill Rajas and imperial forces. *Swayyas* (the praise of the Immortal One) deals with the condemnation of idolatry, rituals and the ephemeral character of worldly things. Mythological tales translated from *Mahabharata* (a Hindu scripture) form the basis of *Gan Probodh* (Dawn of Light). *Triya Charitr* (Wiles of Women) recounts the antics and gimmicks which women are capable of employing. The 404 stories, which cover almost half the collection are designed to warn men against indulging in sensual pleasures.

Not many gurdwaras possess a copy of the Dasam Granth. It is mostly kept in the libraries and scholars keep it for reference. The portions such as the *Jap Sahib, Akal Ustat, Bachitar Natak, Swayyas* and *Zafar Nama* – the authenticity of which is universally accepted – are printed extensively in Sikh anthologies and separately as well. They comprise only about 160 pages of the printed volume which is 1,428 pages long.

The language used in it is mainly Hindi; the *Zafar Nama* however is in Persian, the *Chandi Di War* in Punjabi; but the medium employed throughout is the Gurmukhi script (the written form of Punjabi) in which the Guru Granth Sahib is written. The twofold purpose of uplifting the people spiritually and raising their morale appears to have been the Guru's aim. The book is a store house of Indian mythology and folklore of great literary and poetic merit.

Next to the two Granths in importance come the works of

307

Bhai Gurdas and Bhai Nand Lal. Their writings are approved for recitation in the gurdwaras. Bhai Gurdas (1543-1630) assisted the fifth Guru, Arjan, in the compilation of the Adi Granth. His poems, *Varan* and *Kabit Swayyas* are interpretative and expository in nature. Sikh teachings have been explained in verse form with imagery borrowed from everyday life.

Bhai Nand Lal (1633-1713) was the court poet of Guru Gobind Singh. He wrote mainly in Persian. His poems *Zindgi Nama* and *Ghazaliat* are very popular and are printed in Gurmukhi script. Love of God and devotion to the Guru are the two themes which captured his imagination most.

The Sikh Way of Life

Hindu Influence

The Sikh way of life in India is largely influenced by the prevailing Indian culture with its leaning towards the Hindu customs and conventions. The Sikh faith originated and developed within Hinduism. It parts company and represents an alternative outlook only in places due to the preachings and practices of the Sikh Gurus who tried to wean the Sikhs away from the Hindu fold. However, their approach was basically spiritual and the Hindus who accepted Sikh teaching never thought that they were changing one faith for another. Converts seldom enter Sikhism from Islam and Christianity. Hindus and Sikhs on the other hand are very close in faith and have a common personal law. They have what is termed *Roti Beti di Sanjh*; that is they eat together and intermarry. In many families only a few members become Sikhs while a majority of others stay Hindu in the orthodox way, and in the case of marriage, caste is a more important factor than religion in so far as Hindu-Sikh relationships are concerned. They freely participate in each other's festivities and Hindu religious practices have influenced the Sikh mode of worship as well. Hindu laws of marriage and divorce, adoption and succession are applicable to the Sikhs. The impact of Hindu culture is so dominant over the Sikhs that their leaders have constantly feared their eventual reabsorption in Hinduism. The likelihood of this happening has receded considerably in recent years with the world-wide dispersion of the Sikhs and the emergence of a strong Sikh sense of identity.

The Sikh Gurus and the Caste System

Hindus constitute about 84% of the total population of India, whereas the Sikh total is just under 2%. The most characteristic feature of Hinduism is the concept of *varan-ashrama-dharma*. Broadly speaking it implies that there is a *dharma*, or way of life, appropriate to each class and to each stage in the life of an individual. It gave rise to the emergence of four distinct groups, Brahmins, Kshatriyas, Vaishyas and Shudras, each with its separate duties and distinctive way of life. In the course of time the division became rigid and hierarchical with Brahmins at the top, followed by Kshatriyas and Vaishyas and, at the bottom, the Shudras. This fourfold division with its sub-divisions and sub-sects is known as the caste system. It has been criticized in the past and there are many people who would like to see it end. The caste system is regarded by Sikhs as an instrument of oppression, creating intolerance, perpetuating inequality and developing the spirit of exclusiveness.

The Sikh Gurus were not out to demolish the edifice of this age-old social structure which had served well in the past though changed circumstances and situations have rendered it inefficient and effete. It simply runs counter to the Sikh religious ideology and social approach based on the father-hood of God and the brotherhood of man.

> The Hindu says there are four castes, but they are all of one seed – God. It is like clay of which pots are made, in diverse shapes and forms yet the clay is the same. So are the bodies of men, made of five elements, how can one amongst them be high and another low.
>
> AG 1128

As such, there seems to be no justification for a continuous discrimination against some social groups, dubbed as low-castes and untouchables, on the basis of birth and profession. 'Only those who forget God are low-caste,' said Guru Nanak (AG 10). The Sikh institutions of *Sangat* (congregational worship) and *Pangat* (sitting of all people together for community dining) have gone a long way to enable people to shed belief in inherent and irremovable inferiority and superiority advocated by the caste system.

The Sikh Gurus reacted against caste by including in the Guru Granth Sahib, the hymns of *Namdev* (a washerman) and *Ravidas* (a cobbler) who are regarded as Shudras, or low caste, by the caste-conscious Hindus.

> My message is common for all the four Vanas, Brahman, Khatria, Vaishya and Sudra. In this age all who meditate on the name of God, who pervade all the vessels, will be saved.
>
> Guru Arjan AG 747

Sikh places of worship are open to men of all castes and creeds in contradistinction to the ancient Hindu traditions, which India declared to be illegal in 1951 when its constitution opened all temples to everyone.

The Sikh Gurus never objected to the division of society on the basis of work like the medieval guild system, which arranged the necessary training for its members and encouraged specialization of skills, but they were not in favour of tying down a person permanently to an occupation against his will and aptitude. If a Brahmin cannot subsist by teaching religion, or a Kshatriya has to give up the pursuit of arms, the religion should not stand in their way of taking up the profession of agriculture and tilling the soil themselves instead of depending on the hired labours of Vaishyas and Shudras. A Shudra or Vaishya should not be barred from taking up military service or religious preachings. A Sikh does not hesitate to put his hand to any type of work. Labour is as noble as holding a pen or preaching. 'Every work is noble if performed in the right way' said Guru Amar Das, the third Guru of the Sikhs (AG 568). The Sikhs have proved themselves to be industrious farmers and soldiers, good mechanics and craftsmen. In the gurdwaras you can see men and women, whatever their social status, cleaning cooking utensils, preparing food, or helping repair and decorate the building, as well as keeping it tidy.

Sikhs, however, are sometimes rightly accused of observing caste restrictions in the matters of matrimony. A *jat* will marry a *jat* and a *khatri* will marry a *khatri*. One reason for this is that Sikhs have no personal law of their own. They are covered by the laws made for the Hindus. Each Act of Parliament made for the Hindu community is automatically made applicable to Sikhs, Jains and Buddhists. It was as late as 1909 when the Sikhs were legally allowed to perform marriages without the ministrations of a Brahmin priest and use of Vedic mantras, though the Sikhs had been solemnizing marriages according to regulations legalized by the Anand Marriage Ceremony long before this without much governmental interference. There were cases where caste barriers had also been broken both by Hindus and Sikhs and such marriages were validated by the Hindu Marriage Validity Act 1949. With the passing of the Hindu Marriage Act 1955, the restrictions of caste have been removed and the last block to the Sikh way of life has been cleared, but habits take time to change.

The Role of Women

Socializing with the opposite sex is not customary. Women go to receptions and public meetings with their husbands rather reluctantly as they may feel embarrassed sitting among a mixed audience. They always look for seats reserved for women or huddle together at a public function. Husbands and wives are not supposed to show concern, or feelings of tenderness for one another in public or in the presence of other members of the family, even at home. The woman who walks a few steps behind her husband and takes a meal when the male members of the family and the children have been served is nevertheless supreme in the domain of the household. She is the custodian of the family purse and no decision affecting her sphere of activity can be made without her approval.

Within this male dominated society a Sikh woman has a good measure of protection and independence. She is not regarded as evil, unclean or undesirable:

> It is from woman 'the condemned one', that we are conceived and born. Woman is our life-long friend and keeps the race going.
>
> Why should we revile her who gives birth to great men?
> Guru Nanak AG 473

Guru Nanak exalted the status of women by idealizing the love of a wife for her husband, and holding it up as an example for a devotee of God.

> My beloved Lord is not distant. When my soul was reconciled to the word of the Guru I found God the prop of my life. In this way the bride met God the Bridegroom and became his beloved.
>
> AG 1197

Woman is considered to be indispensable for man's spiritual growth and morality, for the Sikh finds God through married life. For both men and women the rules of conduct and religious duties are identical. Women enjoy equal status with men, unlike their Hindu sisters, who are forbidden to read scriptures. The segregation of sexes while at worship in the Gurdwara is the normal practice, the women, however, are not in *purdah* (veiled) and not relegated to the gallery or made to sit behind a screen. They recite the scriptures, sing the hymns and sometimes lead the congregation in prayer.

Guru Amar Das, the third Guru of the Sikhs, appointed women to act as preachers alongside men.

It is in the social sphere, however, that not much progress has been made. The birth of a daughter in the family is not regarded as a tragedy but is certainly not greeted with the rejoicing and exchange of presents among relations and friends which occurs in the case of a son. The boys have more freedom as they grow older but teenage girls are not allowed to go out unchaperoned. They are not supposed to talk to people who are not related to them. After marriage their fidelity to their husbands should be complete.

A girl has always been considered to be a liability to her parents. Her marriage was an expensive necessity. The social customs did not allow her to go outside the home and she could not earn her keep. In the Middle Ages many Indian parents killed girls at birth. The Sikh Gurus condemned this inhuman practice and forbade Sikhs to have social contact with people who indulged in it. There had always been a shortage of women in the Punjab and many men therefore remained unmarried throughout their life, which gave rise to trafficking in women. The Sikh codes of conduct advised Sikhs not to accept money in return for the hand of a girl. They should only marry their daughters to worthy husbands.

Child marriage is also prohibited in Sikhism. The parents are asked to arrange the marriage only when the boys and girls have matured enough to understand the spiritual significance of a marriage, and the male members should be able to earn enough money to maintain the household:

> When a girl can embroider and stitch her clothes. Only then she should be considered a woman. Ability to manage the household and good conduct endears her to her husband.

> AG 1171

With the emergence of Sikhism the remarriage of widows was also encouraged. The Sikh Gurus issued strong injunctions against *suttee*(the burning of widows with the corpses of their husbands to earn merit after death). In Sikh homes a widow is respected and well looked after.

Looking to the recent past it may be argued that Guru Nanak and his successors, although they spoke boldly in their time against female infanticide, child marriage and immolation of the widows with the deceased husbands, yet they could not completely eradicate these unethical practices

313

without the help of legal sanctions till late in the 19th century. Widow remarriage is definitely popular among the Sikhs but in most cases the service is conducted in a simpler form with less ceremony.

Those widows who did not want to marry again had been allowed only a limited right in the property of their deceased husbands. But there is no denying the fact that Sikhism paved the way for others to work for the emancipation of women and provided the Parliament of India with a moral support to enact laws for the improvement of the social status of women as a whole.

Food

Many religions provide guidelines to their followers regarding the taking of certain foods and the avoidance of others. The choice of food is affected mainly by moral and spiritual considerations, but restrictions are sometimes influenced by temporary conditions, although custom can continue the restriction even when circumstances change. The choice is also dictated by what foods are available in a particular region.

The Punjab, the homeland of the Sikhs, has a surplus in the production of grain, such as wheat, maize and rice, Fresh fruit and vegetables are in abundance. A large variety of pulses are grown by the Punjabi farmers and there is plenty of milk. Naturally, the Sikh diet consists of cereals, fresh vegetables and milk products. The Sikhs do eat meat, but only occasionally, and mostly on ceremonial occasions like weddings and feasts. Meat is not easy to obtain in the countryside where a vast majority of the Sikh population is scattered in villages. Those animals which are kept are raised to supply milk, or to work. The way meat is cooked is also expensive and as such it is only a rare treat for the poor.

To the question whether a Sikh is permitted meat or not, the answer is twofold, i.e. those who eat meat are as good Sikhs as those who abstain from it. Guru Nanak referred to the ancient and current practices in this respect by saying: At Yajnas, marriages and on festive occasions meat is accepted (AG 1290). 'Only fools wrangle about eating or not eating meat' (AG 1289). 'Which food is sinful, the animal food or the vegetable food? (AG 1289). 'The food which causes pain to the body and breeds evil in the mind is baneful' (AG 16). Thus the matter of choice has been left to the discretion of the individual concerned.

Most of the Sikh holy men do not eat meat at all, and they advise others not to. Meat is never cooked in the langar (the free kitchen attached to the gurdwara) and no visitor is embarrassed in consequence. Those who eat meat are, however, commanded not to take *Halal* meat, that is meat cut in accordance with the Muslim religious rites. Sikhism was developed during the Mogul rule in India and Halal meat was used for effecting conversions to Islam. The Hindu method of cutting the neck of the animal with one stroke was banned by the Mogul Emperor Aurangzeb (1681-1707). Guru Gobind Singh (1675-1708) forbade Sikhs to use Halal meat as a protest against this discriminatory treatment against non-Muslims by the State.

A good deal of change is noticed in the dietary habits of the Sikhs in the United Kingdom. Bread, beans and eggs are eaten for breakfast and children like cornflakes and milk. School dinners contain a good portion of meat, with potatoes and peas. Children and young people like fish and chips. Punjabi-type meals are served only in the evenings and at weekends. Meat is used quite often as it is cheaper to buy than the imported Indian vegetables from Indian grocers.

In the gurdwara kitchen there is work for all as they prepare langar, the communal meal. Note the top-knot usually worn by boys until they adopt the turban.

Sikhism does not regard fasting as an act of spirituality: 'Through fasting and penance the soul is softened not' (AG 905). Complete or partial abstinence from food on a particular day of the week or month does not bring the soul nearer to God. It is rather the practice of *Nam-Simran* (God-remembrance) and *Sewa* (selfless service) that accumulates religious merits.

Alcohol and tobacco

In Sikhism there is a strong taboo on the drinking of alcoholic beverages, but the religious injunction against alcohol does not appear to have been heeded by most Sikhs. In the Punjab and the United Kingdom as well, they are found running off-licence shops, public houses and clubs. The widespread use of liquor by the Sikhs on the festive occasions of weddings and birthday parties, together with pub-going, has naturally given rise to the belief among non-Sikhs that Sikhism does not forbid the use of wines and spirits. However, the teaching of the Gurus was that:

> By drinking wine one loses sanity and becomes mad.
> Loses the power of discrimination and incurs the
> Displeasure of God.

> AG 554

The use of drugs and intoxicants of all kinds has, therefore, been condemned outright. The people are advised to avoid these physically harmful and mentally disturbing narcotics and stimulants at all costs, and instead to drink the nectar of God remembrance (AG 399) for the welfare of the soul and society.

The use of tobacco in its various forms, i.e. smoking, chewing and taking snuff is also forbidden to Sikhs. Its harmful effects are too well-known to be discussed here. The strict observance of this religious injunction by the Sikhs has earned the appreciation of all those concerned with anti-smoking campaigns. The ninth Guru, in common with some of the Mogul emperors, regarded this new drug as an encouragement to laziness. Its use was discouraged and finally the tenth Guru prohibited Sikhs from using it. He declared it to be an act of abandonment of religious faith.

Dress

The most distinguishing and eye-catching feature of the dress of a Sikh man is his turban, which is an essential part of his religious and cultural identity.It could be of any colour and style. Less conspicuous, however, are the *kachha* – the under drawers, which both men and women are required to wear by religious command. These signify moral purity and the design provides a befitting and decent covering for the lower parts of the body. Apart from this, the Sikhs enjoy a considerable freedom of choice in the matter of clothes they would like to wear. In the hot climate of the Punjabi countryside, and elsewhere, the working men have preference for pyjamas with a loosely hanging shirt, while in the cities western-style clothes are very popular, especially with the educated class.

A tunic dress and trousers, with a *dupatta* over the head, is the most common form of wear of a Sikh woman; English-style dresses are preferred by the young. Sikh parents do not object to their teenage girls wearing school uniform skirts. The sari, with a short blouse which is hardly more than a covering for the brassière, is becoming increasingly popular with young housewives. Young girls who opt for western trouser suits and jeans have dispensed with the dupatta altogether. Even elderly ladies have been found to throw back the dupatta over one shoulder instead of using it as a head

One of the high points in a Sikh boy's life is the day when he begins to wear the turban. It is often accompanied by a family ceremony.

317

covering to denote modesty. Though Sikhs do not insist that women should not wear tight clothes, they nevertheless require that their womenfolk should dress modestly and keep to the tradition. They view the current trend of tight-fitting clothes as a clear infringement of the injunction which warns against 'wearing clothes which cause pain to the body or breed evil thoughts' (AG 16).

Speakers in the gurdwaras can sometimes be heard reprimanding people who come to the services in unduly showy clothes which invite too much attention and distract worshippers from the service.

Social Concern

Social service is another important aspect of the life of a Sikh.

> A place in God's court can only be attained if we do service to others in the world.
>
> AG 26

It may take the form of reading scriptures for the spiritual comfort of others, of physically tending the sick and disabled, of helping to meet the material needs of the poor and indigent. These activities are positive steps towards the realization of human brotherhood. Community service is centred on the gurdwara which is the property of the Sikh community as a whole and the amount of social service depends on the resources available to the gurdwara committee. In Sikh parlance this voluntary social work is called *sewa*.

As far as wider social work is concerned, the building of orphanages or hospitals, for example, the concept and the need is fairly new in India. Traditionally, the family has provided for those in need, its orphans, its sick. However, Sikhs are now responding to a changing world in which families can no longer meet every need as costs rise and medical care becomes more technical and complex. Sikhs are beginning to build hospitals and similar welfare establishments in Indian cities.

Birth and Childhood

The married state is highly commended by Sikhs in the interest of society and civilized behaviour. If a couple is blessed with children, well and good, otherwise they should resign themselves to the will of God. Family ties, however, do not help man on the path of spirituality and salvation, said Guru Nanak. Only the actions of the individual in this world decide for or against his or her salvation.

> The wife, son, father and brothers, no one shall hold my hand. At last when I shall fall and the time of last prayer shall come, there shall be none to rescue me.
>
> AG 721

Rituals performed on behalf of others, for example one's ancestors, are considered ineffective.

A pregnant woman is well looked after and proper arrangements for the delivery of the child are made at home, or in a hospital. Apart from this no pre-natal ceremony of any kind whatsoever is called for. Sometimes after the birth of the child they are both taken to the gurdwara for thanksgiving and naming the child.

It is not obligatory in India to give a name to the child within six weeks of his or her birth. The date of the birth, with the sex of the child and father's name, are considered sufficient for the purpose of registration of birth. The child is called by a 'pet name' till then, which the family may continue to use throughout his or her life. When a day for naming the child is fixed the family gathers in front of the Guru Granth Sahib in their home or in the gurdwara. After prayer the Guru Granth is opened at random and a lesson is read. The first letter of the first word of the hymn which is read forms the initial letter of the name to be proposed for the child. Suppose the letter is 'G', the name could be Gurmukh (God-oriented) and the word 'Singh' is added to it in the case of a boy and 'Kaur' if the child is female. The names Gurmukh Singh or Gurmukh Kaur are announced to the congregation. A *romalla* (an embroidered silk cloth) is offered for the Guru Granth Sahib and after *Ardas,* the prayer for grace, *karah prashad* is distributed to the congregation. In the United Kingdom and elsewhere the ceremony usually forms a part of the regular weekly worship in the gurdwara and the parents are thus spared the trouble of making any special arrangements for it.

It is incumbent upon the parents and the community as a whole to bring up the children according to the discipline of the faith. The hair of the child should not be cut and the boys should be encouraged to wear a turban as soon as they can tie one. A *kara* (steel wrist band) is provided at the time of the naming ceremony, or soon after. The children should be

319

taught to read and write Gurmukhi if there is no provision for the teaching of the language at school. They should be taken to the gurdwara as often as possible and provided with religious teachings. Habits of saying or listening to prayers should be inculcated. Most of the Sikh parents in the Punjab and Delhi prefer to send their children to Sikh schools, where adequate facilities for the teaching of the language and the faith are available. At the age of 16 or so when they can shoulder religious responsibilities they should be prepared for the initiation ceremony, called *Amrit Pahul*. Initiation, in fact, marks the culmination of the teachings so far received and practised. A solemn pledge is made to correct deviations, if any, in their observance.

Initiation (Amrit Pahul)

Whenever and wherever there are candidates for initiation the ceremony can be arranged. It begins with the installation of the Guru Granth Sahib in the gurdwara, or in an enclosure with no access to the people who are not directly involved in the ceremonial. The candidates and five good Sikhs called the *Panj Pyaras* and a Granthi form the congregation. All the participants take a full bath and equip themselves with the five Ks before joining in. A steel bowl, the two-edged sword (*khanda*), water and some sugar pellets are kept at hand for the preparation of the *amrit* (ceremonial nectar). Karah prashad is also brought in and is distributed at the close of the ceremony. When everything is made ready, all stand facing the Guru Granth Sahib. One of the Panj Pyares then explains the Sikh principles and beliefs to the initiates. On obtaining their consent he recites the Ardas to seek the grace of God, and this is followed by the reading of a lesson from the Guru Granth Sahib by the Granthi.

The actual process of the preparation of amrit then begins. Water is poured into the bowl and sugar pellets are added to it. The Panj Pyaras hold the bowl jointly and recite the five prescribed scriptural compositions, one each in turn, while stirring the water with the double-edged sword. When the recitations are over, the amrit is ready. A prayer of thanksgiving is offered. The candidates are asked to come forward one by one to receive the amrit in their cupped hands, drink it, and say '*Wahe guru ji ka khalsa. Wahe guru ji ki feteh*' (The khalsa is dedicated to God. Victory ever is of the Almighty God). It is repeated five times, five times the amrit is sprinkled on their eyes and hair. If some amrit is left in the bowl, they are asked to drink from it in turn. The Sikh creed (Mool Mantra) is repeated five times and the initiates are reminded once again to abide by the Sikh code of conduct. With the sharing of *karah prashad* (ceremonial sweetmeat) by the assembly the ceremony is concluded. This is also the procedure used for making converts.

Amrit initiation, which Sikhs may take at any age (but not as a young child), is not regarded as a sacrament. It is an act voluntarily undertaken by a Sikh who wishes to identify himself with the community formed by the tenth Guru in 1699. Reinitiation is permitted if a woman or man who has broken the vows (by cutting the hair, eating Halal meat, smoking, or committing adultery) but only if it is clear that the applicant's penitence is sincere.

The Five Ks

These are the five symbols of the Sikh faith which in Punjabi begin with the letter 'K'. They are:
Kesh – the uncut hair and beard
Kangha – comb
Kara – steel wrist band
Kaccha – short trousers
Kirpan – sword.

An observant Sikh man or woman is careful to wear all these. The first two represent the householder (*grhastha*) way of life, the second two, moral restraint and sexual continence, and the last symbolizes readiness to fight in the defence of the faith, of truth and of oppressed people.

Marriage

A chance encounter at a dance, or a momentary acquaintance while travelling on a train, between a young boy and a girl is not the starting point of an Indian marriage. The parents of the girl will look for a suitable boy in the community. They may have recourse to public advertisement, or seek assistance from a marriage bureau. The final selection is the result of a hard-headed process of discussion between parents and relatives of the prospective partners. Social status, financial prospects and the backgrounds of families concerned are subjected to close scrutiny. The age, health, complexion and accomplishments of the marriage partners are also considered.

321

All the broad factors, religious and cultural, supposed to be conducive to the stability of a happy married life are taken into consideration before joining the hands of the couple in the sacred marriage ceremony called *Anand Karaj* (the ceremony of bliss). In most cases the decision taken by the parents, after the necessary consultations, of course, is welcomed by the couple. If otherwise, an opportunity is provided to enable them to meet and talk, under the watchful eyes of the close relations, to say yes or no to the proposal. The Sikh community is extremely alarmed by the increasing popularity of mixed or inter-religious marriages. A Sikh girl who 'marries out' causes great distress to the family and the community as a whole. She is virtually cast off for bringing shame on the family. A Sikh boy who brings in a wife from the folds traditionally barred by the community also gives rise to disapproval. The bride is tolerated if she undergoes conversion, and is respected if she agrees to abide by the social and cultural norms of their communal behaviour.

No two persons are alike. There are differences of taste and temper, ideals and interests, owing to the circumstances in which an individual is brought up. The marriage partners are relatively strange to each other at first so have to make every effort to reconcile their differences by subordinating private interests and inclinations for the sake of stability and growth of love in the marital bond. The perfect relationship is not found, it has to be created. Relations and friends are there to advise and assist the newly weds. Marriage is not the union of only two individuals: husband and wife are a link between the two families. It is therefore the loving concern of the families to see the couple happy and well settled.

In spite of the general climate of moral laxity and the social mixing of sexes in schools and colleges, in factories and offices, chastity is demanded of women, though custom does not demand the same strict continence from men. Virginity is a virtue and a badge of respectability for a bride. Her words, looks, deportment and dress are all important. A slight suspicion about these essentials will jeopardise her chances of finding a good husband. Youthful love affairs are very much the exception in the Sikh community. The Sikh Gurus refused to countenance the commonly held view which overlooked moral lapses in men. They condemned such conduct:

Do not cast your eyes on the beauty of another's wife.

AG 274

322

The man of lust is satisfied not with any number of women, and breaks into other homes, He sins and then regrets, so he withers away by sorrow.

AG 672

The modern trend by young couples of living together without marriage for as long as they like one another and then quietly separating, has no place in Sikhism. It is the very negation of the idea of the indissolubility of marriage and is an easy passport to promiscuity.

They are not husband and wife
Who only live together
Rather they are husband and wife
Who have one spirit in two bodies.

AG 788

For a Sikh, marriage is not a social contract to be dissolved at will but a religious bond in which a man and a woman are tied together permanently for physical, social and spiritual purposes in the presence of the scriptures – the Guru Granth Sahib. The holy Granth is regarded as a witness to the marriage and it is thought that a marriage document is unnecessary. In Britain, however, a civil ceremony conducted by a registrar, or an equivalent official appointed for the purpose in a gurdwara is necessary to comply with the law.

Marriage is generally preceded by betrothal. This may take place anytime after the arrangements related to the proposal have been made, up to just before the actual marriage ceremony. The bridegroom, accompanied by his parents and friends, goes to the place arranged by the parents of the bride for the solemnization of the marriage, on a date fixed after mutual consultations. The place could be a gurdwara, a hall in a club or school hired for the purpose, or the house of the bride's parents. The gurdwara is preferred for the simple reason that the facilities required for the occasion are easily made available by the management. On coming together, a formal meeting (*milni*) takes place when the boy's father, grandfather and maternal uncle are introduced to their counterparts on the girl's side. Light refreshments are served and everybody moves to the place set aside for the performance of the marriage ceremony. The couple sit facing the Guru Granth Sahib. The relatives and guests form the congregation. A few hymns appropriate to the occasion are sung and a prayer is offered. The person officiating at the

323

function tells the couple about the obligations of married life. The father or the guardian of the bride comes forward to tie the edge of her dupatta, the long head-dress, to the bridegroom's sash. This is called tying the knot. It signifies that henceforth they should stick together through thick and thin. The granthi reads the marriage hymn from the Guru Granth Sahib. The same hymn is sung by the musicians while the couple walk round the Guru Granth Sahib in a clockwise direction. The action is repeated four times in response to the four hymns called the Lavans. The Lavans convey the highest moral and spiritual ideals to the couple. A final prayer is offered and after the distribution of karah prashad the congregation disperses for entertainments and lunch. In the evening the bride leaves for her new home with the bridegroom and his party to be welcomed by her in-laws.

In days gone by polygamy was legal in India, but with the Sikhs 'one man one wife' has been the rule. Only in rare cases when the wife proved barren, or failed to produce a male child, a second marriage was conducted. This loophole has now been stopped by law.

Sikh attitudes to family planning and the use of methods of

At a Sikh wedding the couple being married sit in front of the Guru Granth Sahib. The bride's father-in-law can be seen coming forward to welcome her into his family after the religious ceremony.

birth control by married couples are favourable. There is no religious opposition to such measures.

Divorce has no place in the idea of a marriage for life. If however, a marriage breaks down, the parents quietly arrange another marriage for their children with the approval of their community. This practice has now been legalized. It provides for both judicial separation and divorce in difficult cases. The proceedings for divorce are, however, allowed to go on for some time to enable the members of the community to bring about a reconciliation if possible.

> If the wife and husband break off
> Their concern for their children re-unites them
>
> AG 143

The community has never objected to the marriage of a divorcee in the gurdwara on social or religious grounds.

Death

As the moment approaches the dying person is encouraged to say *Wahe Guru, Wahe Guru* (Wonderful Lord) a few times, and one of those present by his side will recite *Sukhmani* (the hymn of peace) or some other text, such as the *Japji Sahib*, from the scripture. The near and dear ones of the dead person are dissuaded from weeping and wailing by quoting scripture to them, for example, 'He who is born shall die. It is God's will. We must abide by his will.' The cremation takes place as soon as possible. The corpse is bathed and dressed in the symbols of faith by the relatives and the members of the community and carried on a bier to the cremation grounds. A prayer for the peace of the soul of the deceased is said and the pyre is lit by a close relative. Death is regarded as a short sleep and the mourners recite the bedtime prayer while the corpse is cremated. The people who have been handling the corpse take a bath and others wash their faces, hands and feet before returning home. A reading of the Guru Granth Sahib is commenced, only a few pages are read to begin with, *karah prashad* (ceremonial food) distributed and the mourners take leave of the bereaved family. The ashes are collected the following day and thrown into the flowing water of a nearby stream or a river.

The friends and relatives continue to visit the family for condolence for a number of days. They sit on mats or carpets spread on the floor. The reading of the scripture is completed

325

in about ten days when a final gathering takes place and the period of condolence closes.

In countries where facilities for cremation are not available, the Sikhs bury their dead. In western countries the facilities provided by undertakers, including the use of coffin and crematorium in the disposal of the body, are fully utilized. The distribution of karah prashad after the funeral signifies that the social life should continue as usual. The reading of the scripture at the house of the deceased is meant to provide spiritual support and mental consolation to the family and friends of the deceased. Sikhs are forbidden to build monuments for the dead. The words and deeds of the righteous are their true memorials:

> The dead keep their link with the living
> Through their virtuous deeds.
>
> AG 143

No prayers to, or for the dead, are ordained in the Guru Granth Sahib.

Fairs and Festivals

In the annual cycle of fairs and festivals people are provided with opportunities to rediscover the fundamental beliefs of their faith and to re-dedicate themselves to the observance of it in their day-to-day lives. They are supplementary to regular daily worship but far exceeding it in pomp and splendour. The Sikhs individually, and sometimes in groups, used to visit Guru Nanak and his successors to pay homage and seek spiritual guidance. Guru Amar Das, the third Guru of the Sikhs, asked all his followers to gather in his presence twice a year at the time of *Baisakhi* and *Diwali* – the two famous Hindu festivals. Guru Gobind Singh, the tenth Guru of the Sikhs, ordered a third annual gathering on the occasion of the spring festival of *Holi*. The tradition of these annual assemblies has survived the Gurus, but in a slightly changed form. The celebrations now mostly take place in the local gurdwaras and in the homes of the Sikhs, except Hola Mohalla which is still held at Anandpur Sahib, the venue of its first gathering in 1700. Over a period of time the celebrations of the birth and death anniversaries of the Gurus, along with a score of events relating to the development of the Sikh religion and history, have been added to the religious calendar of the Sikhs.

The origin of Holi, Baisakhi and Diwali is embedded in the Hindu religious and cultural traditions. The Sikh Gurus started parallel functions only to wean Sikhs from Hindu influences to begin with. In the course of time, however, the Sikh accretions changed their context and character altogether.

The dates of festivals are calculated by the light and dark phases of the lunar months, while the months and years are reckoned by the sun. A lunar year is only about 354 days long and to make it fall in line with the solar year of 365 days an extra lunar month is added to it every thirty months. As such the dates of festivals differ from year to year and move forward and backward within the lunar moth.

Baisakhi is the only fixed festival, being based on the solar

327

calendar. It falls on 13 April and marks the beginning of the Sikh religious year.

Diwali is observed on the last day of the dark half of the lunar month of Kartik (October/November).

Hola Mohalla occurs on the first day of the dark half of the lunar month of Chaitra (March).

We shall now consider each of these in detail.

Baisakhi (April)

From time immemorial Baisakhi has been observed as new year's day in north India. It marks the commencement of the Bikram era which is used by Sikhs for dating their religious calendar. Early in the morning people start wending their way to a nearby river for a ceremonial bath, though a Sikh would prefer to have a dip in the holy tank attached to a gurdwara instead.

Baisakhi marks a turning point in the development of the Sikh religion. On this day in 1699 Guru Gobind Singh brought into being a new brotherhood of saint-soldiers – the Khalsa – to fight against political and social injustice and to uphold the freedom of worship and religious liberty. The emergence of a distinctive physical appearance of a Sikh with uncut hair and turban became instrumental in the establishment of Sikhism as a separate religion with its own public symbols of faith, rituals and code of conduct. The day is commemorated by arranging the initiation of the prospective candidates of the faith, though there is no objection to such arrangements being made at any other time of the year.

Diwali (October/November)

Diwali is another all-India festival, the celebrations of which are shared by the Sikhs. Houses are given a spring cleaning and decorated, not of course to extend a welcome to Lakshmi the goddess of wealth and prosperity, but to get rid of mosquitoes and insects before moving beds indoors at the approach of winter. Trade is brisk for a few days. People buy new clothes, jewellery and household goods. Children enjoy themselves with sweetmeats and fireworks. Presents are exchanged among friends and relations. Gurdwaras and homes are illuminated with candles and devas (clay lamps with wick and oil). Everything looks beautiful in the totally moonless Diwali night. A few events that took place on this

328

day are recollected and recounted. Guru Ram Das had on this day laid the foundation of the City of Amritsar in 1577. Guru Hargobind who was imprisoned by the Emperor Jehangir was released on this day. Diwali also marks the day of martyrdom of Bhai Mani Singh in 1738.

Hola Mohalla (March)

The seasonal festival of Holi is very popular in north India, and is the precursor of Hola Mohalla, the Sikh festival. Children and young people enjoy themselves in bright, sunny weather by squirting coloured water and powder at one another. However, much of the fun is lost when people resort to the use of mud and rubbish in place of colours, or when an unwilling stranger is sprayed with coloured water and made the target of fun. In a multi-racial and multi-religious country like India, very often this sort of excess provokes communal riots. The feast is also associated with Krishna and his sports with the Gopis – the milkmaids. Its celebration is marked by a good deal of horseplay and ribaldry. The identification of the festival with the god of love provides an excuse for unrestrained merrymaking and obscenity. Guru Gobind Singh planned an alternative three-day celebration for Sikhs, at Anandpur Sahib, with religious gatherings, musical and poetical contests, feats of power and martial display. It was named Hola Mohalla owing to the predominance of military manoeuvres and mock fights in the programme. The literal meaning of Hola Mohalla is 'attack and place of attack'.

Gurpurbs

The festivals which are purely of Sikh origin and nature are called Gurpurbs – the holy days in honour of the Gurus. The birthdays of Guru Nanak and Guru Gobind Singh, and the martyrdom day of Guru Arjan Dev, are celebrated by the Sikhs all over the world, wherever they are. There are some others, the celebrations of which are confined to the places where the original events took place, such as the martyrdom day of Guru Tegh Bahadur at Delhi; the anniversary of the installation of the Adi Granth at Amritsar and the martyrdoms of Guru Gobind Singh's sons at Chamkaur and Fatehgarh Sahib.

A few days before the date of the actual function, groups of devout people start with the pre-dawn hymn singing rounds

(*Prabhat-Pheries*) in their villages and towns. Nobody will accuse them of being an early morning nuisance, such is the attitude of Indians to religious celebrations of every kind. Another important preliminary is the collection of funds and food from the local community which they also accept with pleasure. Two days before the function, a continuous public reading of the Guru Granth Sahib, by a relay of readers, is commenced, to be completed in the early hours of the day of the celebration. This is called *Akhand Path*. Marquees and awnings are erected for accommodating the congregation and for the cooking and serving of food to the public at large. On the evening of the celebration and sometimes on the afternoon of it, the Guru Granth Sahib is taken out in procession through the main streets.

This is becoming increasingly popular. The Guru Granth Sahib, under a canopy, is placed on a decorated float which is guarded by five Sikhs with drawn swords. The speakers and musicians are also provided with suitable conveyances and equipment to enable them to address the crowd gathered on the crossroads and the street corners. Brass bands are hired and the children of Sikh schools and colleges are invited to participate in the procession. People show their love for the Gurus by putting up temporary arches on the route of the procession and making arrangements for the distribution of free snacks and refreshments to those taking part.

The birthday of Guru Nanak is celebrated on the day of the full moon in the month of November. After the conclusion of the usual morning service the congregation is told of the religious situation that existed at the time of his birth and the regeneration brought about by Guru Nanak with his message of the fatherhood of God and the brotherhood of man.

The martyrdom of Guru Arjan is commemorated in midsummer (May/June). He is credited with the editing and compilation of the Sikh scriptures and providing the Sikh community with a central place of worship. The extreme sacrifice of his life highlights the belief that truth cannot be suppressed with torture and high-handedness and man has to suffer sometimes for his religious convictions. The recalling of the tragic incidents is not an invitation to mourning but to strengthening the resolve of the Sikh community to meet new challenges to human rights and dignity.

The birthday of Guru Gobind Singh is usually celebrated in January, but sometimes in December. Guru Gobind Singh is chiefly remembered for imparting a martial colouring to the

330

Sikh movement in his efforts to overcome the political tyranny and religious persecutions let loose by the Muslim rulers of India. Programmes are geared to emphasize the necessity of wearing the five Ks, as well as the turban, to keep the Sikh identity from being eroded.

The Sikhs in Britain

Britain is no longer a strange country for the Sikhs. It has become a second home for many of them. The people who initially came for employment and a temporary stay have been joined by their families and they now intend to remain. Perhaps they will never return. Improved standards of living and the facilities afforded by a developed state, such as Britain, are sufficient reasons to keep them here permanently. It is a free country and people enjoy complete freedom of worship and belief. Sikh studies have become popular in schools and colleges. The misunderstandings in the past about the Sikh way of life, which caused so much conflict between the transport authorities of various towns and the turban-wearing Sikhs, appear to have vanished. There has been a slight change, however, in the practice of religious obser-vances. As Sunday is a public holiday in Britain it makes the day convenient for Sikhs to attend the gurdwara. The celebration of a festival if it falls during the week is moved to the weekend to enable as large a number of people as possible to join in the festivities. The religious street processions which are an integral part of Gurpurb Celebra-tions in the Punjab have been totally discontinued here. Occasionally, however, when a new gurdwara is opened the Guru Granth Sahib is carried there in a procession from the old building where the congregational worship used to be held.

Gurdwaras are used far more in Britain for the solemniza-tion of weddings and for funeral rites. Perhaps the availability of the necessary facilities in the gurdwaras and the incle-mency of the English weather make it difficult to arrange functions in the open air.

Socially, Sikhs have not always been able to adjust themselves to the English way of life. They only have a working relationship with the host community. It is through their children that they have started feeling the impact of western culture. Indian customs do not allow adolescent girls and boys to mix and talk freely together, but the boys, and particularly the girls, in Britain find it irksome when they find their school friends enjoying a freedom which they are denied. Sometimes in extreme cases of conflict the girls run away from home. The joint family system is also breaking down. Houses originally built for one family unit are not big enough to accommodate the married sons and their families. Divorce, which was rarely heard of among Sikhs, has become fairly common among the young couples married here, just as it is in British society as a whole. The younger generation is slowly but steadily losing faith in Sikhism and its traditions. The sooner the leaders of the community look into the problems faced by their second generation the better.

Sikhs and Other Faiths

Sikhs have never claimed that their religion is the best, or the only way of approaching God. Rather, they will concede that there is more than one way in which man expresses his beliefs and attitudes in the pursuit of a universal quest for truth and goodness. The Sikh Gurus stood for harmony and concord. 'Those who are united with God are the friends of all men', (A.G. 238) said Guru Arjan. The true vocation of a religious preceptor therefore is to 'Unite all with the Lord' (A.G. 72, Guru Nanak).

There may be differences of colour, dress, diet and appearance but in reality there is only one caste, humanity. One may be a Hindu, a Muslim, or a Christian but all human beings belong to one brotherhood of mankind: 'Know the whole human species as one' said Guru Gobind Singh.

God will judge a person by the purity of his/her mind and sincerity of their worship irrespective of the credal statements of one kind or the other.

> The Universe is burning
> Be merciful O God.
> By whatever path anyone approaches you,
> Lift him and accept him!

> AG 853

This is one of the many utterances of the Sikh Gurus that have crystallized the Sikh attitude into one of acceptance of the validity of other faiths.

Further Reading

Hinduism

Hinnels, J. and Sharpe, E.J., *Hinduism*, Routledge & Kegan Paul.

Hopkins, T.J., *The Hindu Religious Tradition*, Dickenson.

Kanitkar, V.P., (Hemant) and Cole, W.O., *Hinduism*, (Teach Yourself Series), Hodder & Stoughton.

Kinsley, D.R., *Hinduism*, Prentice-Hall.

O'Flaherty, W.D., *Hindu Myths*, Penguin.

Younger, R & S., *Hinduism*, Argus Publications.

Judaism

Asheri, M., *Living Jewish*, Jewish Chronicle Publications, 1978.

Fisherman, I., *Introduction to Judaism*, Vallentine, Mitchell.

Trepp, L., *A History of the Jewish Experience*, Behrman.

Guide to Jewish Festivals, Jewish Chronicle Publications.

Buddhism

Batchelor, Stephen, *The Jewel in the Lotus*, Wisdom.

Bechert, Prof. H. and Gombrich, Prof. R. (eds), *The World of Buddhism*, Thames and Hudson, London.

Harvey, Dr. Peter, *An Introduction to Buddhism*, Cambridge University Press.

Kitagawa, Joseph M. and Cummings, Mark D. (eds), *Buddhism and Asian History*, (Articles from Encyclopedia of Religion) Macmillan, New York.

Narada Maha Thera, Ven., *The Buddha and his Teachings*, Buddhist Publication Society, Sri Lanka.

Rahula, Ven. Dr. Walpola, *What the Buddha Taught*, Gordon Fraser, London.

Snelling, John, *The Buddhist Handbook*, Rider, London.

The Buddhist Society, *Buddhism for Schools and Colleges*, London.

Christianity

Banks, R. et al., *The Quiet Revolution*, Lion.

Cole, W.O. and Mantin, R.M., *Teaching Christianity*, Heinemann. Teachers at all levels might find this a helpful guide.

Cole, W.O. and Sambhi, P.S., *Sikhism and Christianity: A Comparative Study*, Macmillan.

Dodd, C.H., *The Founder of Christianity*, Fontana.

Moore, P., *Christianity*, Ward Lock.

Islam

El-Droubie, R., *Islam*, Ward Lock Educational.

Gibb, H.A.R., *Muhammadanism*, Oxford University Press (A good introduction, despite the title which Muslims find unacceptable).

Watt, W.M., *Muhammad, Prophet and Statesman*, Oxford University Press.

Sikhism

Cole, W.O., *Sikhism* (Teach Yourself Series), Hodder & Stoughton. More for the student looking for the next step than the following book may be.

Cole, W.O. and Sambhi, P.S., *The Sikhs, Their Religious Beliefs and Practices*, (second, fully revised edition) Sussex Academic Press, Brighton.

McLeod, W.H., *Textual Sources for the Study of Sikhism*, Manchester University Press. More recent edition, University of Chicago Press.

General

Cole, W.O., (ed.) *World Faiths in Education*, Allen & Unwin. This is a book in which many of the issues raised by teaching comparative religion are discussed.

Photographic Acknowledgements

Thanks are due to Mrs Nila Pancholi who provided a photograph in the Hindu section; to Rabbi Douglas Charing and the Jewish Education Bureau, Leeds, for the photographs in the Judaism section; to Mr Piara Singh Sambhi for photographs in the Sikh section; and to Dr Anil Goonewardene who provided photographs for the Buddhism section. The photograph on p. 215 is reproduced courtesy of Church House. Other photographs were taken by Mr Nick Hedges – our thanks to him.

Index

344